SCIENCE COMICS

D1648779

POLAR BEARS

Survival on the Ice

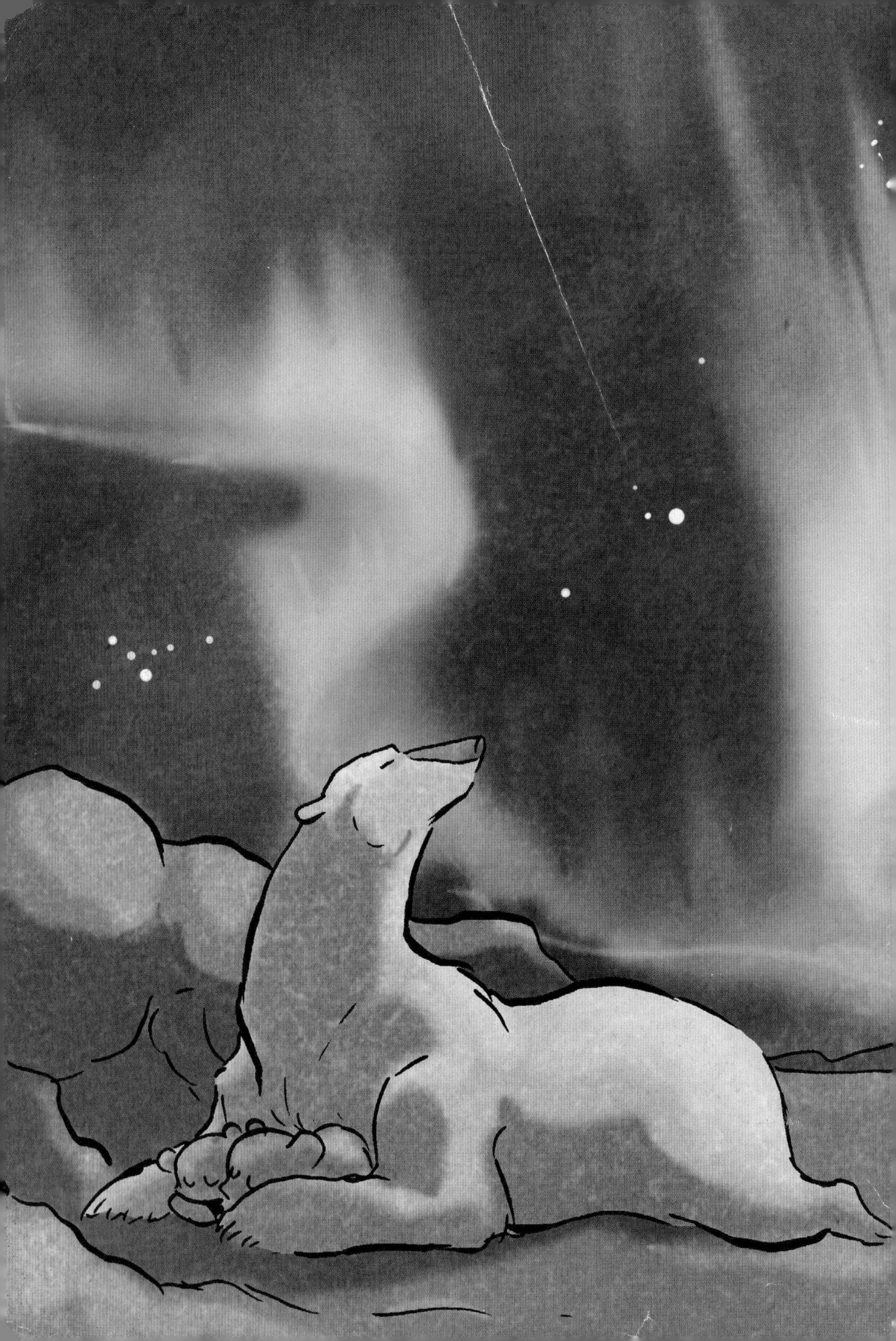

POLAR BEARS

Survival on the Ice

written by
JASON VIOLA

illustrated by
ZACK GIALLONGO

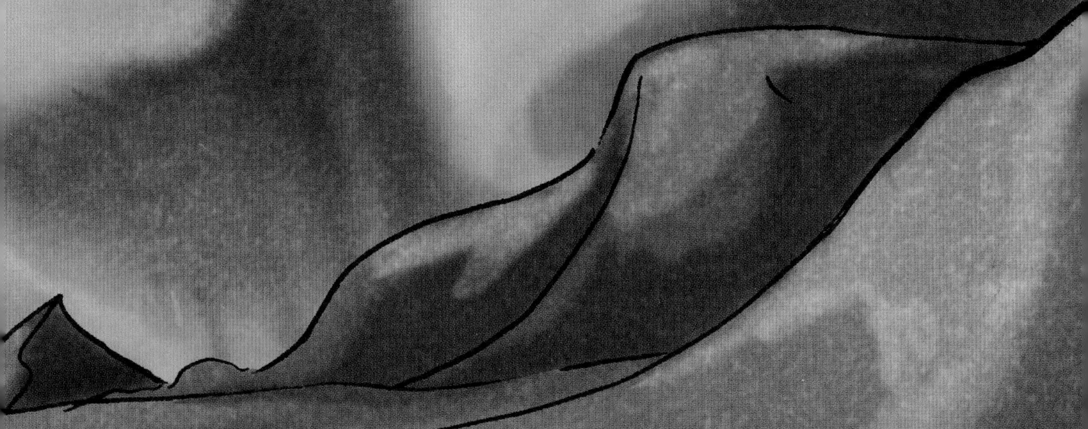

First Second
New York

To my Hunewill family. Thanks for all the oatmeal.
—Jason

To the protectors
—Zack

First Second

Text copyright © 2019 by Jason Viola
Illustrations copyright © 2019 by Zack Giallongo

Penciled in blue lead and inked with Tombow brush pens on Strathmore smooth Bristol. Colored and lettered digitally in Photoshop. Lettered with Comicrazy font from Comicraft.

Published by First Second
First Second is an imprint of Roaring Brook Press,
a division of Holtzbrinck Publishing Holdings Limited Partnership
175 Fifth Avenue, New York, NY 10010
All rights reserved

Library of Congress Control Number: 2018938083

Paperback ISBN: 978-1-62672-824-0
Hardcover ISBN: 978-1-62672-823-3

Our books may be purchased in bulk for promotional, educational, or business use. Please contact your local bookseller or the Macmillan Corporate and Premium Sales Department at (800) 221-7945 ext. 5442 or by e-mail at MacmillanSpecialMarkets@macmillan.com.

First edition, 2019
Edited by Dave Roman
Book design by John Green
Polar bear consultant: Thea Bechshoft

Printed in China by Toppan Leefung Printing Limited, Dongguan City, Guandong Province
Paperback: 10 9 8 7 6 5 4 3 2 1
Hardcover: 10 9 8 7 6 5 4 3 2 1

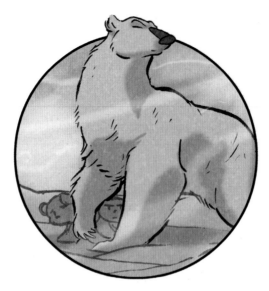

I bet that if someone suddenly showed you a picture of a polar bear and asked you what it was, you would know the answer right away. In fact, probably the great majority of kids your age could answer that question because the polar bear is one of the most admired and widely recognized animals in the whole world. Although you may not have specifically thought about it, you likely also know a few important facts about polar bears as well, such as they are white, they live in the Arctic, and they walk around on the ice to find and hunt the seals they eat. In fact, before I started doing research on polar bears all over the Canadian Arctic, over forty-five years ago, I probably didn't know much more about their life in the wild myself. However, with all the wonderful information on nature that is so easily available these days in books, on the internet, and in TV documentaries, most kids like you have probably already learned lots of neat stuff about these amazing bears. Even so, as you read this exciting comic, you will find yourself going on a new journey of scientific exploration. In fact, you will be like a scientist yourself, going out into the Arctic for the first time to observe and learn about a family of these wonderful bears. With your new knowledge about the lives of wild polar bears, you will be able to understand some of the big conservation issues now affecting the bears all over the Arctic, and more importantly, you will learn about a few things we can all do to help them.

But now . . . stop reading. Don't start turning pages yet. Imagine that *you* are a scientist, and you are going out to study polar bears for the very first time ever, anywhere! Just for a moment, pretend you could just float silently in the air above the bears in the vast expanse of the Arctic Ocean, watch everything they did all day long, listen to them talking to each other, and understand what they were saying. What kinds of things would you want to find out about the life of polar bears if you really were a scientist? For example, you might wonder how the cubs learn about what they must do on a day-to-day basis to find something to eat, to locate a place to den and have their own cubs, to avoid danger, to find a mate, and to survive in one of the coldest places on the planet. Some of the answers might surprise you. And of course, to the cubs in the story, Anik and Ila, the Arctic isn't a cold, desolate place at all—it is just home . . . and a very comfortable one at that! I think you might be pleased to read how many of the answers to your questions are waiting for you in the pages ahead. You will probably also be amazed to learn some of the neat things you didn't have

any idea about before this. It is the discovery of new things that makes science so interesting to us all!

Polar bear cubs must spend a long time with their mothers—two and a half years—before they are ready to try to survive on their own. So, they have to watch, study, and practice over and over. It is a little like you and your friends being in school. And, as you will see, sometimes polar bear cubs are not very good at sitting still and being quiet for long periods either!

It is also important to remember that as we learn more about any wild animals and the areas they live in, we also become aware that there can be concerns for their future. It may surprise you to learn that even in somewhere as far away and remote as the Arctic, humans are responsible for problems with issues such as contaminants and climate change. By the time you finish this comic, you will understand why both of these threats are important, and how they were both caused by humans. However, probably the most important thing to remember is that if we work hard, humans can solve these problems as well. That is where we will need the scientists of the future, like you! Read on and enjoy.

—Ian Stirling, PhD,
Canadian polar bear scientist,
author of *Polar Bears: The Natural History of a Threatened Species*

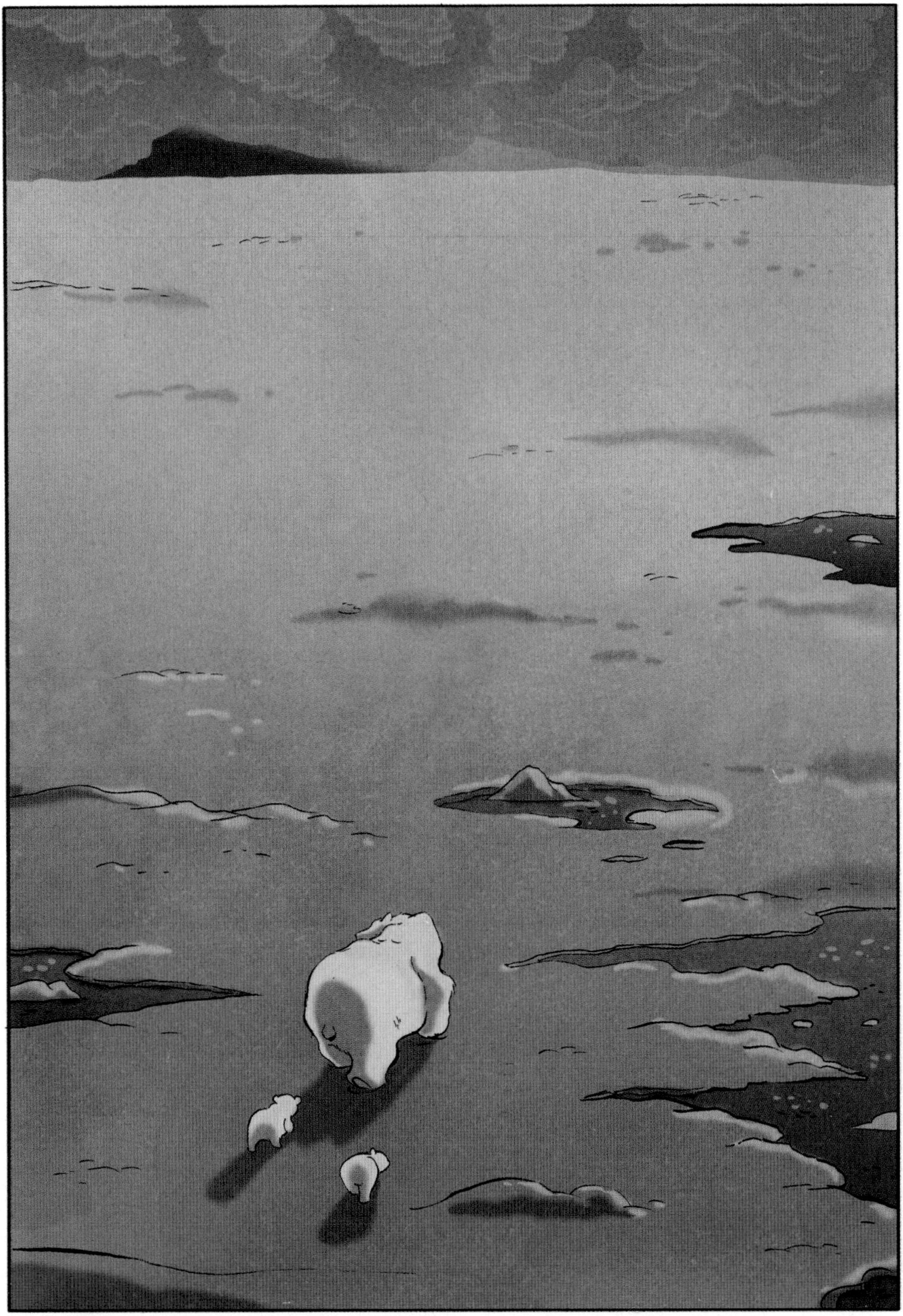

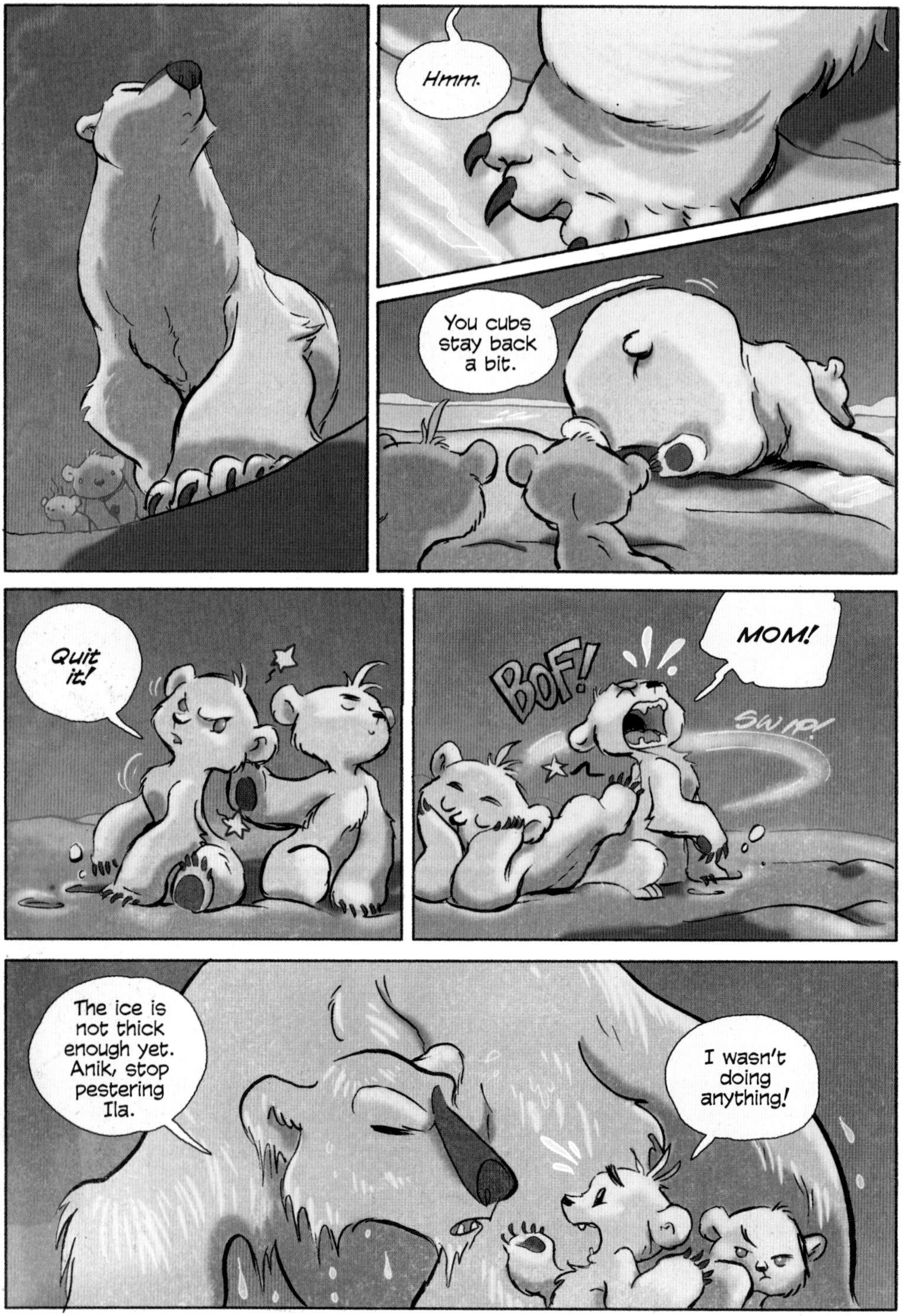
Hmm.
You cubs stay back a bit.
Quit it!
BOF!
MOM!
SWIP!
The ice is not thick enough yet. Anik, stop pestering Ila.
I wasn't doing anything!

I'm hungry, Mama.

I just fed you.

I want *real* food.

What's "real" food?

SEALS.

First, tell me what kind of ice this is?

Nilas ice!

Very good, Ila.

The long strips are formed by *grease ice* in calmer waters. Grease ice is from frazil ice and it's too thin to—

You are such an ice nerd.

And what does all that grease ice mean, Ila?

It means it's *autumn!*

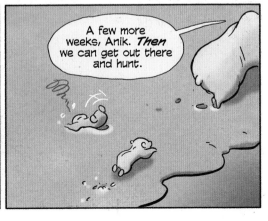

A few more weeks, Anik. *Then* we can get out there and hunt.

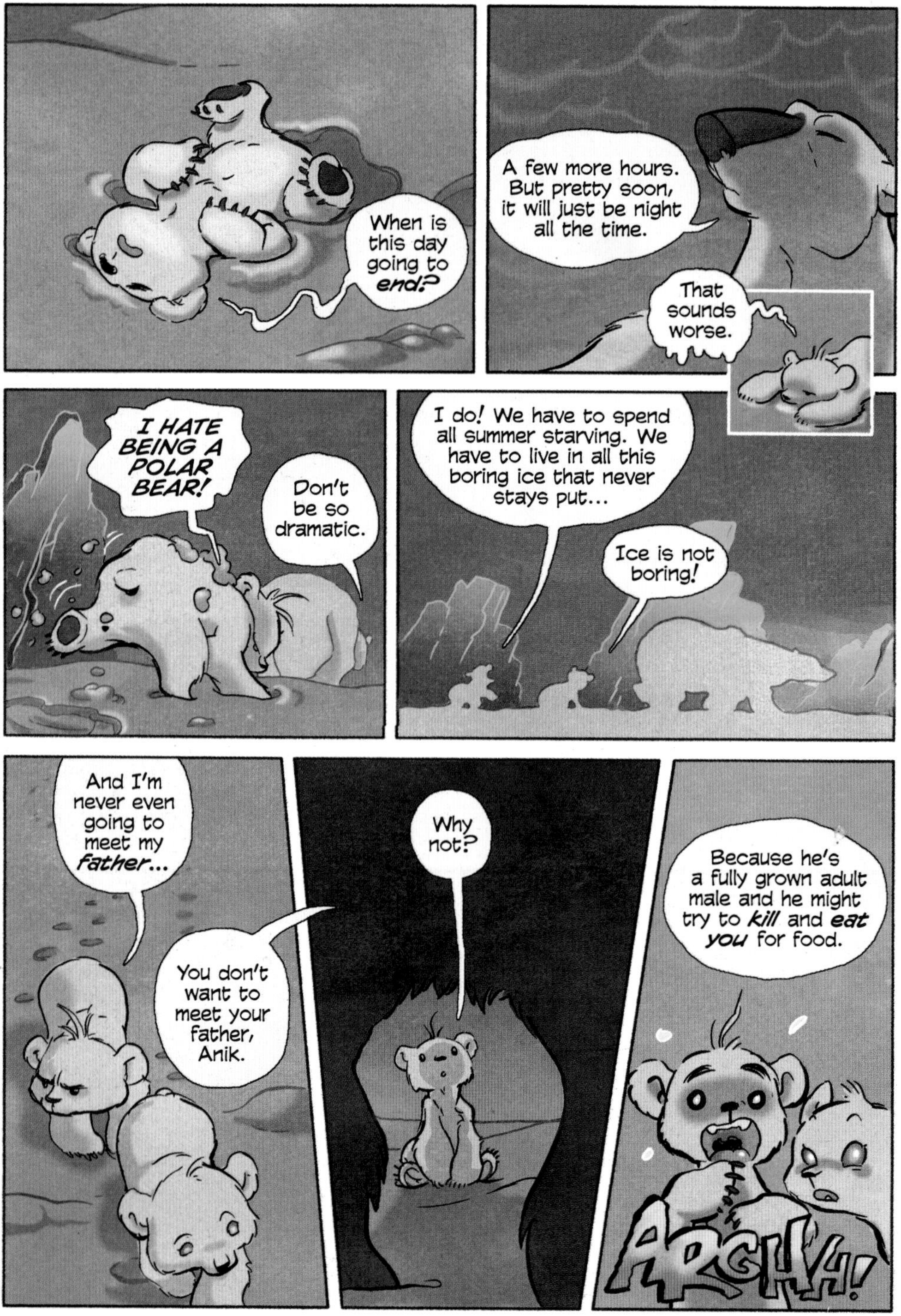
When is this day going to *end?*
A few more hours. But pretty soon, it will just be night all the time.
That sounds worse.
I HATE BEING A POLAR BEAR!
Don't be so dramatic.
I do! We have to spend all summer starving. We have to live in all this boring ice that never stays put...
Ice is not boring!
And I'm never even going to meet my *father*...
You don't want to meet your father, Anik.
Why not?
Because he's a fully grown adult male and he might try to *kill* and *eat you* for food.
ARGHH!

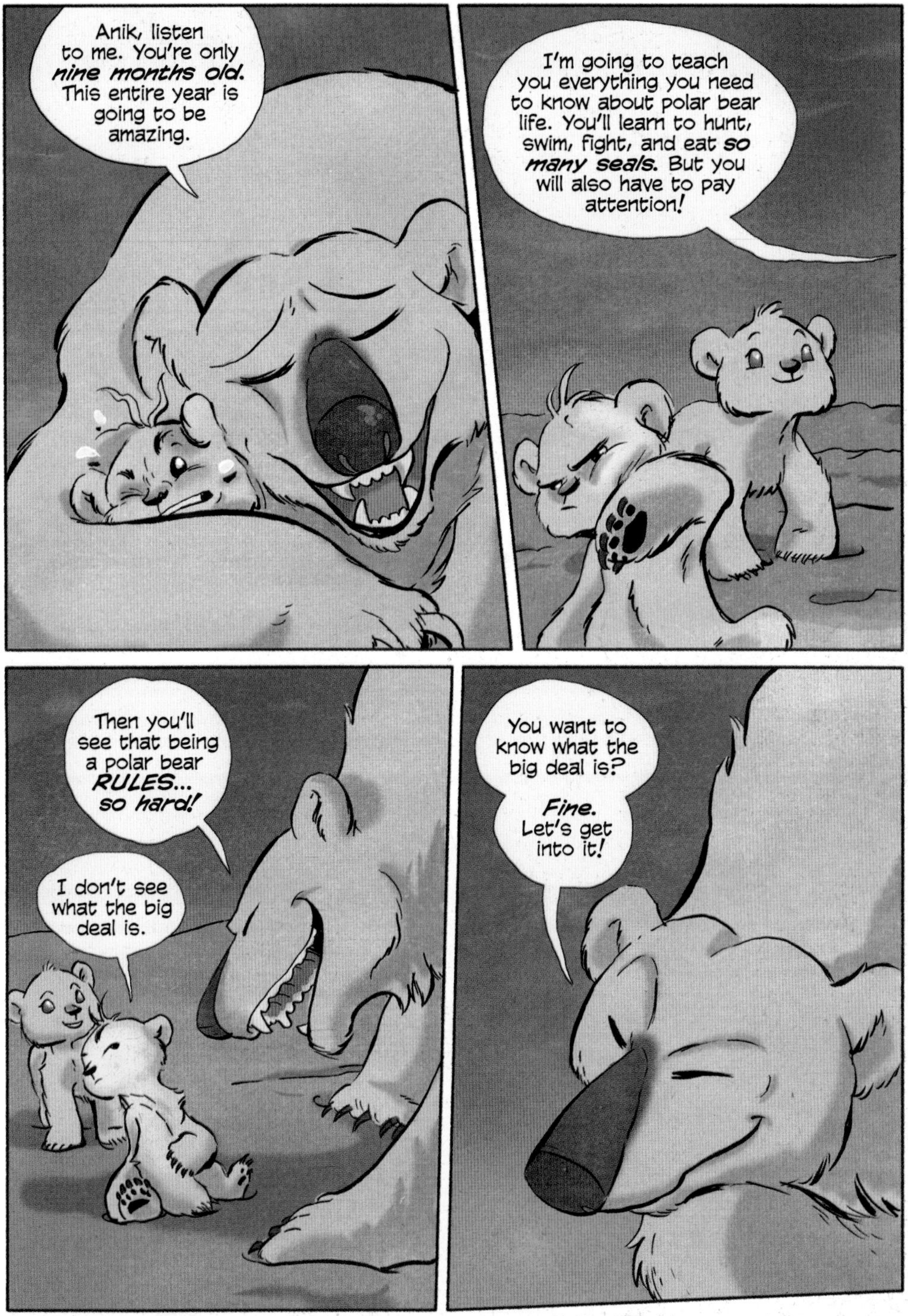
Anik, listen to me. You're only *nine months old.* This entire year is going to be amazing.
I'm going to teach you everything you need to know about polar bear life. You'll learn to hunt, swim, fight, and eat *so many seals.* But you will also have to pay attention!
Then you'll see that being a polar bear *RULES... so hard!*
I don't see what the big deal is.
You want to know what the big deal is?
Fine. Let's get into it!

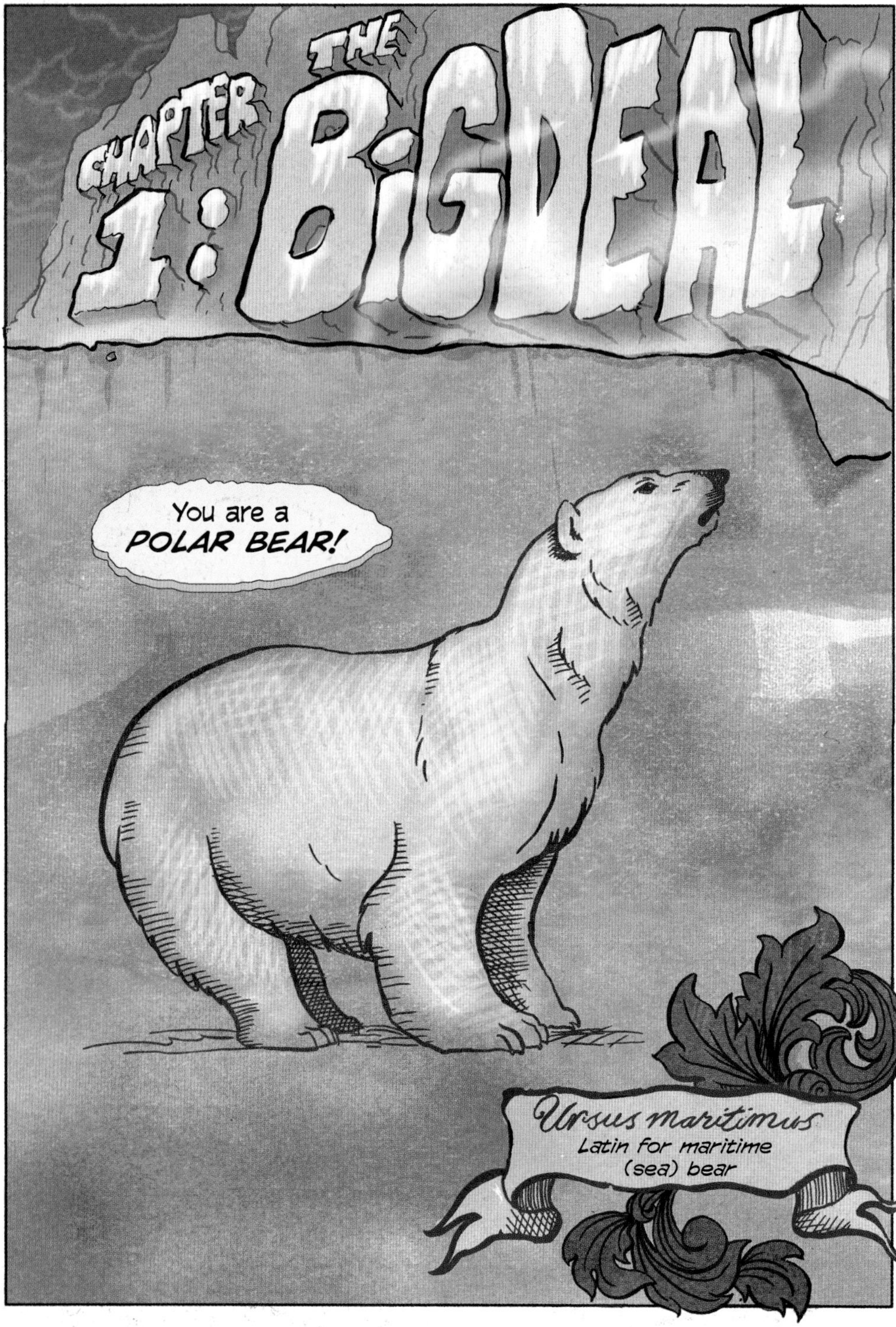
CHAPTER 1: THE BiG DEAL
You are a POLAR BEAR!
Ursus maritimus
Latin for maritime (sea) bear

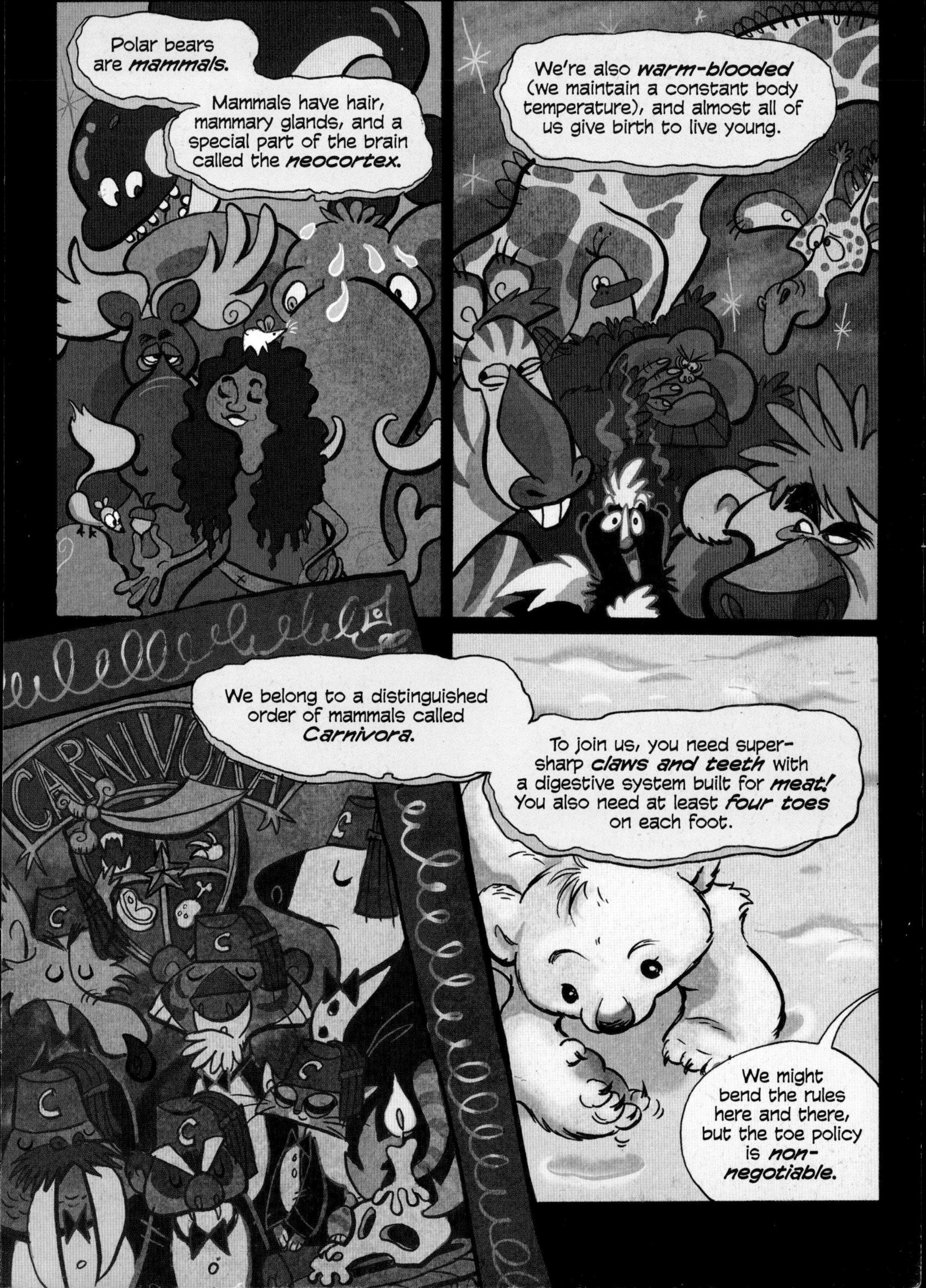
Polar bears are *mammals.*
Mammals have hair, mammary glands, and a special part of the brain called the *neocortex.*
We're also *warm-blooded* (we maintain a constant body temperature), and almost all of us give birth to live young.
We belong to a distinguished order of mammals called *Carnivora.*
CARNIVORA
To join us, you need super-sharp *claws and teeth* with a digestive system built for *meat!* You also need at least *four toes* on each foot.
We might bend the rules here and there, but the toe policy is *non-negotiable.*

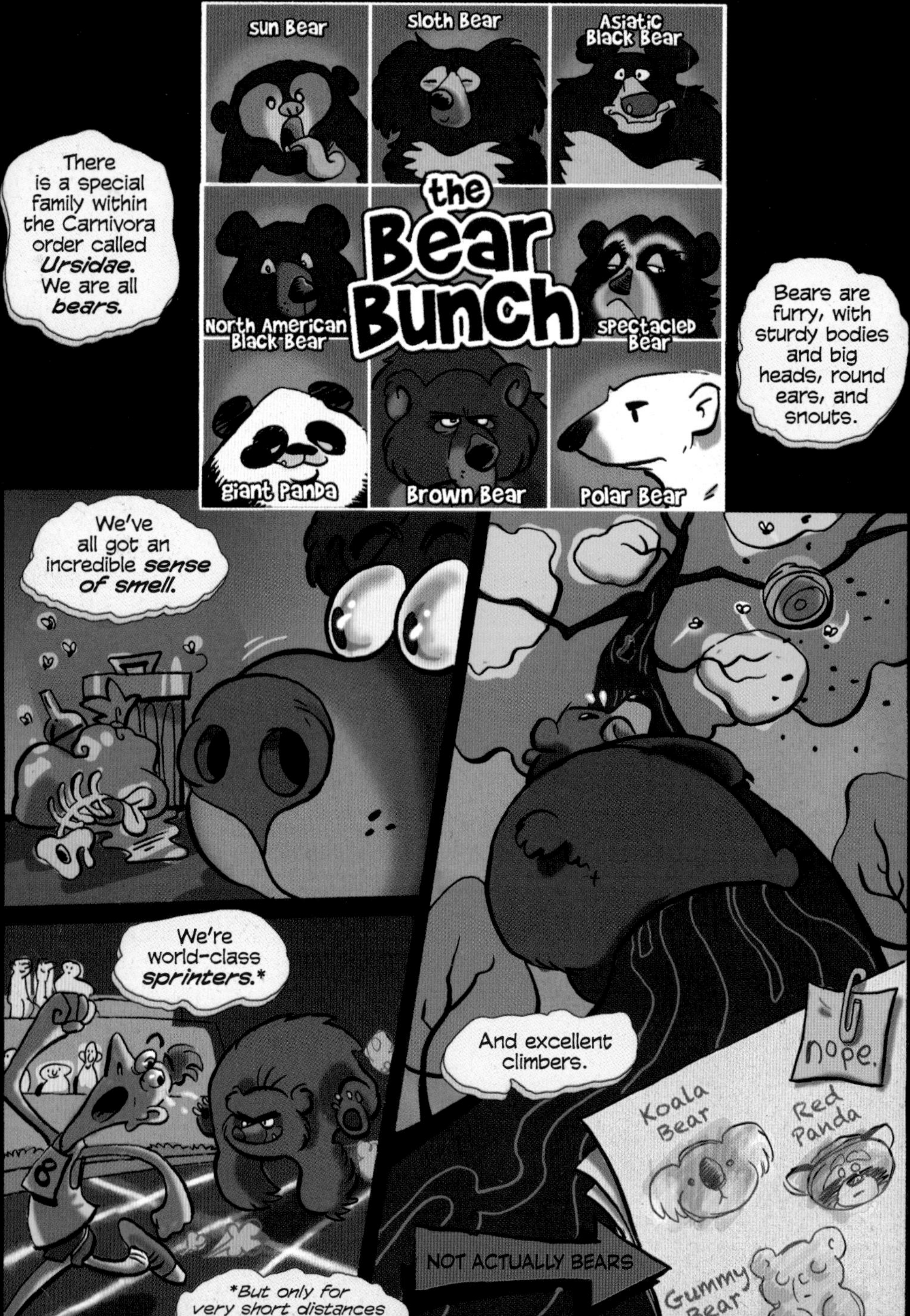

the Bear Bunch
sun Bear
Sloth Bear
Asiatic Black Bear
North American Black Bear
Spectacled Bear
giant Panda
Brown Bear
Polar Bear
There is a special family within the Carnivora order called *Ursidae*. We are all *bears*.
Bears are furry, with sturdy bodies and big heads, round ears, and snouts.
We've all got an incredible *sense of smell*.
We're world-class *sprinters*.*
*But only for very short distances because we overheat fairly quickly.
8
And excellent climbers.
nope.
Koala Bear
Red Panda
Gummy Bear
NOT ACTUALLY BEARS

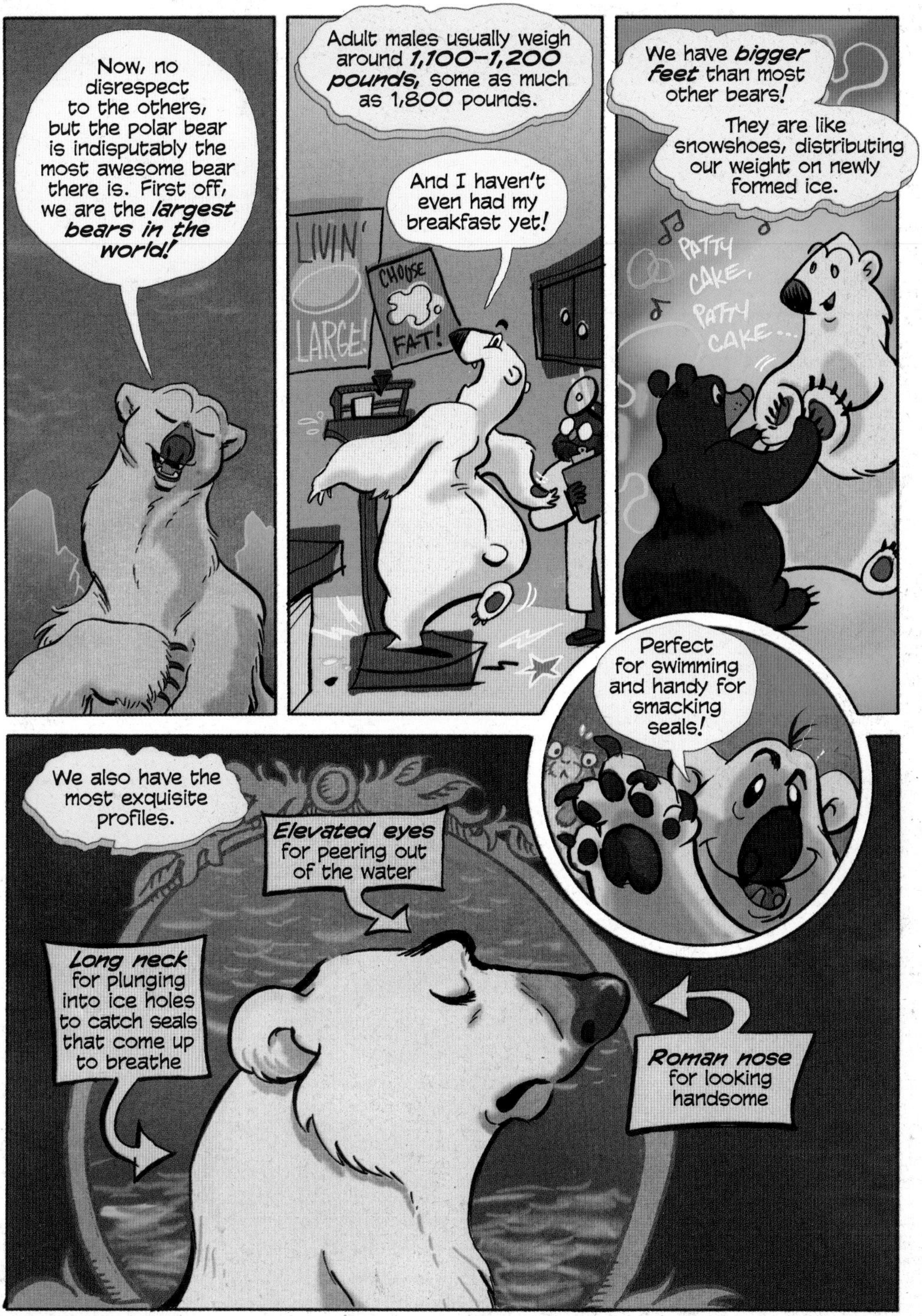
Now, no disrespect to the others, but the polar bear is indisputably the most awesome bear there is. First off, we are the *largest bears in the world!*
Adult males usually weigh around *1,100–1,200 pounds,* some as much as 1,800 pounds.
And I haven't even had my breakfast yet!
LIVIN' LARGE!
CHOOSE FAT!
We have *bigger feet* than most other bears!
They are like snowshoes, distributing our weight on newly formed ice.
PATTY CAKE, PATTY CAKE...
Perfect for swimming and handy for smacking seals!
We also have the most exquisite profiles.
Elevated eyes for peering out of the water
Long neck for plunging into ice holes to catch seals that come up to breathe
Roman nose for looking handsome

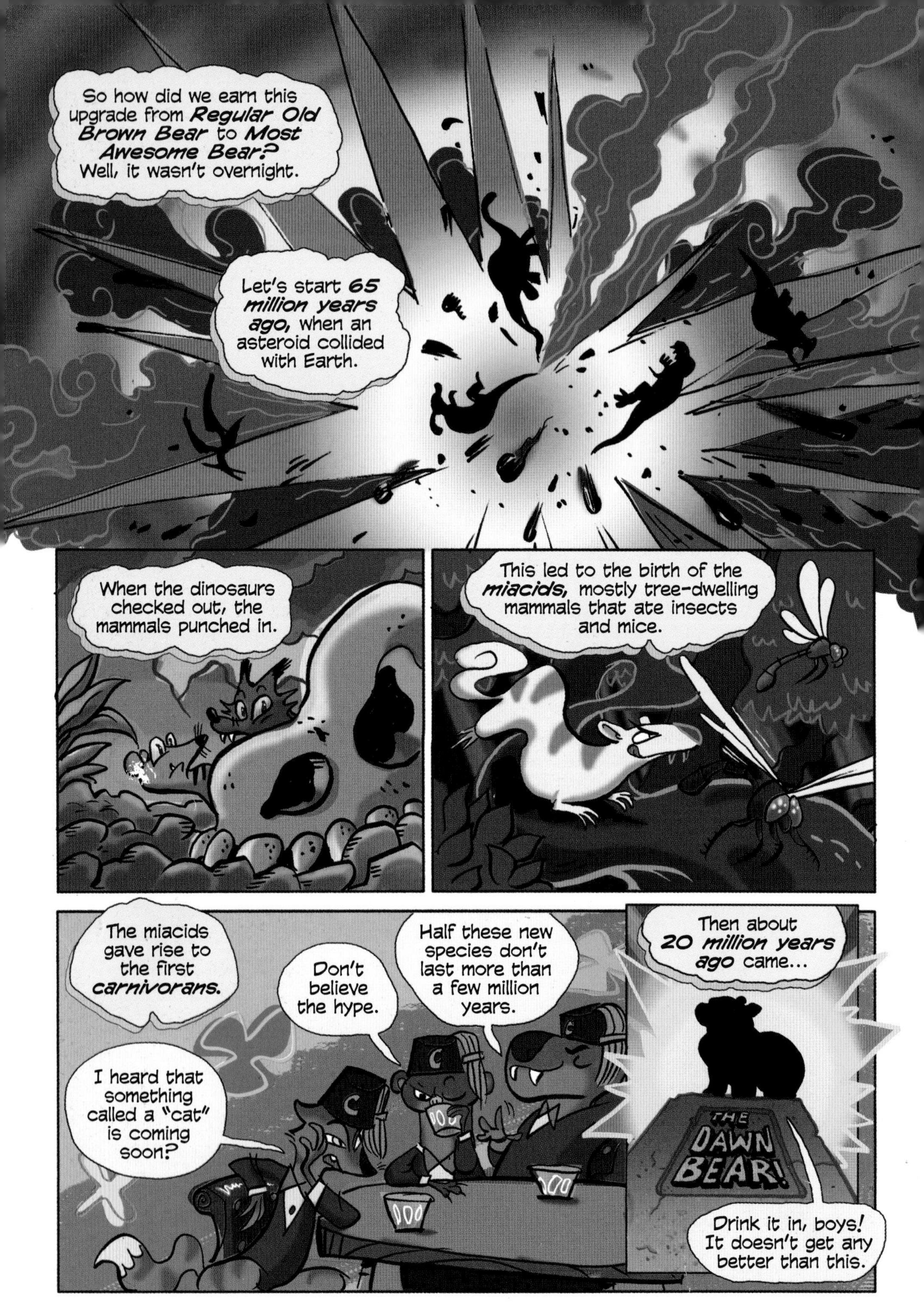
So how did we earn this upgrade from *Regular Old Brown Bear* to *Most Awesome Bear?* Well, it wasn't overnight.
Let's start *65 million years ago,* when an asteroid collided with Earth.
When the dinosaurs checked out, the mammals punched in.
This led to the birth of the *miacids,* mostly tree-dwelling mammals that ate insects and mice.
The miacids gave rise to the first *carnivorans.*
Don't believe the hype.
Half these new species don't last more than a few million years.
I heard that something called a "cat" is coming soon?
Then about *20 million years ago* came...
THE DAWN BEAR!
Drink it in, boys! It doesn't get any better than this.

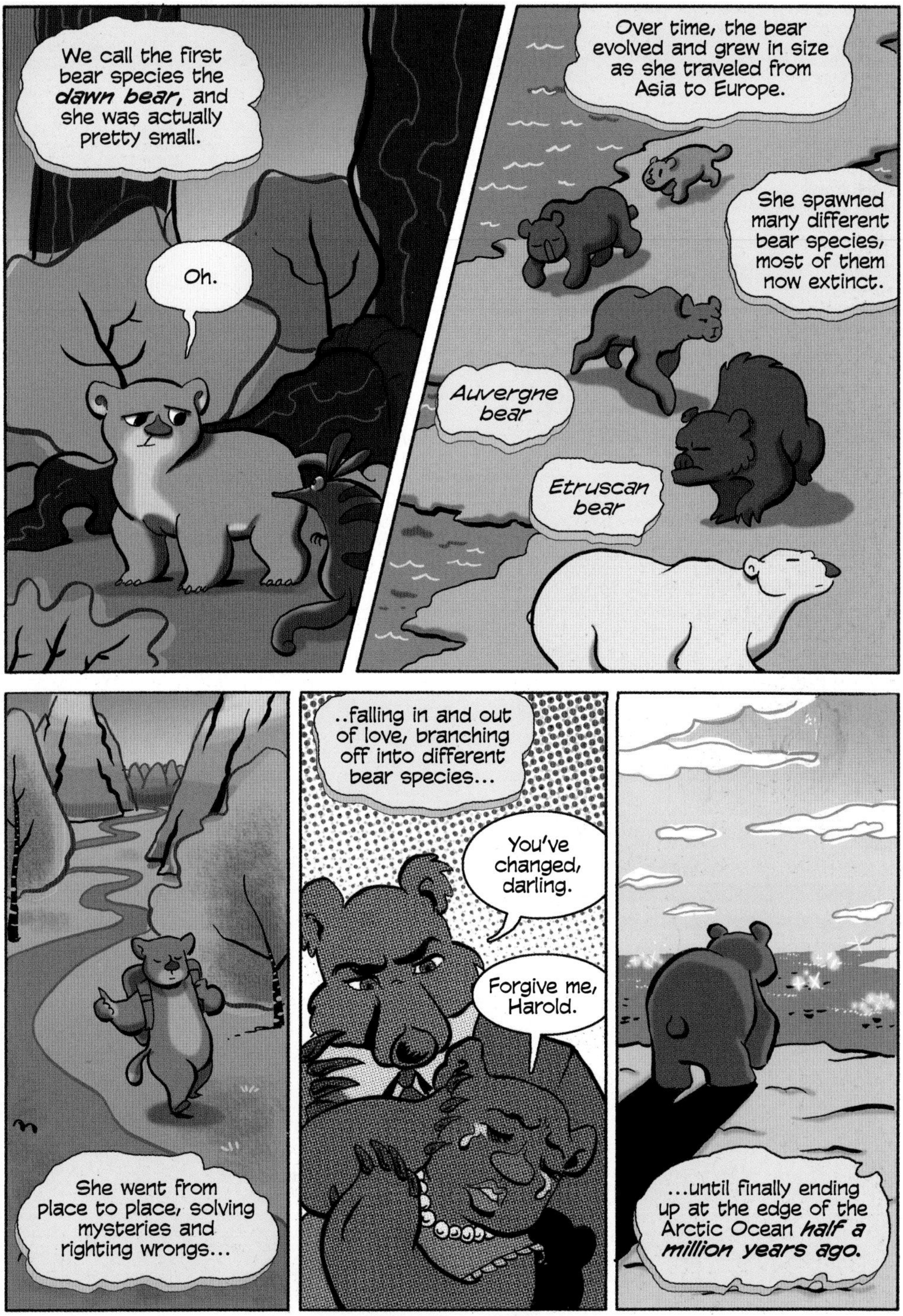
We call the first bear species the *dawn bear,* and she was actually pretty small.
Oh.
Over time, the bear evolved and grew in size as she traveled from Asia to Europe.
She spawned many different bear species, most of them now extinct.
Auvergne bear
Etruscan bear
She went from place to place, solving mysteries and righting wrongs...
..falling in and out of love, branching off into different bear species...
You've changed, darling.
Forgive me, Harold.
...until finally ending up at the edge of the Arctic Ocean *half a million years ago.*

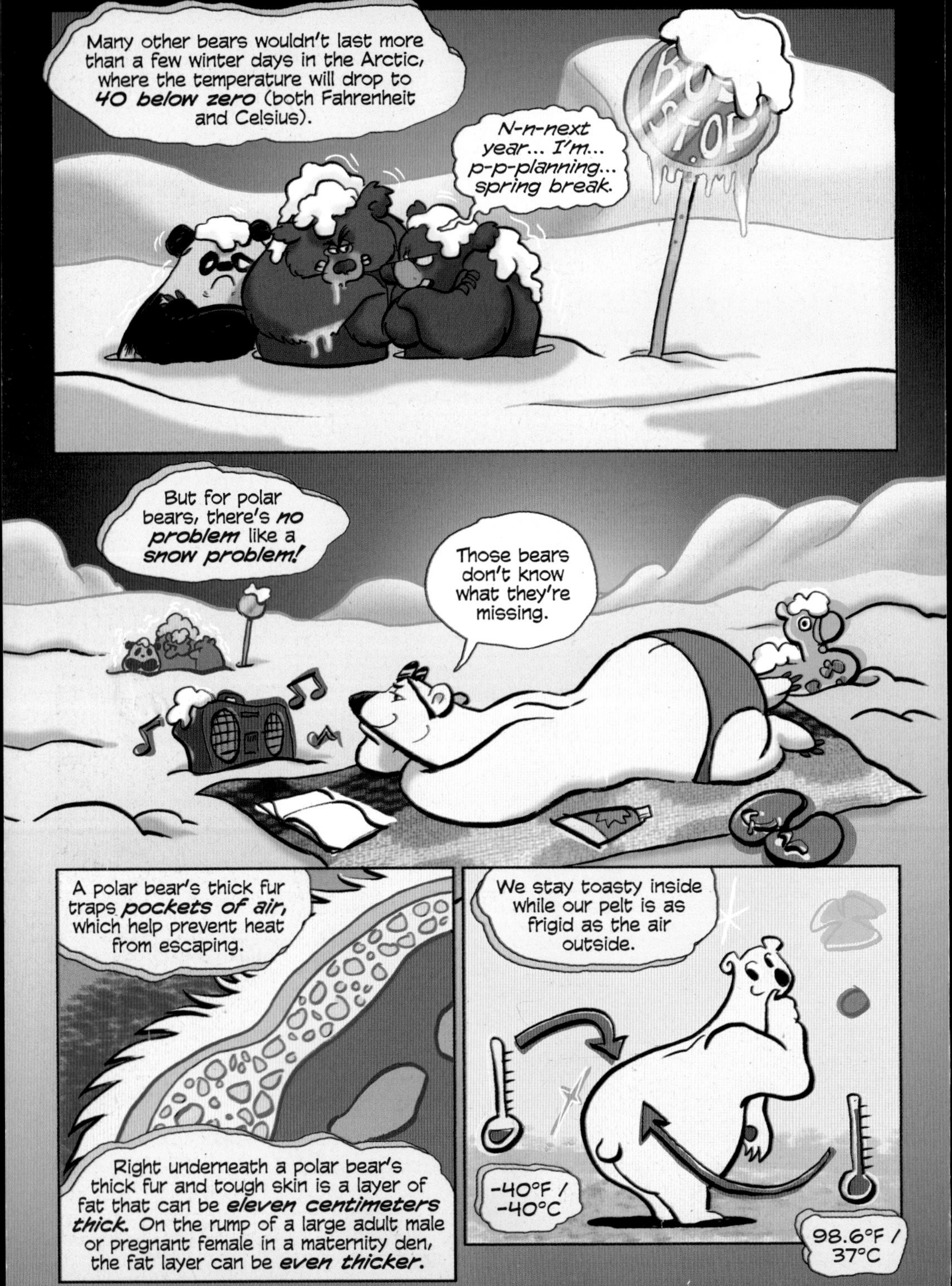
Many other bears wouldn't last more than a few winter days in the Arctic, where the temperature will drop to **40 below zero** (both Fahrenheit and Celsius).
N-n-next year... I'm... p-p-planning... spring break.
But for polar bears, there's **no problem** like a **snow problem!**
Those bears don't know what they're missing.
A polar bear's thick fur traps **pockets of air,** which help prevent heat from escaping.
Right underneath a polar bear's thick fur and tough skin is a layer of fat that can be **eleven centimeters thick.** On the rump of a large adult male or pregnant female in a maternity den, the fat layer can be **even thicker.**
We stay toasty inside while our pelt is as frigid as the air outside.
-40°F / -40°C
98.6°F / 37°C

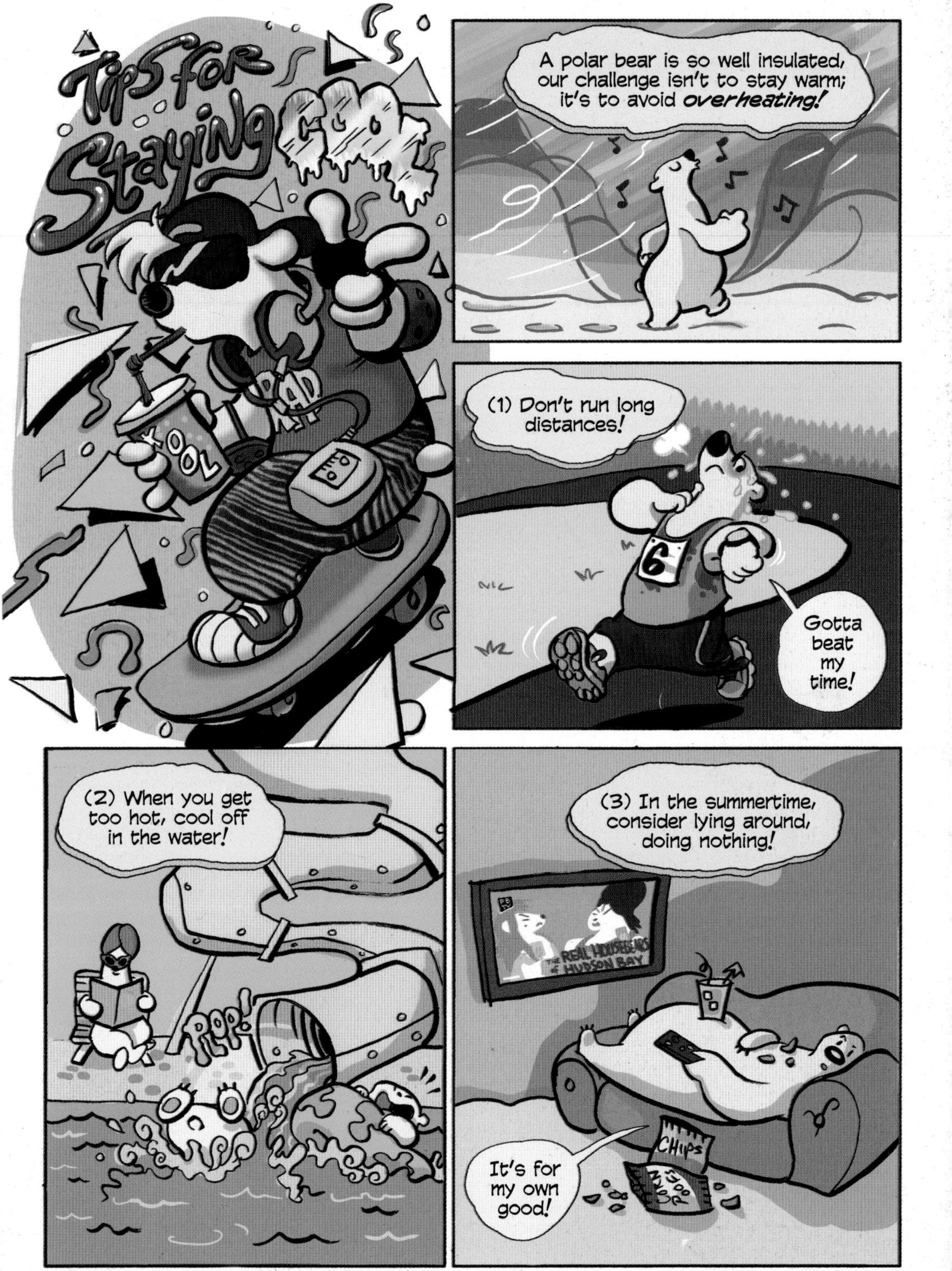
Tips for Staying Cool
KOOL
RAD
A polar bear is so well insulated, our challenge isn't to stay warm; it's to avoid ***overheating!***
(1) Don't run long distances!
Gotta beat my time!
6
(2) When you get too hot, cool off in the water!
POP!
(3) In the summertime, consider lying around, doing nothing!
THE REAL HOUSEBEARS OF HUDSON BAY
It's for my own good!
CHIPS

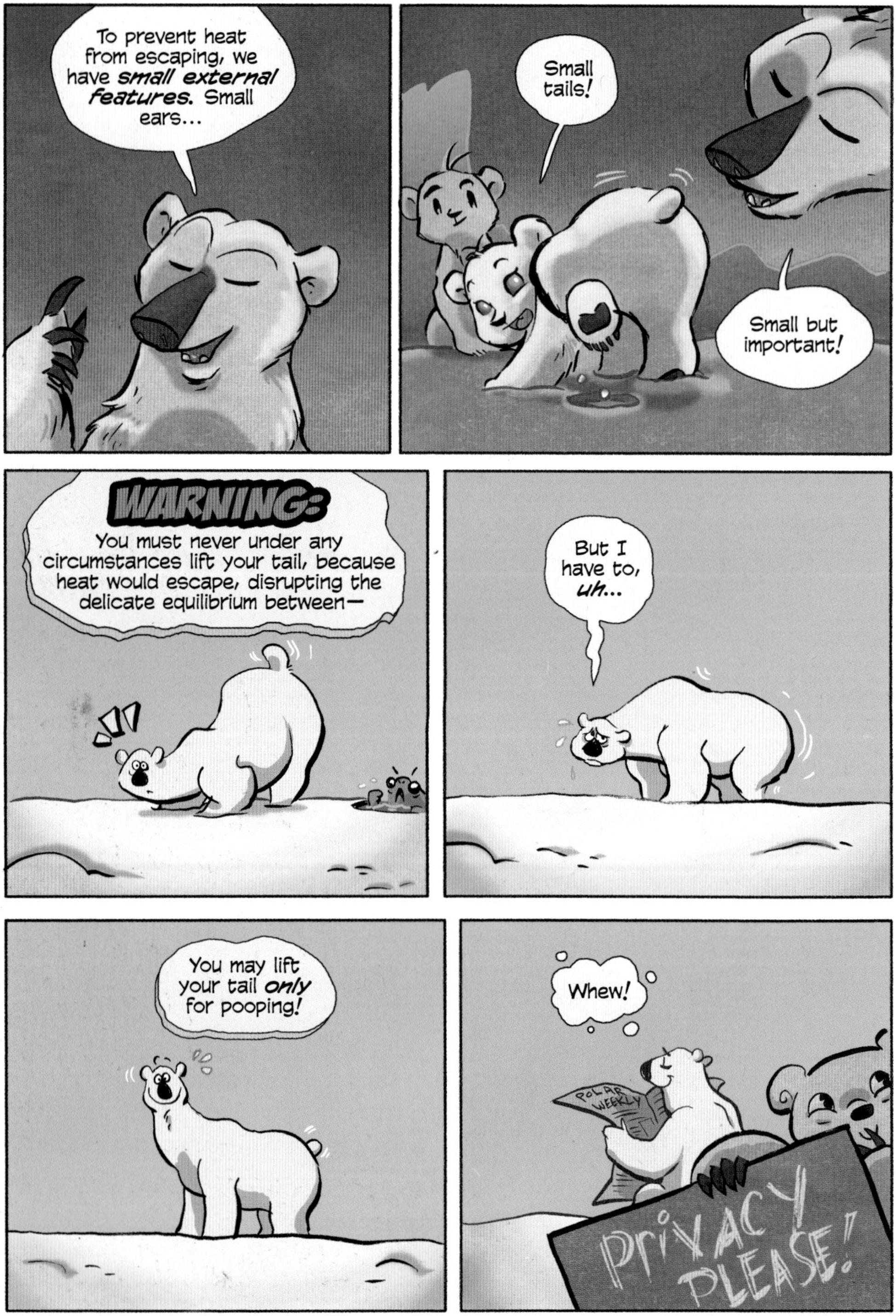
To prevent heat from escaping, we have *small external features.* Small ears...
Small tails!
Small but important!
WARNING:
You must never under any circumstances lift your tail, because heat would escape, disrupting the delicate equilibrium between—
But I have to, *uh*...
You may lift your tail *only* for pooping!
Whew!
POLAR WEEKLY
PRIVACY PLEASE!

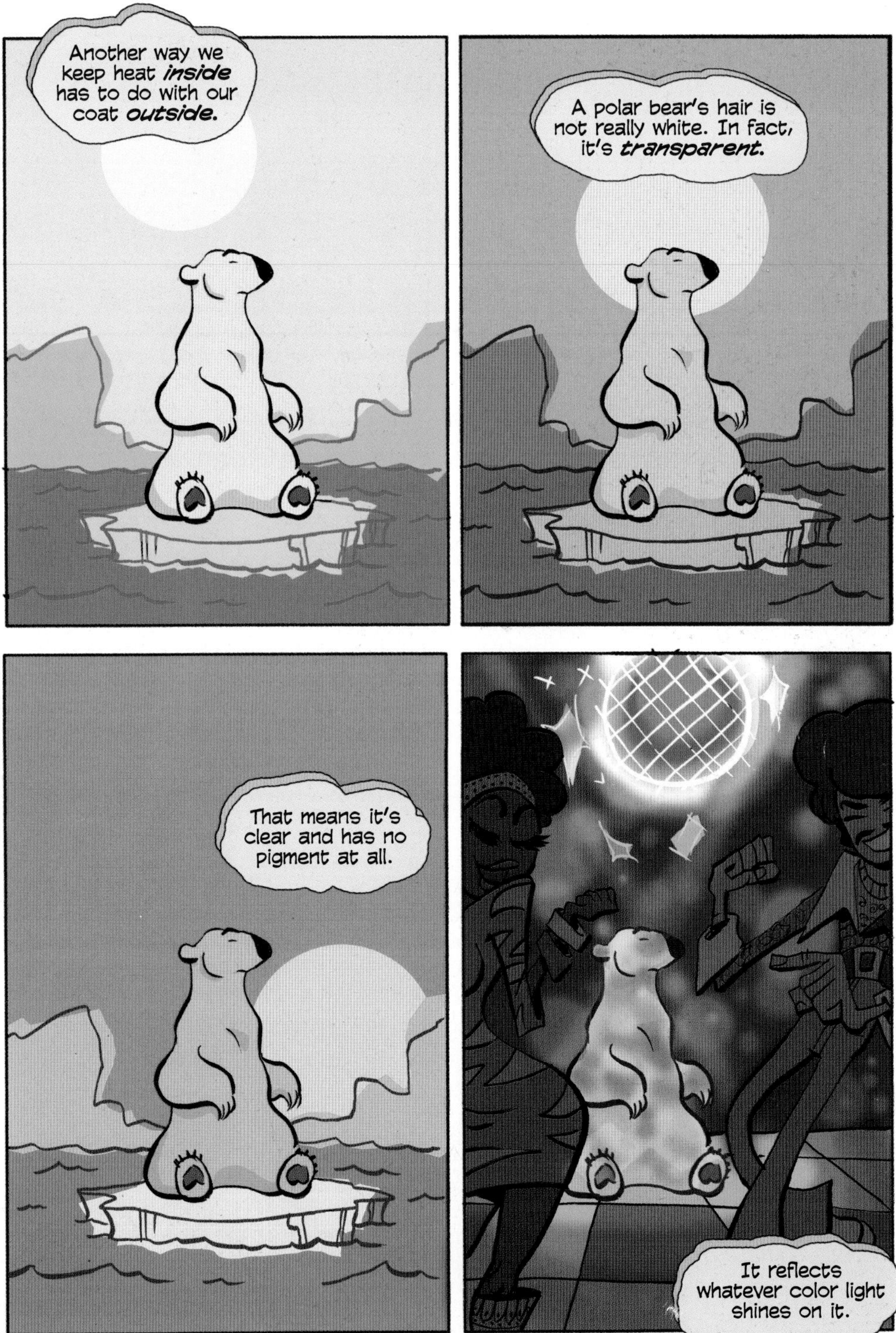
Another way we keep heat *inside* has to do with our coat *outside*.
A polar bear's hair is not really white. In fact, it's *transparent*.
That means it's clear and has no pigment at all.
It reflects whatever color light shines on it.

Underneath a polar bear's hair...

...his skin is completely black.

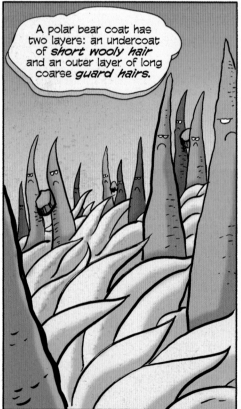

A polar bear coat has two layers: an undercoat of *short wooly hair* and an outer layer of long coarse *guard hairs*.

Scientists think that when heat escapes from the body, the transparent hairs reflect it. The black skin easily re-absorbs the reflected radiation.

YOU SHALL NOT PASS!

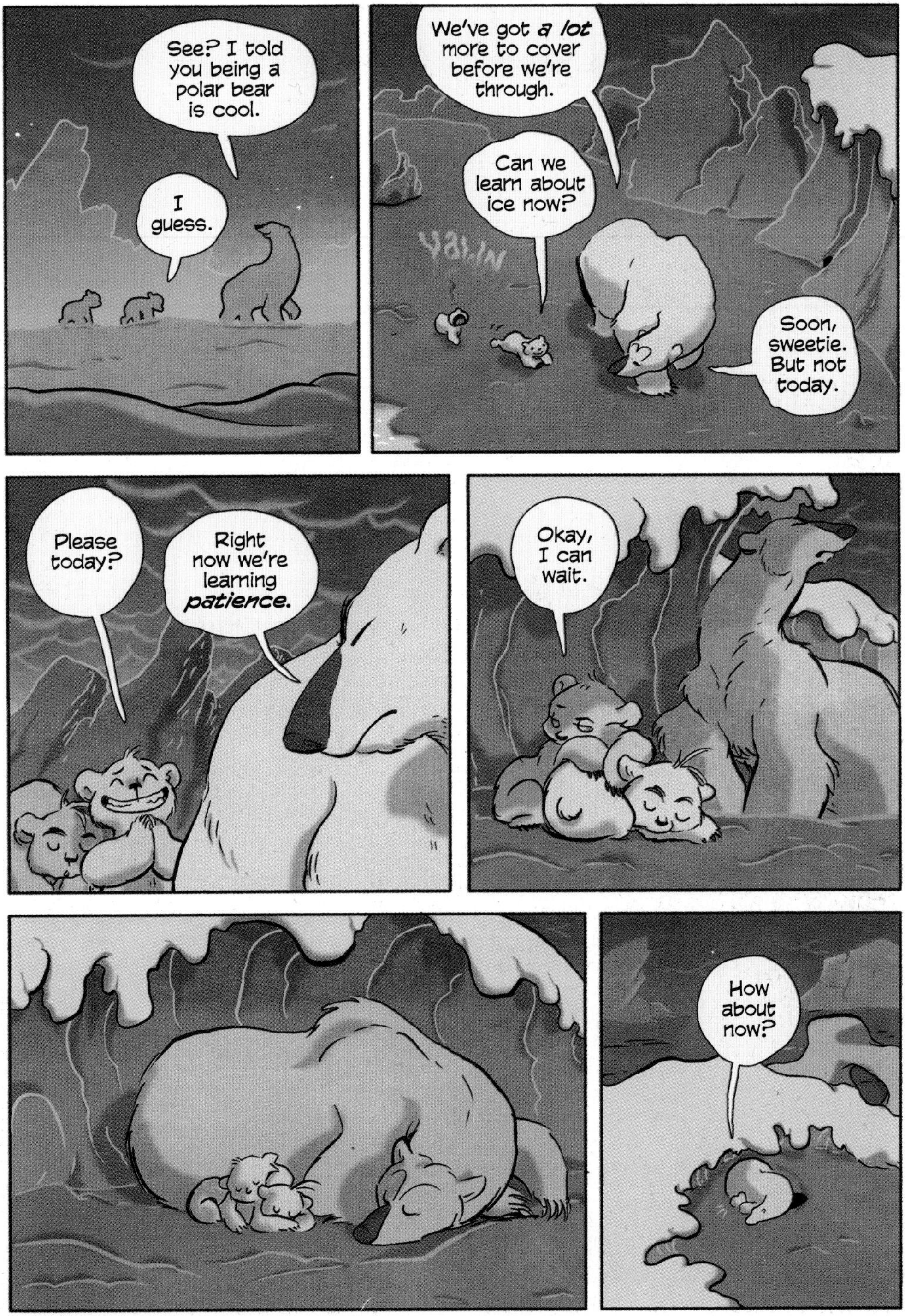

See? I told you being a polar bear is cool.
I guess.
We've got *a lot* more to cover before we're through.
Can we learn about ice now?
Soon, sweetie. But not today.
Please today?
Right now we're learning ***patience.***
Okay, I can wait.
How about now?

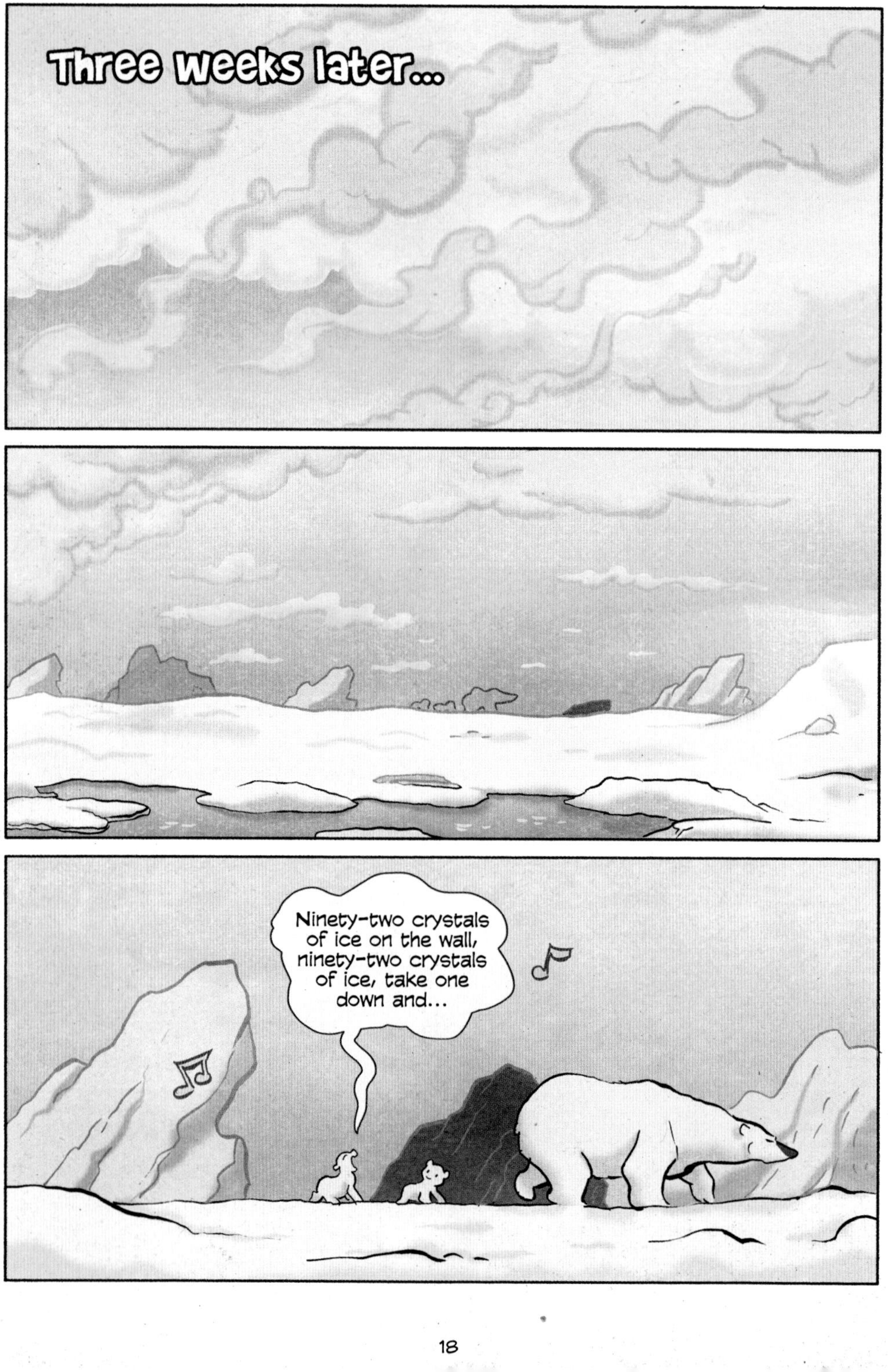
Three weeks later...
Ninety-two crystals of ice on the wall, ninety-two crystals of ice, take one down and...

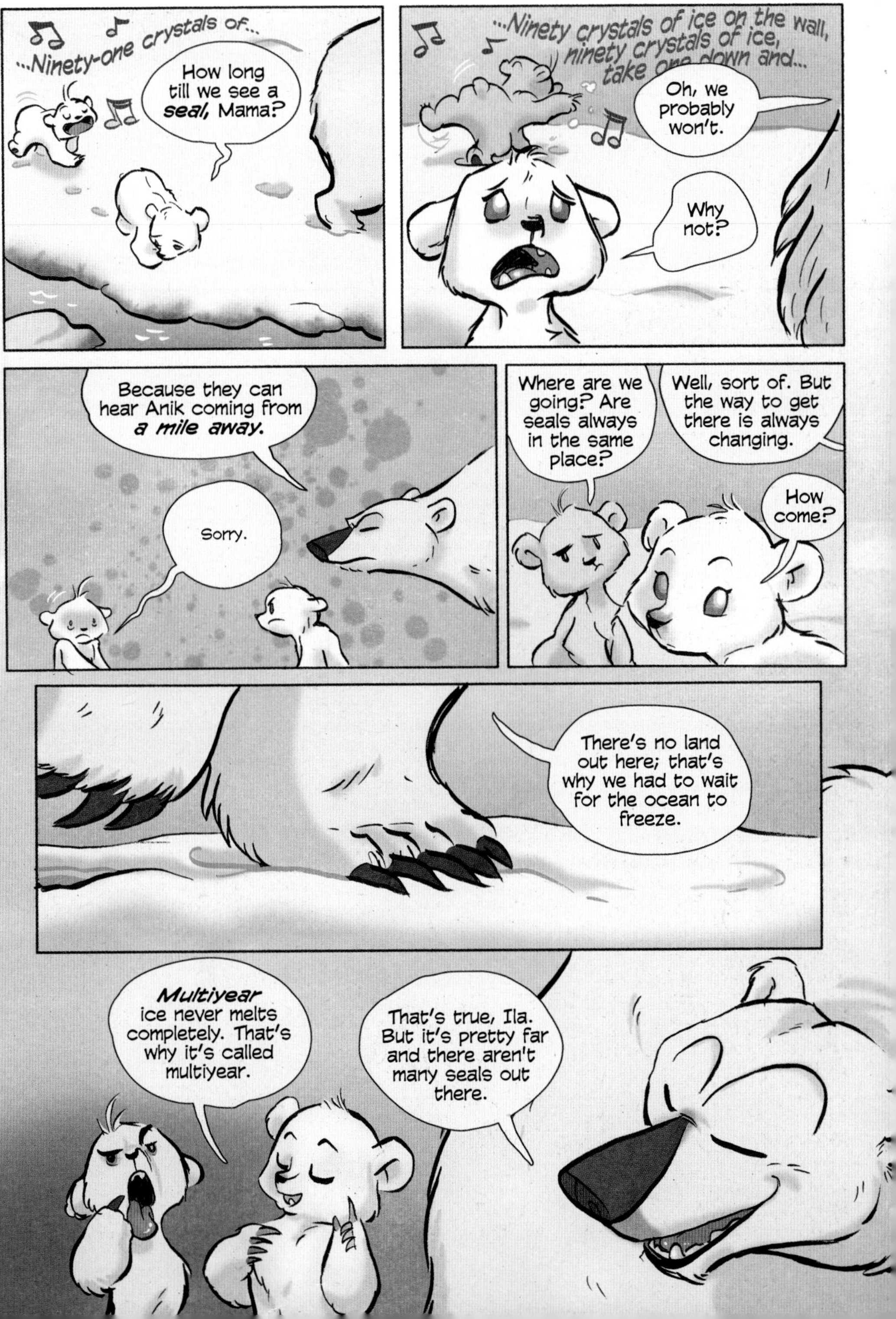
...Ninety-one crystals of...
How long till we see a *seal,* Mama?
...Ninety crystals of ice on the wall, ninety crystals of ice, take one down and...
Oh, we probably won't.
Why not?
Because they can hear Anik coming from *a mile away.*
Sorry.
Where are we going? Are seals always in the same place?
Well, sort of. But the way to get there is always changing.
How come?
There's no land out here; that's why we had to wait for the ocean to freeze.
Multiyear ice never melts completely. That's why it's called multiyear.
That's true, Ila. But it's pretty far and there aren't many seals out there.

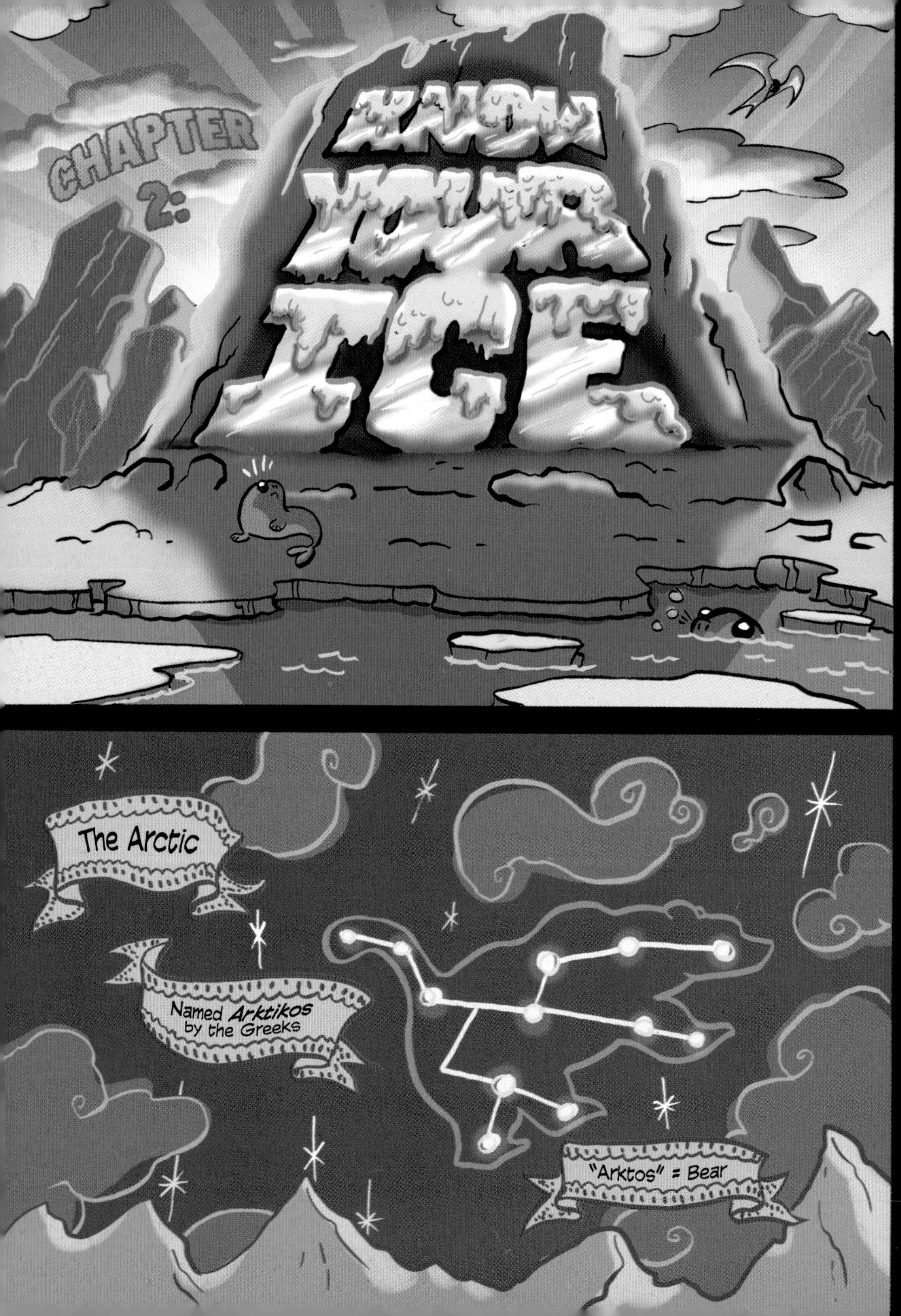

CHAPTER 2: KNOW YOUR ICE
The Arctic
Named *Arktikos* by the Greeks
"Arktos" = Bear

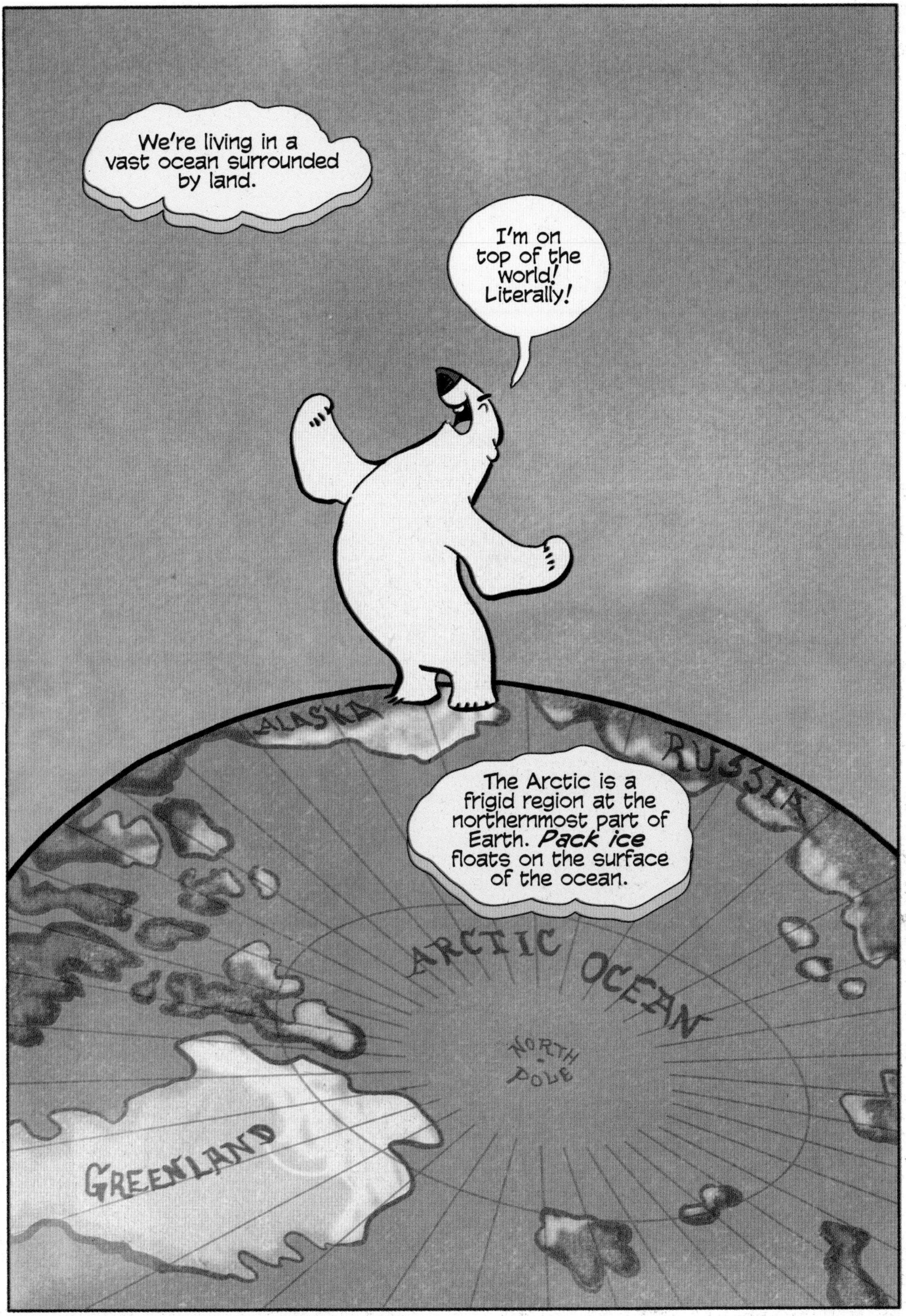
We're living in a vast ocean surrounded by land.
I'm on top of the world! Literally!
ALASKA
RUSSIA
The Arctic is a frigid region at the northernmost part of Earth. *Pack ice* floats on the surface of the ocean.
ARCTIC OCEAN
NORTH POLE
GREENLAND

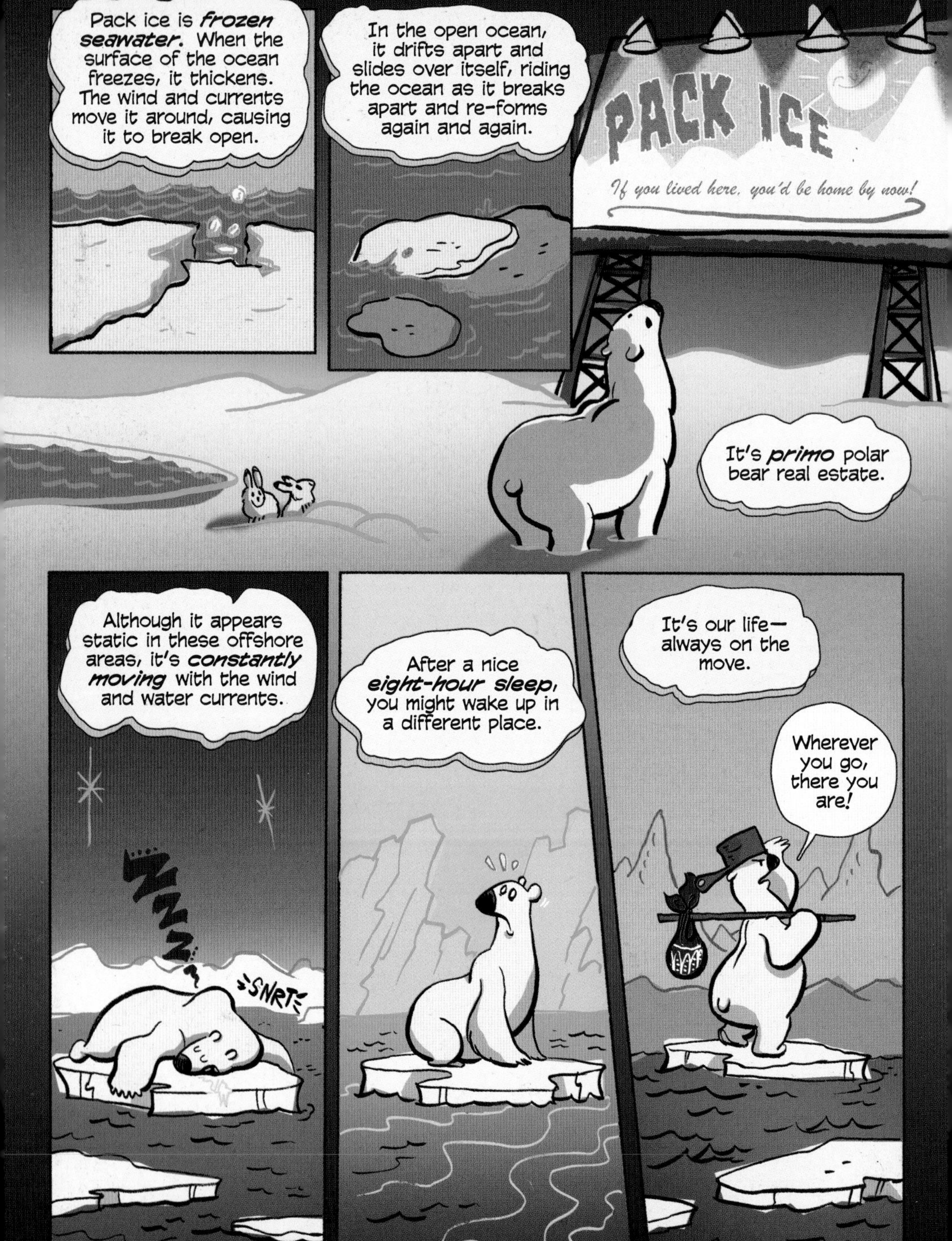
Pack ice is *frozen seawater.* When the surface of the ocean freezes, it thickens. The wind and currents move it around, causing it to break open.
In the open ocean, it drifts apart and slides over itself, riding the ocean as it breaks apart and re-forms again and again.
PACK ICE
If you lived here, you'd be home by now!
It's *primo* polar bear real estate.
Although it appears static in these offshore areas, it's *constantly moving* with the wind and water currents.
ZZZ
SNRT
After a nice *eight-hour sleep,* you might wake up in a different place.
It's our life—always on the move.
Wherever you go, there you are!

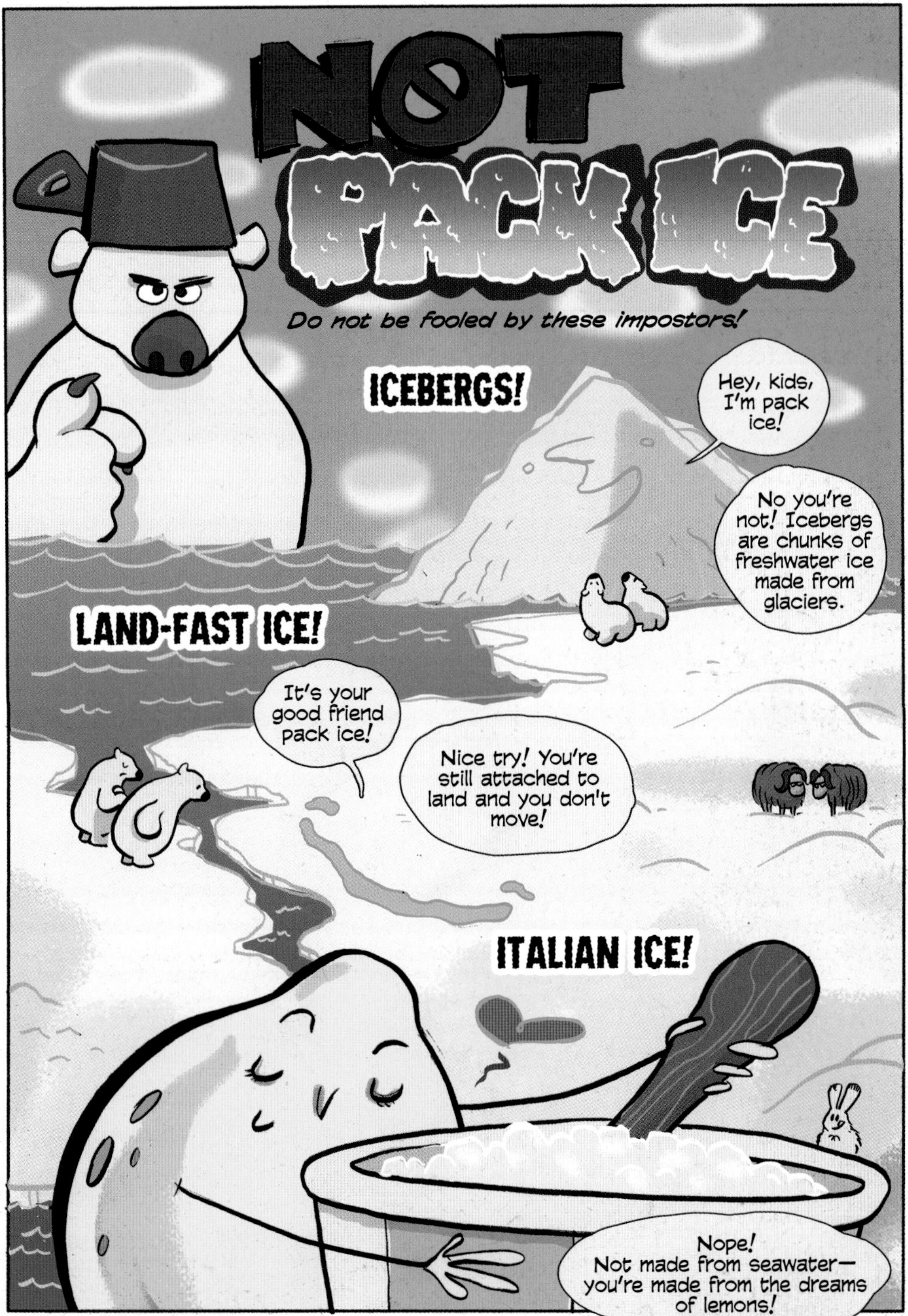
NOT PACK ICE
Do not be fooled by these impostors!
ICEBERGS!
Hey, kids, I'm pack ice!
No you're not! Icebergs are chunks of freshwater ice made from glaciers.
LAND-FAST ICE!
It's your good friend pack ice!
Nice try! You're still attached to land and you don't move!
ITALIAN ICE!
Nope! Not made from seawater— you're made from the dreams of lemons!

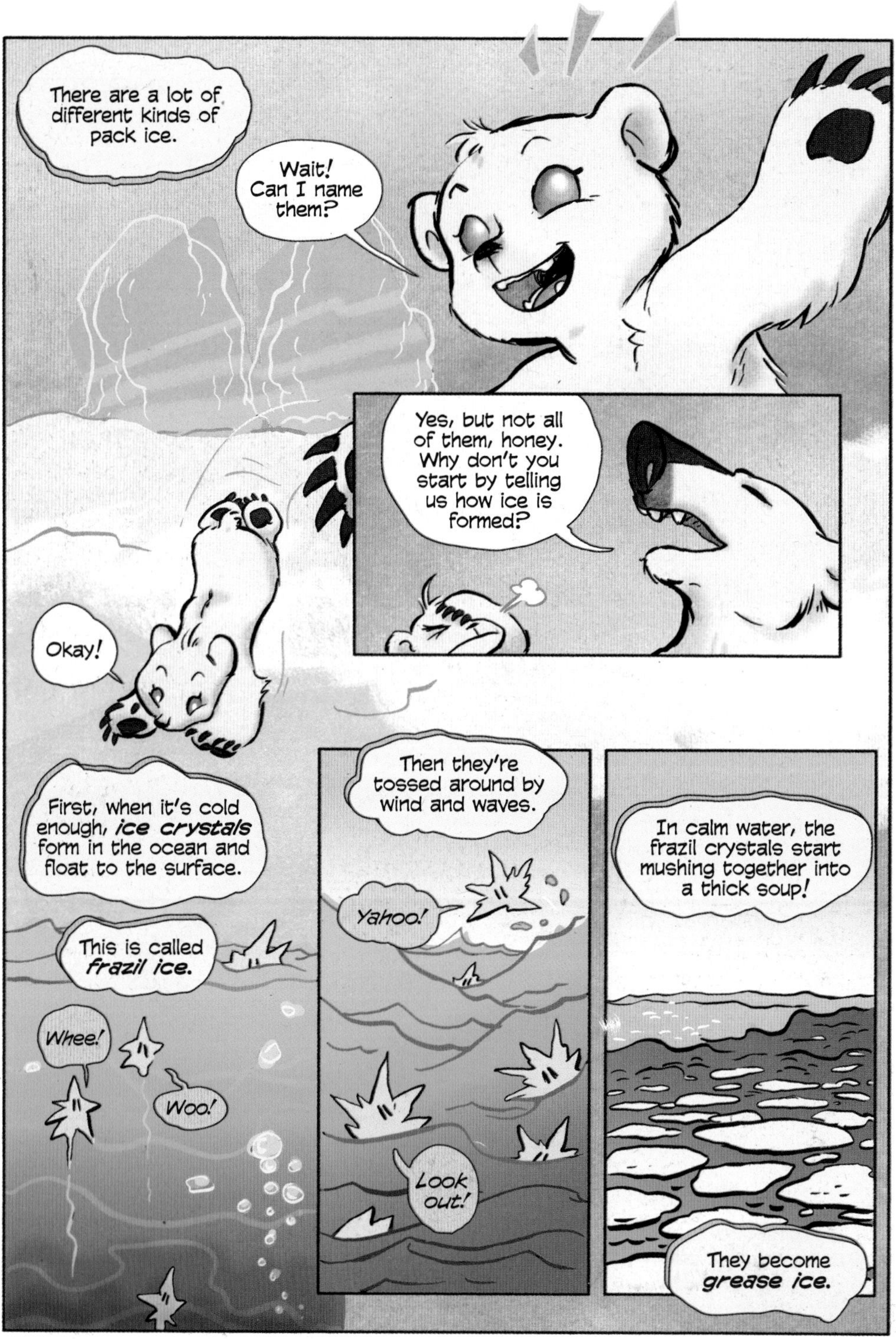
There are a lot of different kinds of pack ice.
Wait! Can I name them?
Yes, but not all of them, honey. Why don't you start by telling us how ice is formed?
Okay!
First, when it's cold enough, ***ice crystals*** form in the ocean and float to the surface.
This is called ***frazil ice.***
Whee!
Woo!
Then they're tossed around by wind and waves.
Yahoo!
Look out!
In calm water, the frazil crystals start mushing together into a thick soup!
They become ***grease ice.***

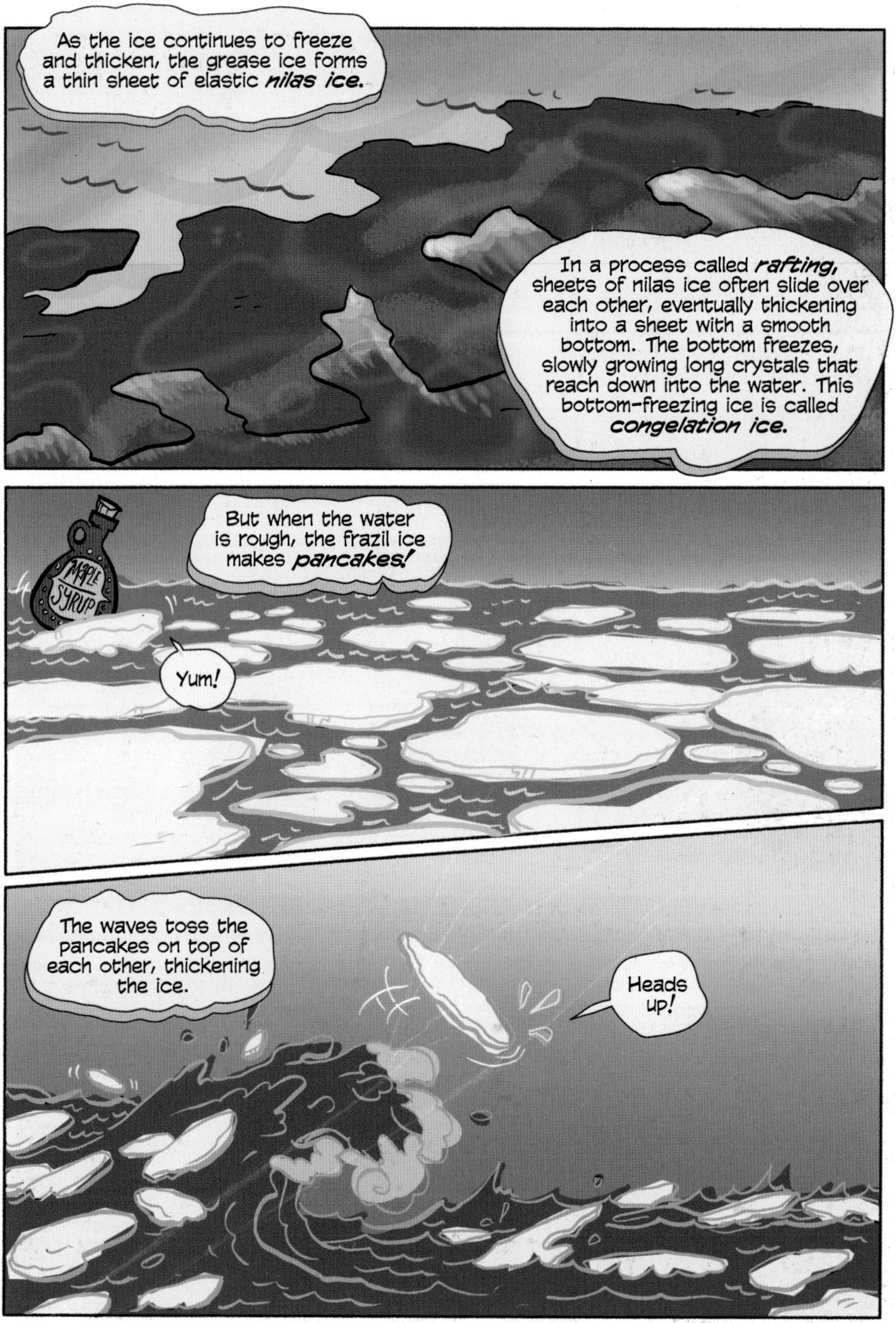

As the ice continues to freeze and thicken, the grease ice forms a thin sheet of elastic nilas ice.
In a process called rafting, sheets of nilas ice often slide over each other, eventually thickening into a sheet with a smooth bottom. The bottom freezes, slowly growing long crystals that reach down into the water. This bottom-freezing ice is called congelation ice.
MAPLE SYRUP
But when the water is rough, the frazil ice makes pancakes!
Yum!
The waves toss the pancakes on top of each other, thickening the ice.
Heads up!

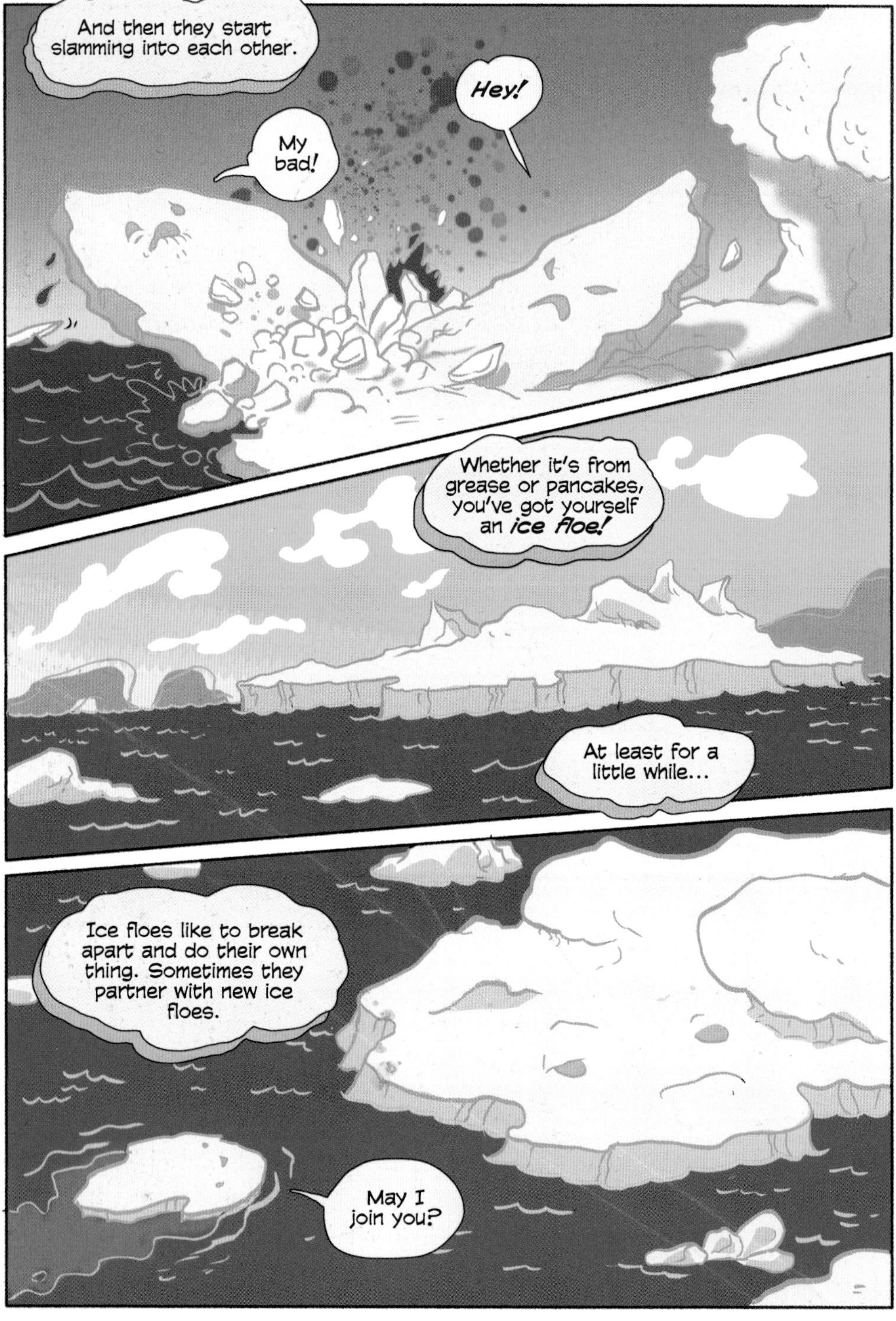
And then they start slamming into each other.
My bad!
Hey!
Whether it's from grease or pancakes, you've got yourself an *ice floe!*
At least for a little while...
Ice floes like to break apart and do their own thing. Sometimes they partner with new ice floes.
May I join you?

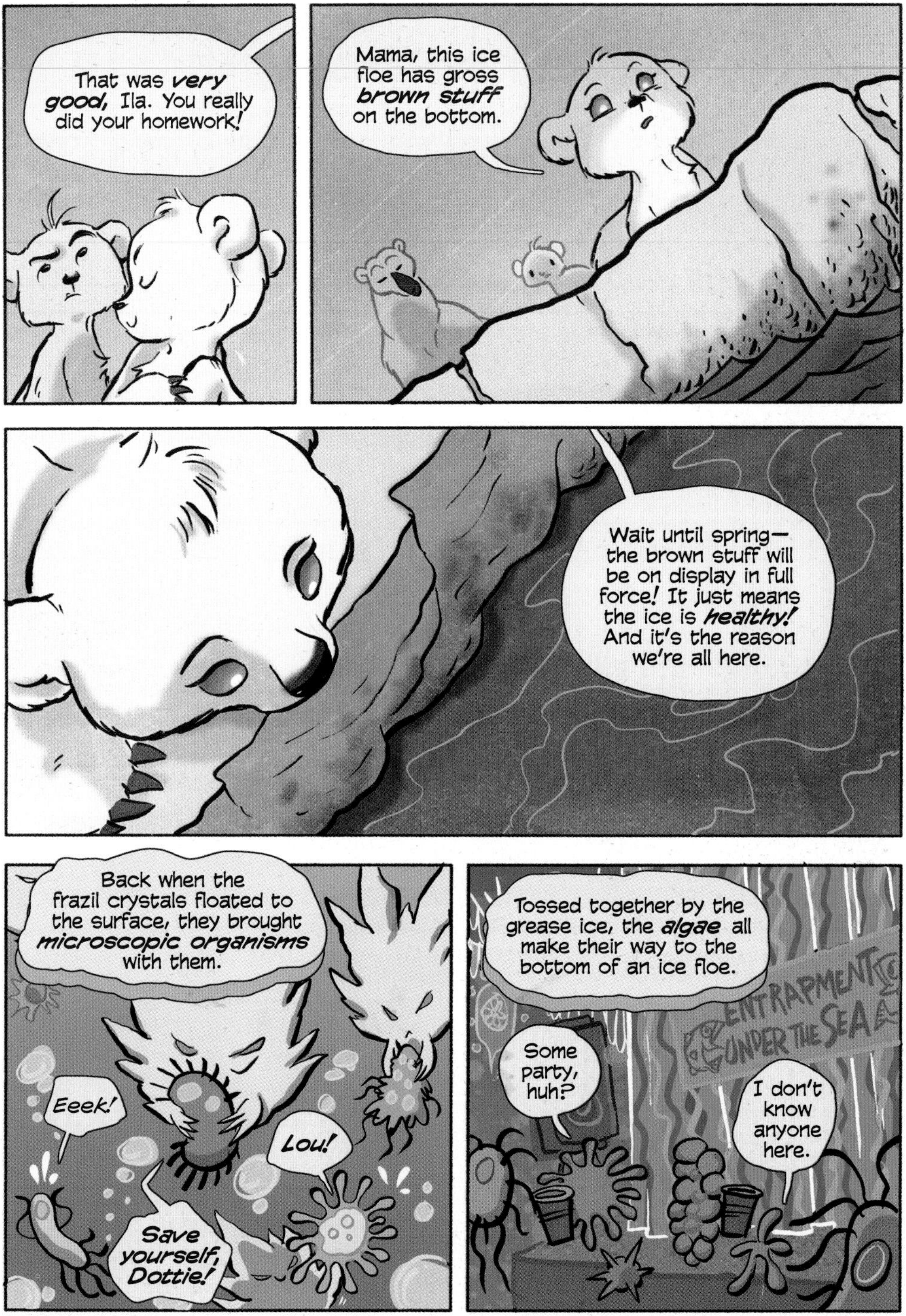
That was *very good,* Ila. You really did your homework!
Mama, this ice floe has gross *brown stuff* on the bottom.
Wait until spring—the brown stuff will be on display in full force! It just means the ice is *healthy!* And it's the reason we're all here.
Back when the frazil crystals floated to the surface, they brought *microscopic organisms* with them.
Eeek!
Lou!
Save yourself, Dottie!
Tossed together by the grease ice, the *algae* all make their way to the bottom of an ice floe.
ENTRAPMENT UNDER THE SEA
Some party, huh?
I don't know anyone here.

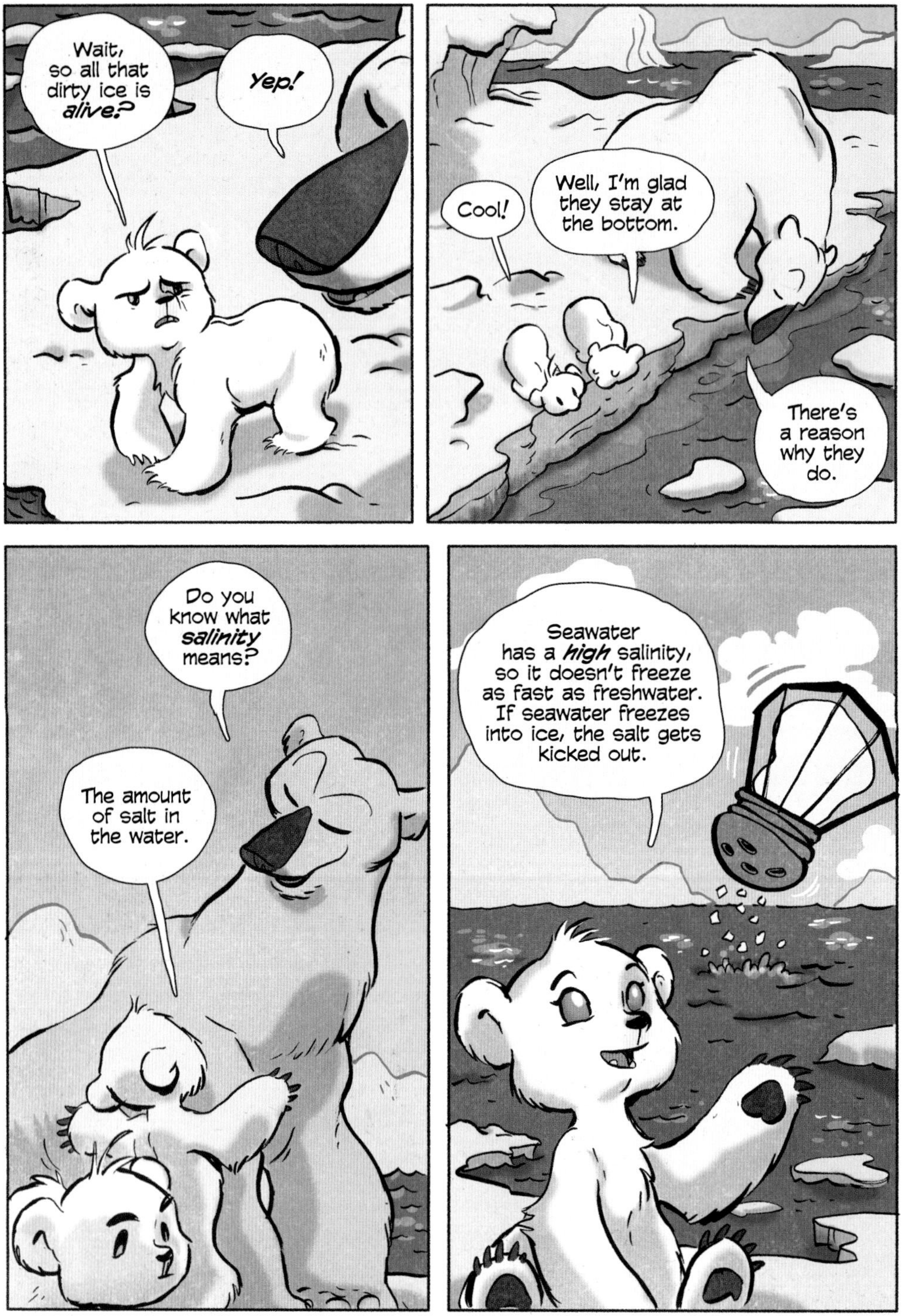
Wait, so all that dirty ice is alive?
Yep!
Cool!
Well, I'm glad they stay at the bottom.
There's a reason why they do.
Do you know what salinity means?
The amount of salt in the water.
Seawater has a high salinity, so it doesn't freeze as fast as freshwater. If seawater freezes into ice, the salt gets kicked out.

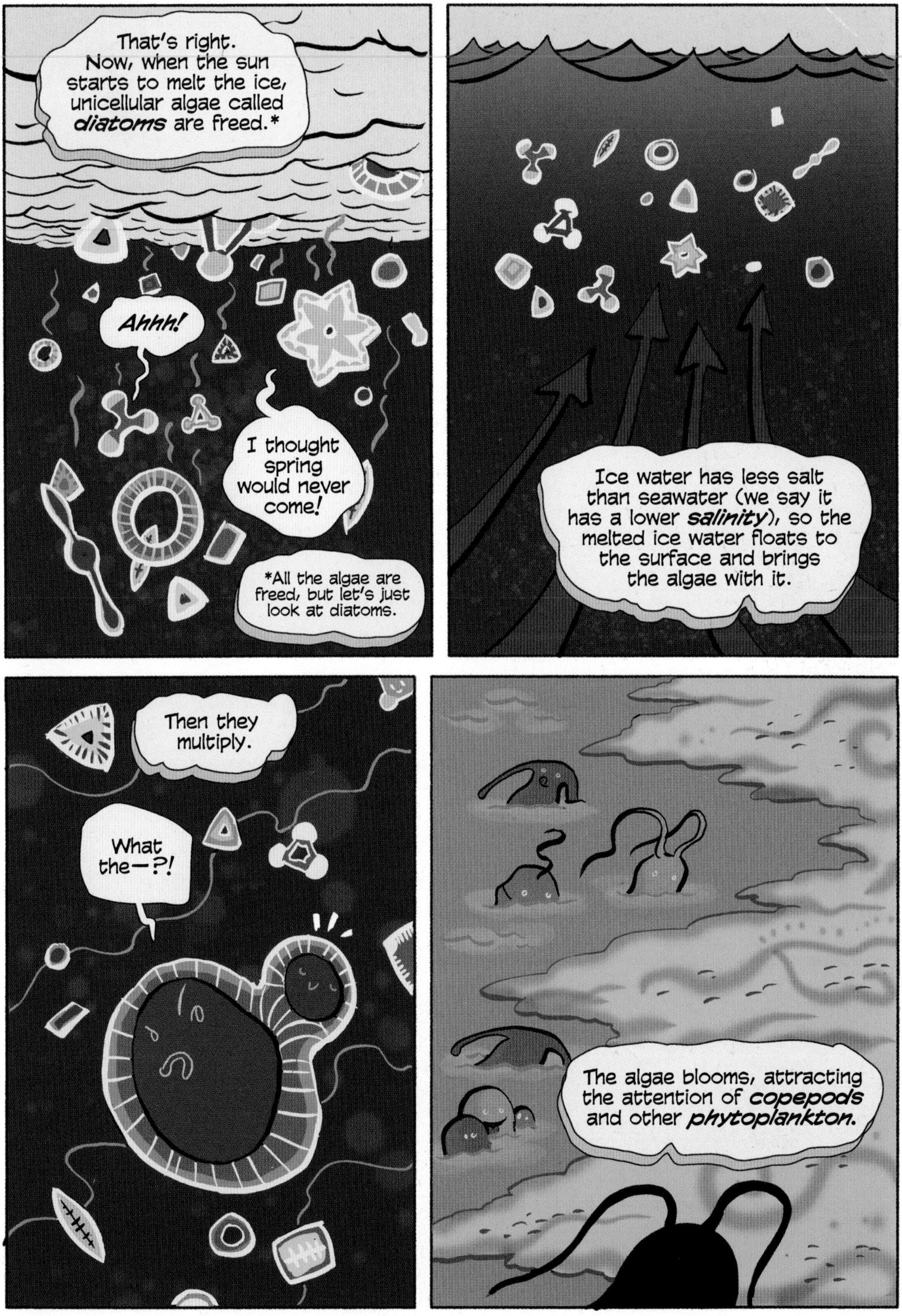
That's right. Now, when the sun starts to melt the ice, unicellular algae called *diatoms* are freed.*
Ahhh!
I thought spring would never come!
*All the algae are freed, but let's just look at diatoms.
Ice water has less salt than seawater (we say it has a lower *salinity*), so the melted ice water floats to the surface and brings the algae with it.
Then they multiply.
What the—?!
The algae blooms, attracting the attention of *copepods* and other *phytoplankton*.

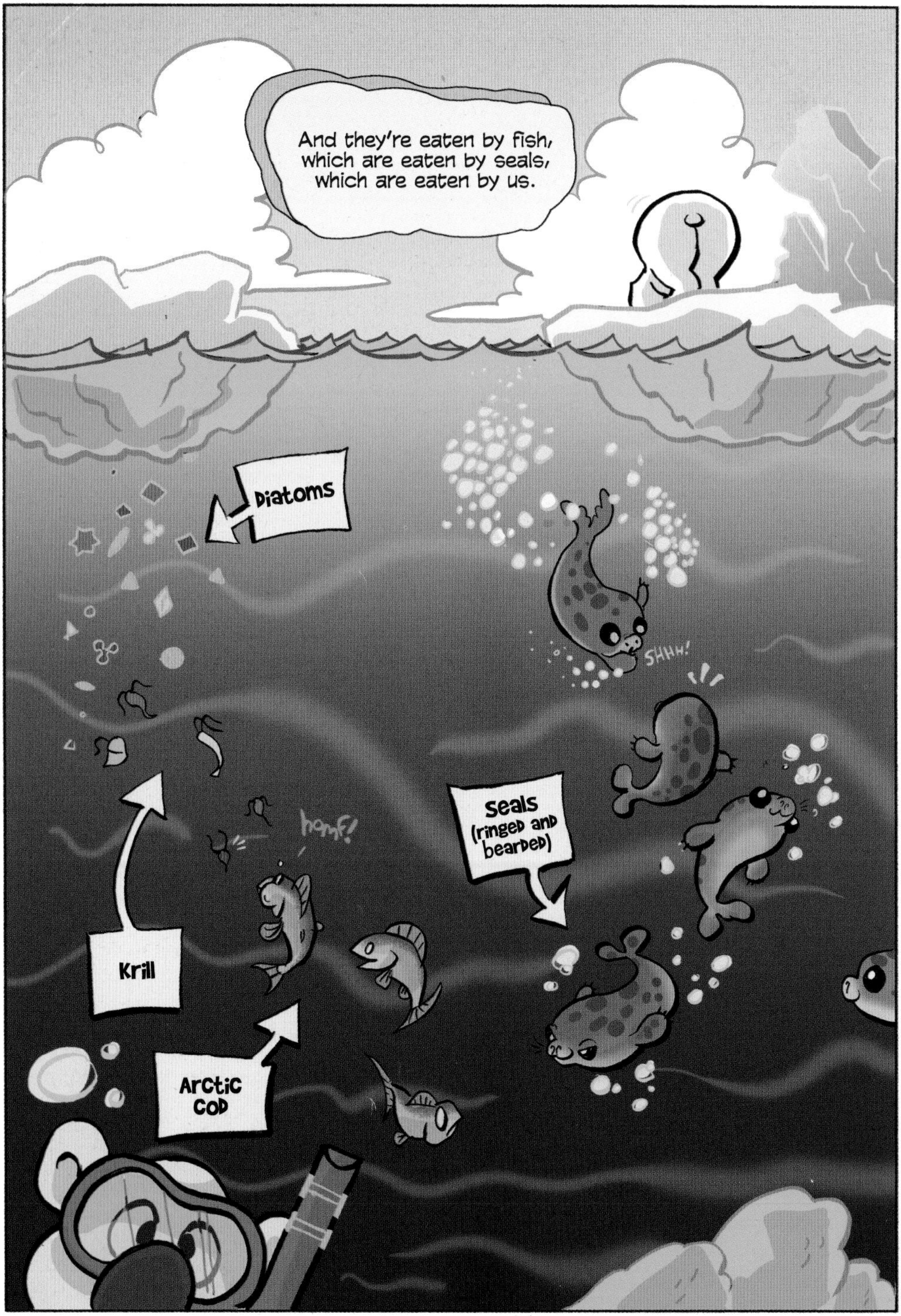
And they're eaten by fish, which are eaten by seals, which are eaten by us.
Diatoms
SHHH!
Seals (ringed and bearded)
Krill
Arctic Cod

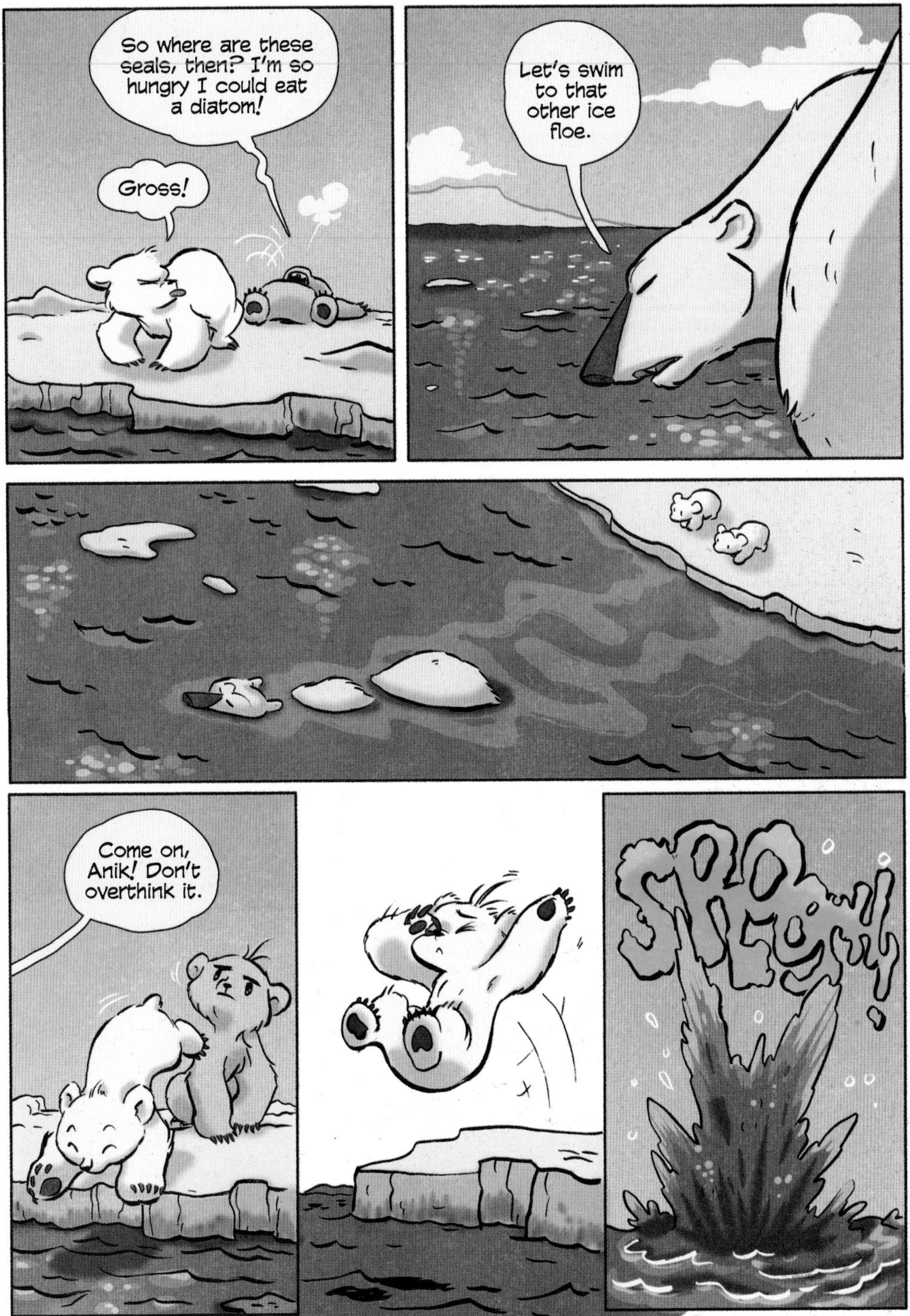
So where are these seals, then? I'm so hungry I could eat a diatom!
Gross!
Let's swim to that other ice floe.
Come on, Anik! Don't overthink it.
SPLOOSH!

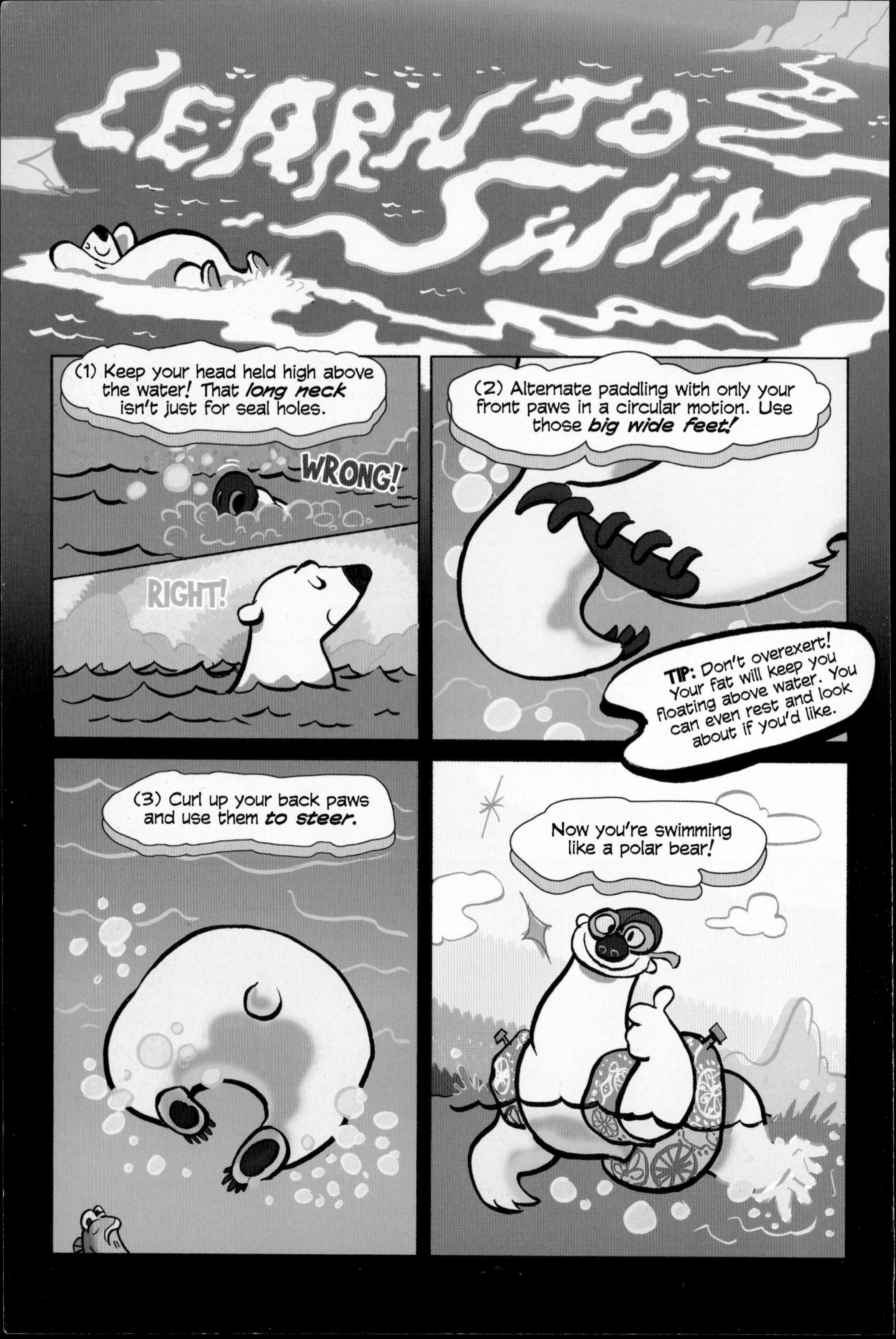
LEARN TO SWIM
(1) Keep your head held high above the water! That long neck isn't just for seal holes.
WRONG!
RIGHT!
(2) Alternate paddling with only your front paws in a circular motion. Use those big wide feet!
TIP: Don't overexert! Your fat will keep you floating above water. You can even rest and look about if you'd like.
(3) Curl up your back paws and use them to steer.
Now you're swimming like a polar bear!

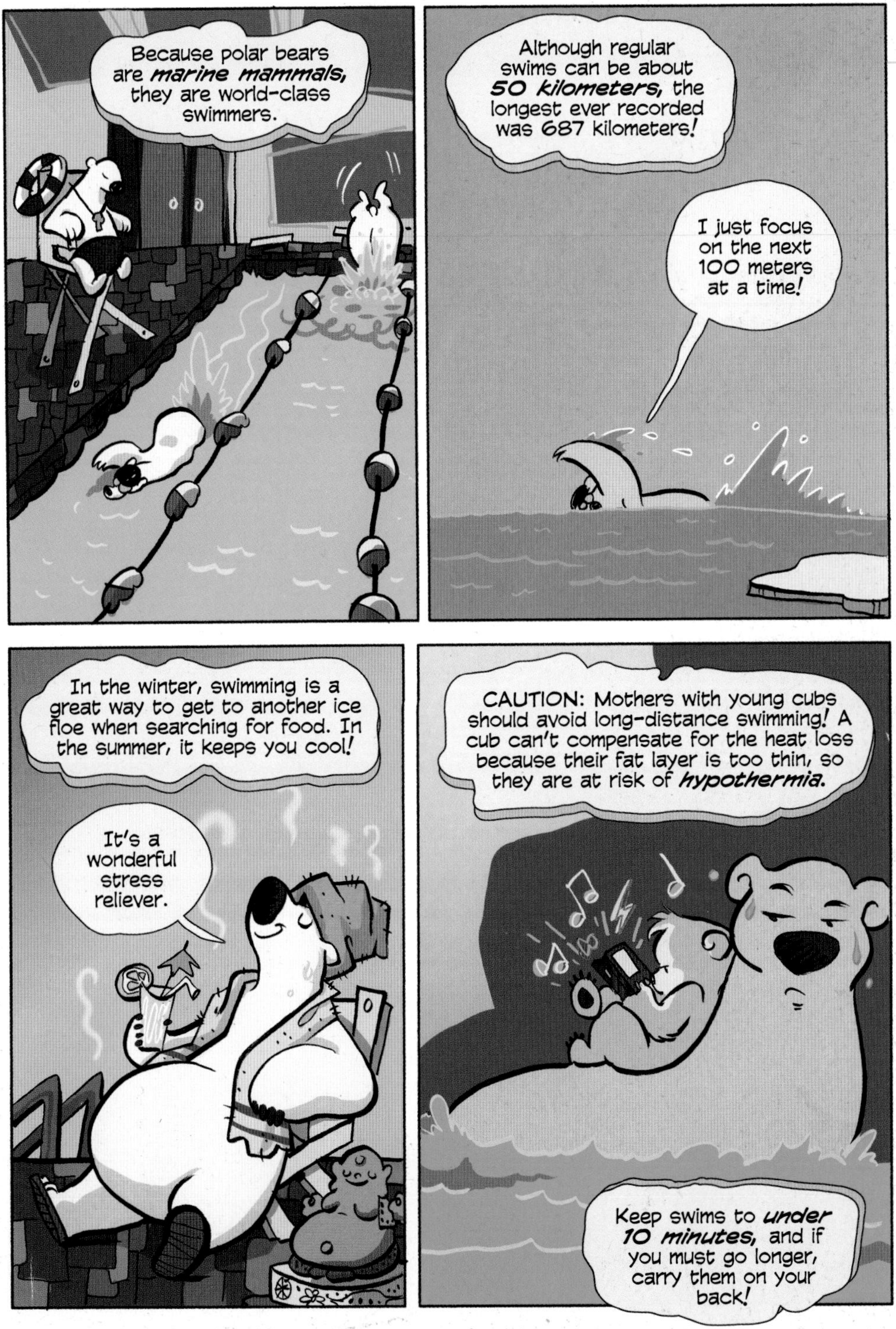
Because polar bears are ***marine mammals,*** they are world-class swimmers.
Although regular swims can be about ***50 kilometers,*** the longest ever recorded was 687 kilometers!
I just focus on the next 100 meters at a time!
In the winter, swimming is a great way to get to another ice floe when searching for food. In the summer, it keeps you cool!
It's a wonderful stress reliever.
CAUTION: Mothers with young cubs should avoid long-distance swimming! A cub can't compensate for the heat loss because their fat layer is too thin, so they are at risk of ***hypothermia.***
Keep swims to ***under 10 minutes,*** and if you must go longer, carry them on your back!

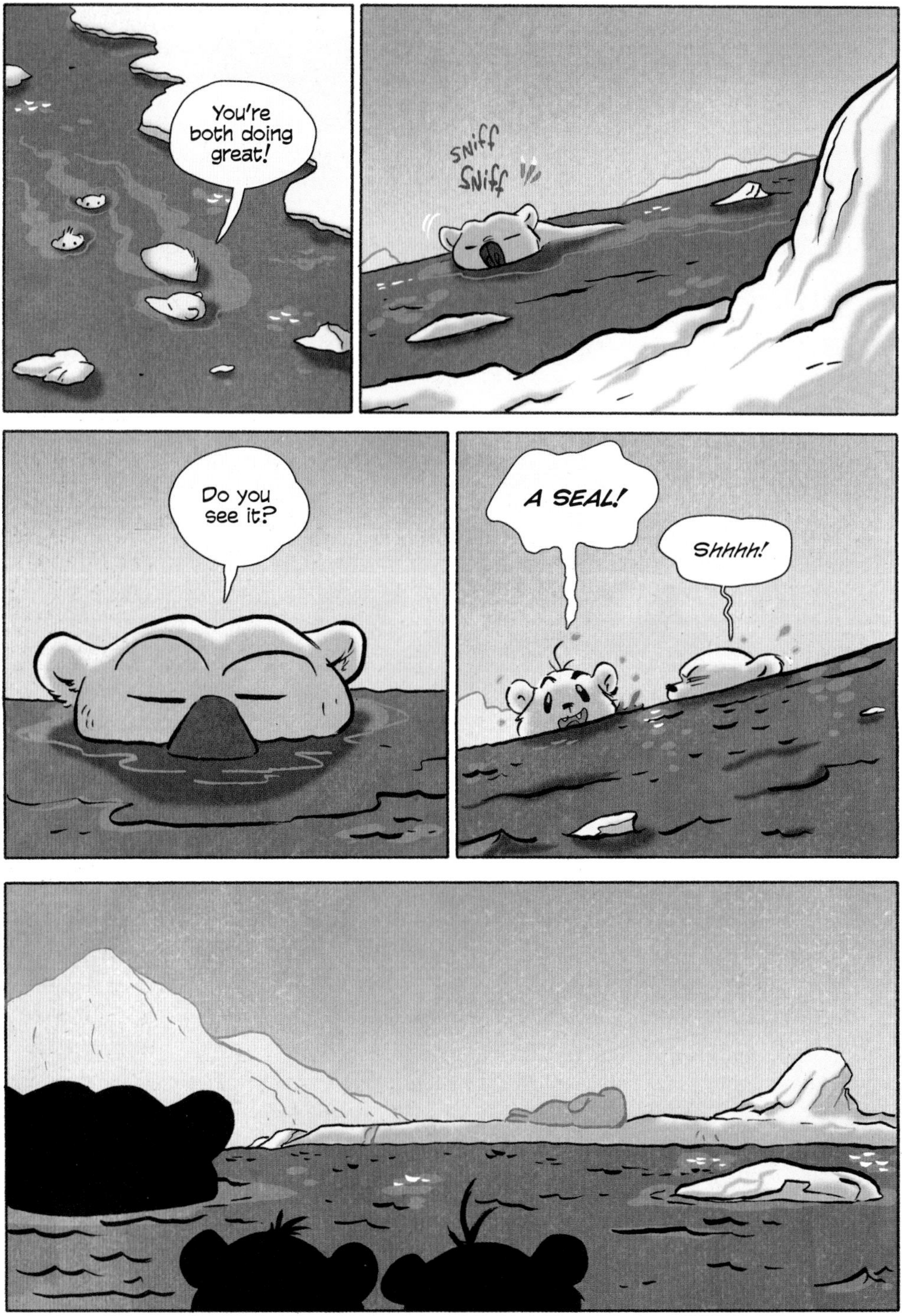
You're both doing great!
SNiff
SNiff
Do you see it?
A SEAL!
Shhhh!

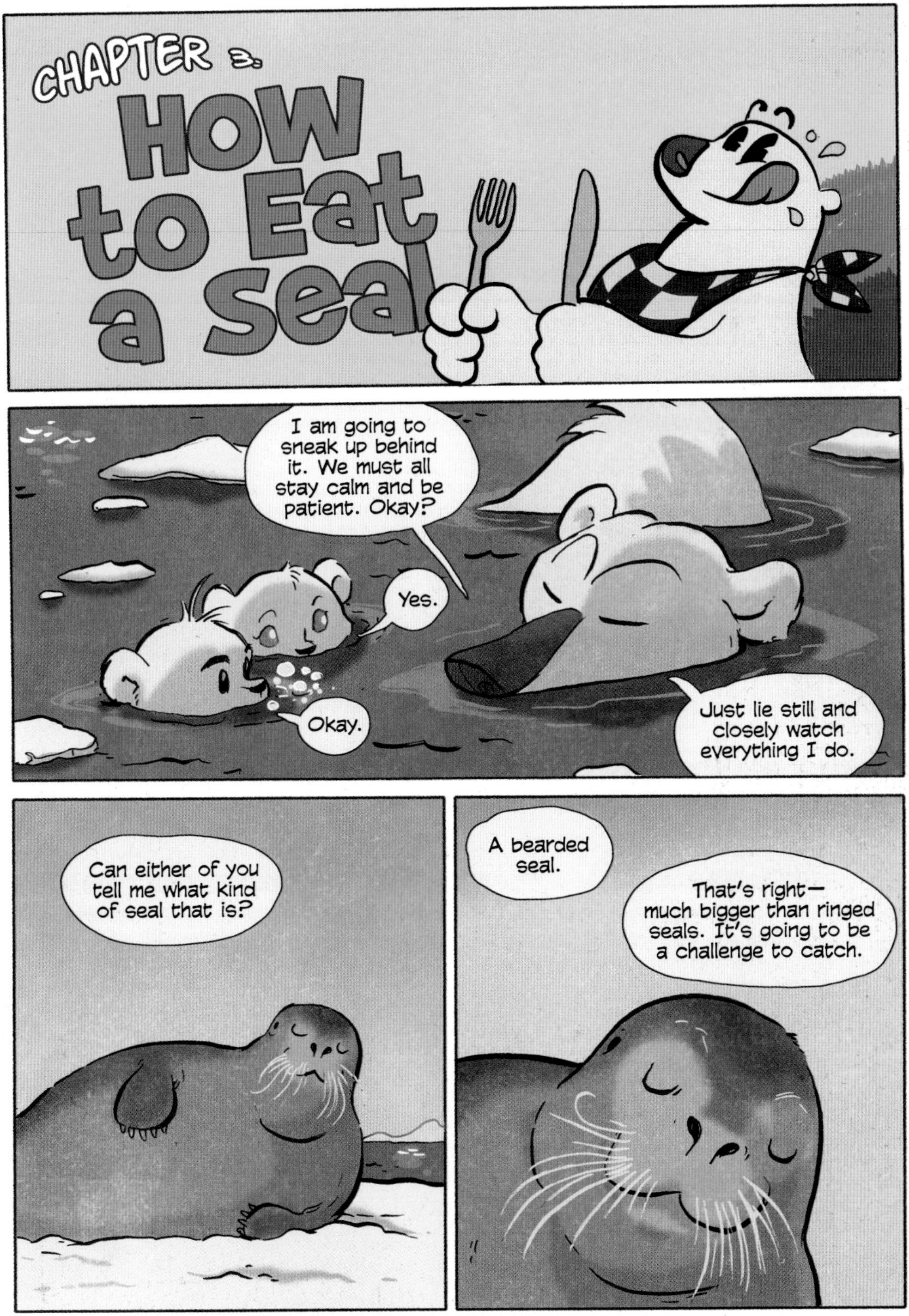
CHAPTER 3:
HOW to Eat a Seal
I am going to sneak up behind it. We must all stay calm and be patient. Okay?
Yes.
Okay.
Just lie still and closely watch everything I do.
Can either of you tell me what kind of seal that is?
A bearded seal.
That's right— much bigger than ringed seals. It's going to be a challenge to catch.

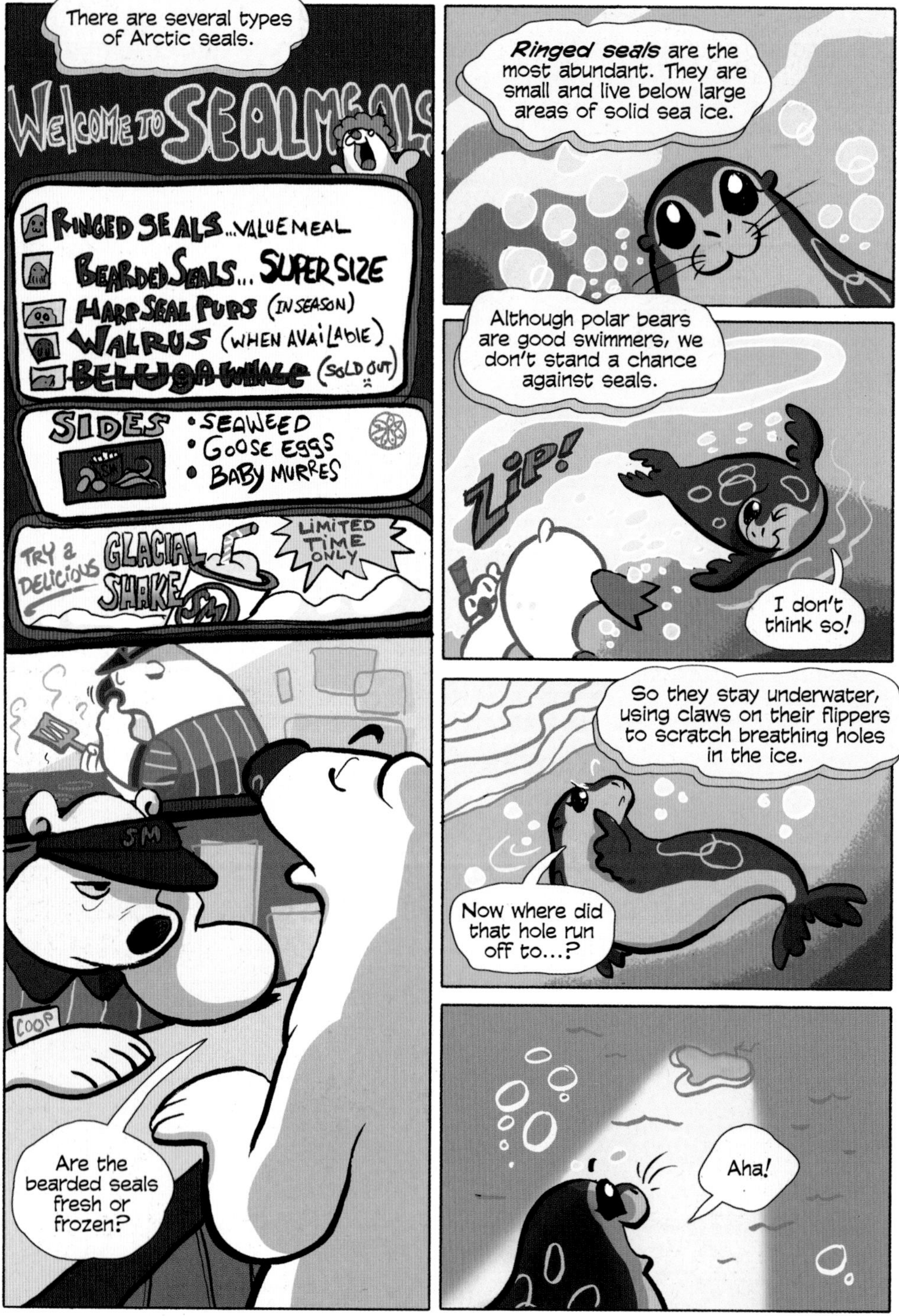

There are several types of Arctic seals.
WELCOME TO SEALM
RINGED SEALS...VALUE MEAL
BEARDED SEALS... SUPER SIZE
HARP SEAL PUPS (IN SEASON)
WALRUS (WHEN AVAILABLE)
BELUGA WHALE (SOLD OUT)
SIDES
• SEAWEED
• GOOSE EGGS
• BABY MURRES
TRY a DELICIOUS GLACIAL SHAKE
LIMITED TIME ONLY
SM
COOP
Are the bearded seals fresh or frozen?
Ringed seals are the most abundant. They are small and live below large areas of solid sea ice.
Although polar bears are good swimmers, we don't stand a chance against seals.
ZIP!
I don't think so!
So they stay underwater, using claws on their flippers to scratch breathing holes in the ice.
Now where did that hole run off to...?
Aha!

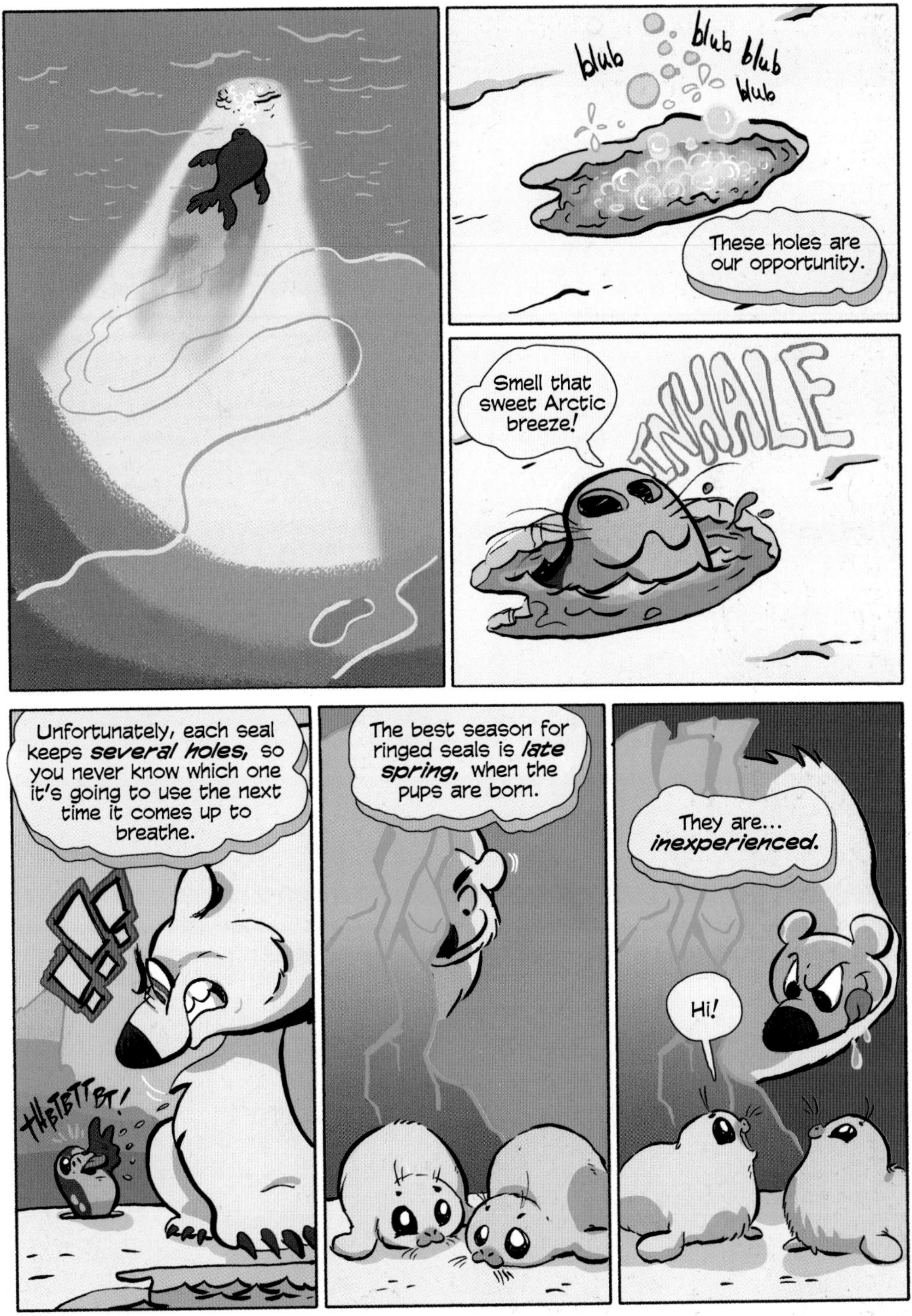

blub
blub blub
blub
These holes are our opportunity.
Smell that sweet Arctic breeze!
INHALE
Unfortunately, each seal keeps *several holes,* so you never know which one it's going to use the next time it comes up to breathe.
THBTBTTBT!
The best season for ringed seals is *late spring,* when the pups are born.
They are... *inexperienced.*
Hi!

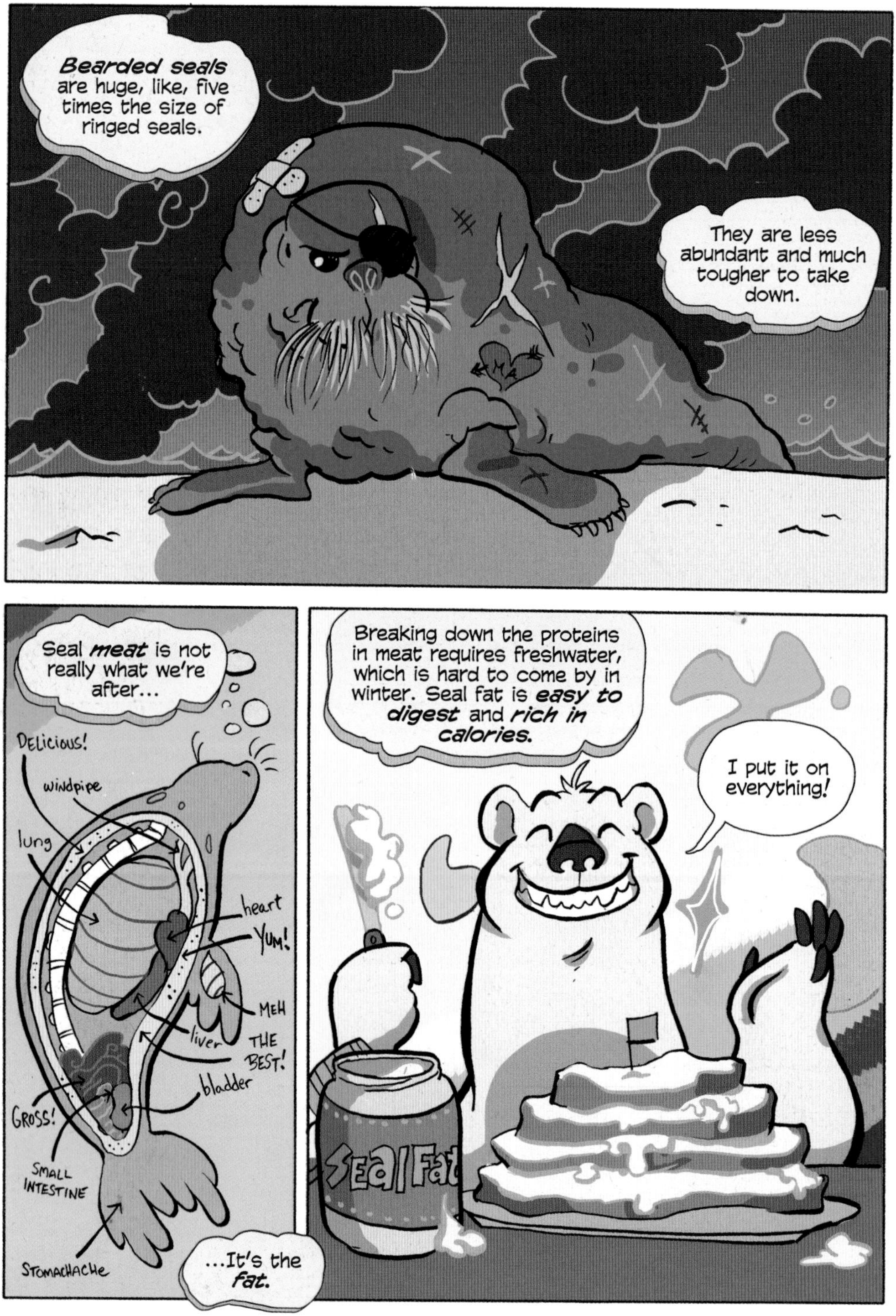
Bearded seals are huge, like, five times the size of ringed seals.
They are less abundant and much tougher to take down.
Seal meat is not really what we're after...
DELICIOUS!
windpipe
lung
heart
YUM!
MEH
liver
THE BEST!
bladder
GROSS!
SMALL INTESTINE
STOMACHACHE
...It's the fat.
Breaking down the proteins in meat requires freshwater, which is hard to come by in winter. Seal fat is easy to digest and rich in calories.
I put it on everything!
SealFat

All right, you two wait right here. Stay hidden and quiet.

Prip!

SpsHH

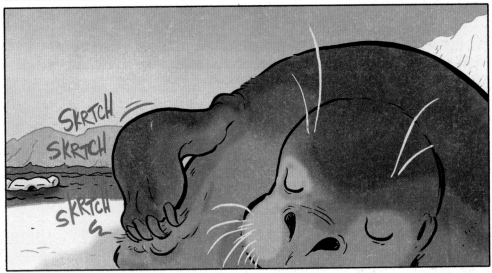

SKRTCH
SKRTCH
SKRTCH

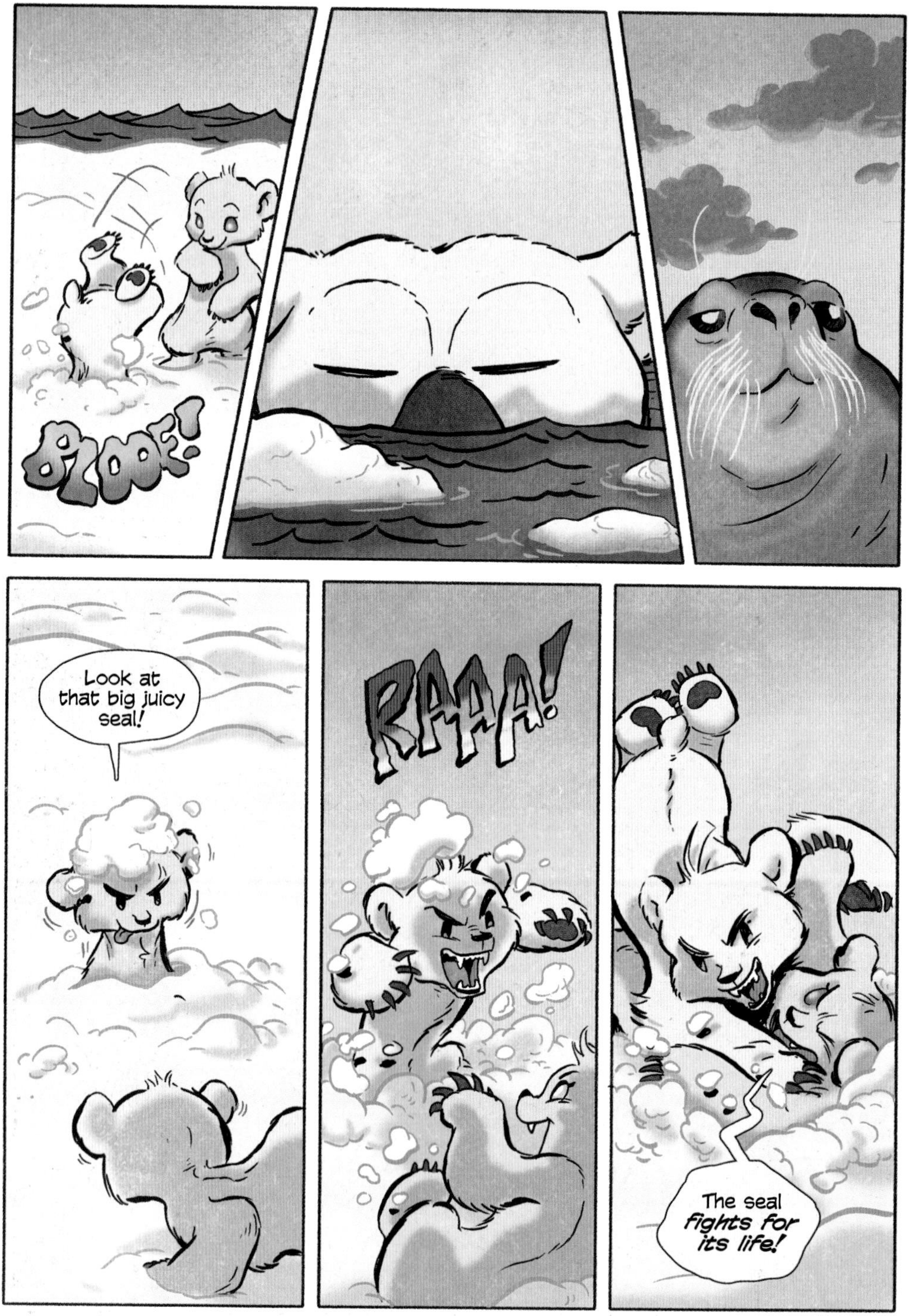
BLOOF!
Look at that big juicy seal!
RAAA!
The seal fights for its life!

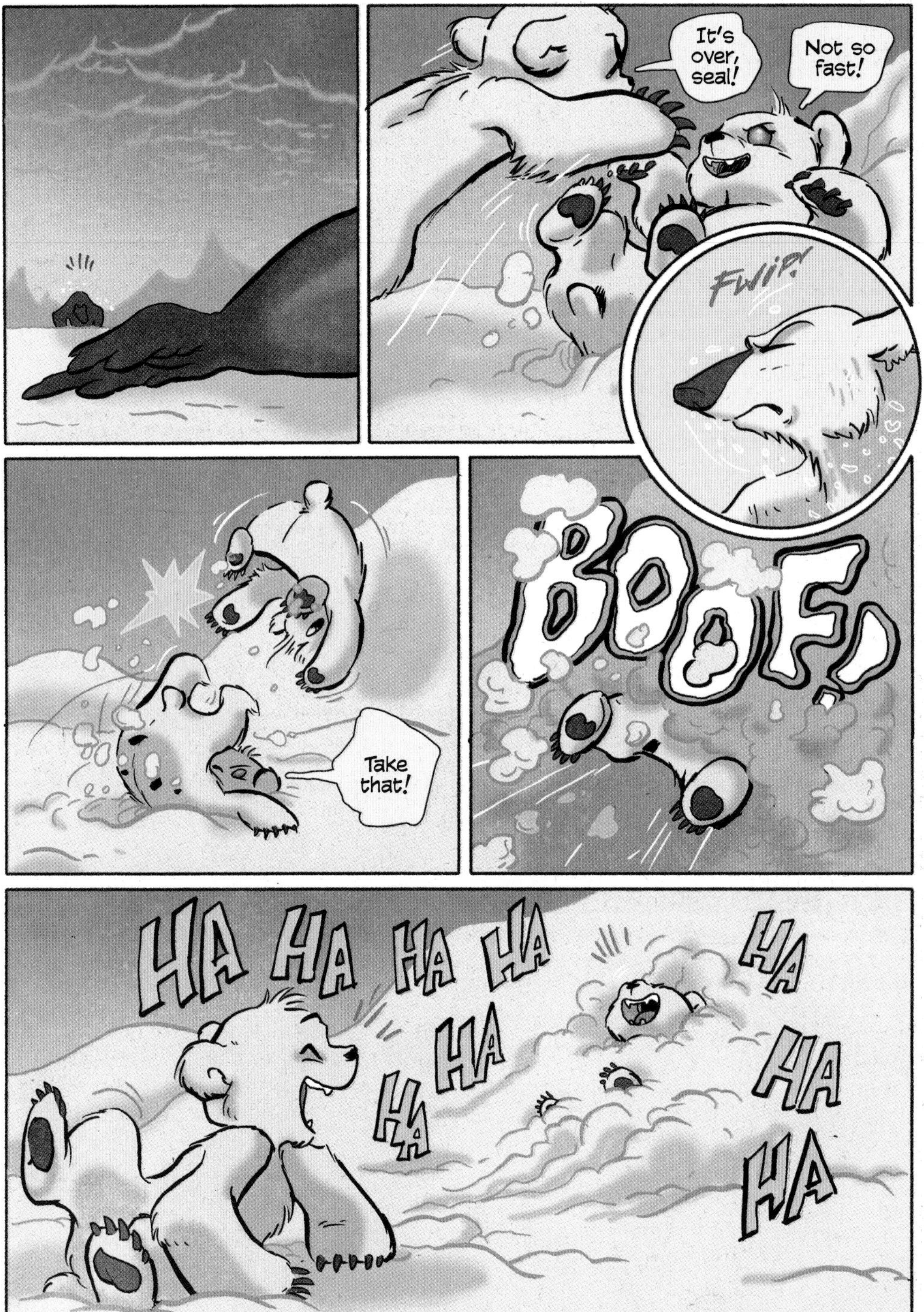
It's over, seal!
Not so fast!
FWIP!
Take that!
BOOF!
HA HA HA HA
HA HA
HA
HA
HA HA HA

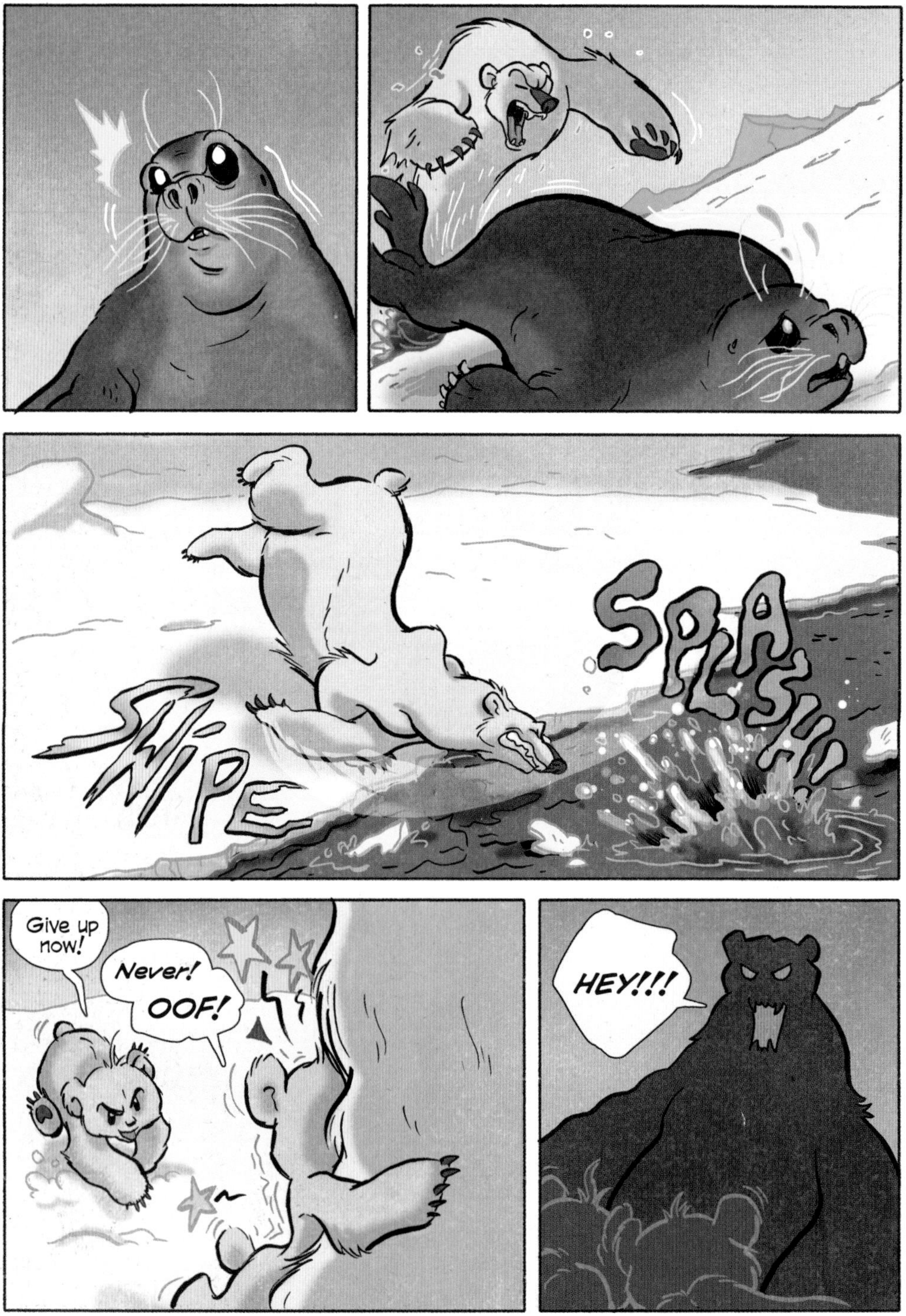
SWIPE
SPLASH!!
Give up now!
Never!
OOF!
HEY!!!

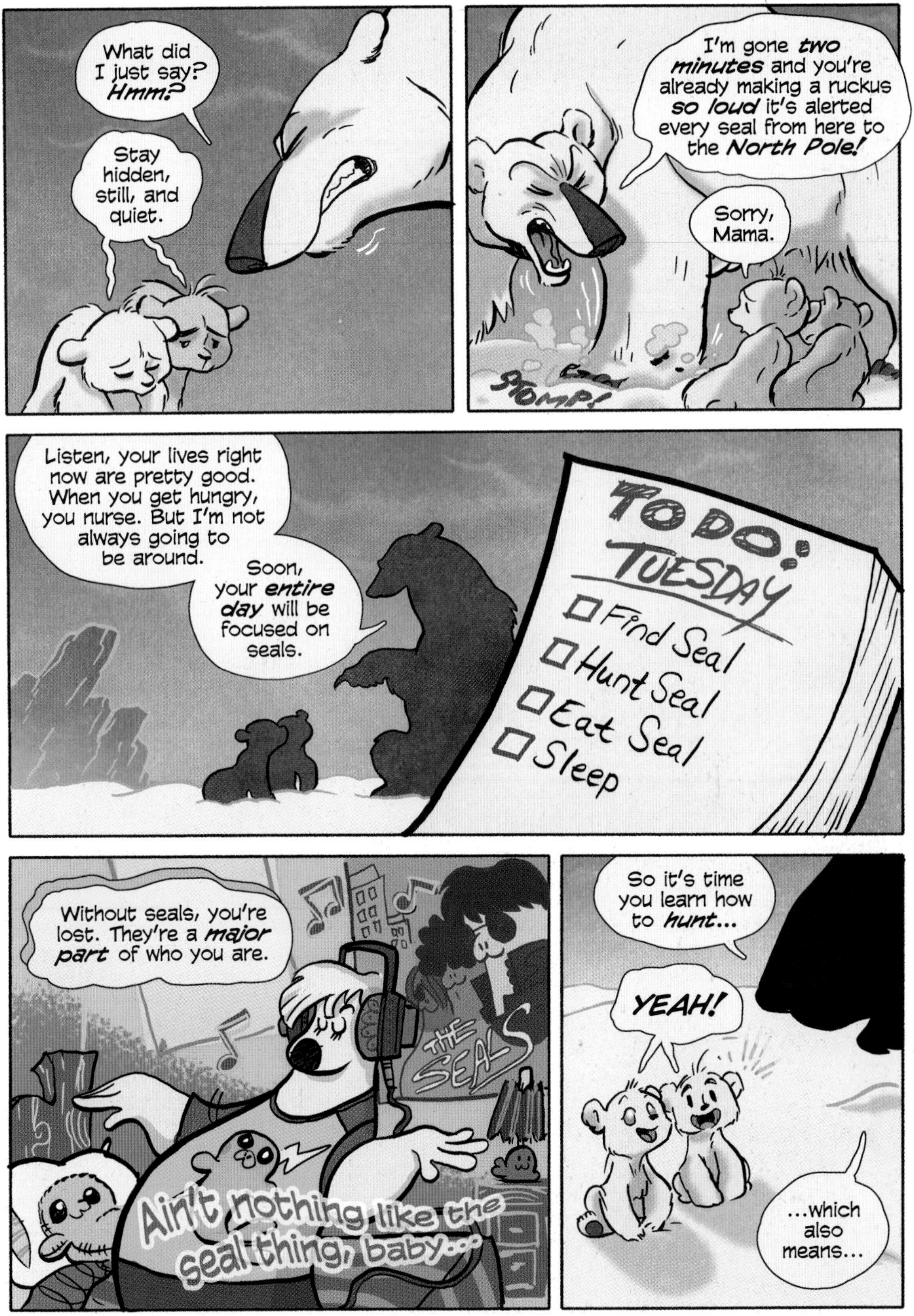
What did I just say? *Hmm?*
Stay hidden, still, and quiet.
I'm gone **two minutes** and you're already making a ruckus **so loud** it's alerted every seal from here to the **North Pole!**
STOMP!
Sorry, Mama.
Listen, your lives right now are pretty good. When you get hungry, you nurse. But I'm not always going to be around.
Soon, your **entire day** will be focused on seals.
TO DO:
TUESDAY
Find Seal
Hunt Seal
Eat Seal
Sleep
Without seals, you're lost. They're a **major part** of who you are.
THE SEALS
Ain't nothing like the seal thing, baby...
So it's time you learn how to **hunt**...
YEAH!
...which also means...

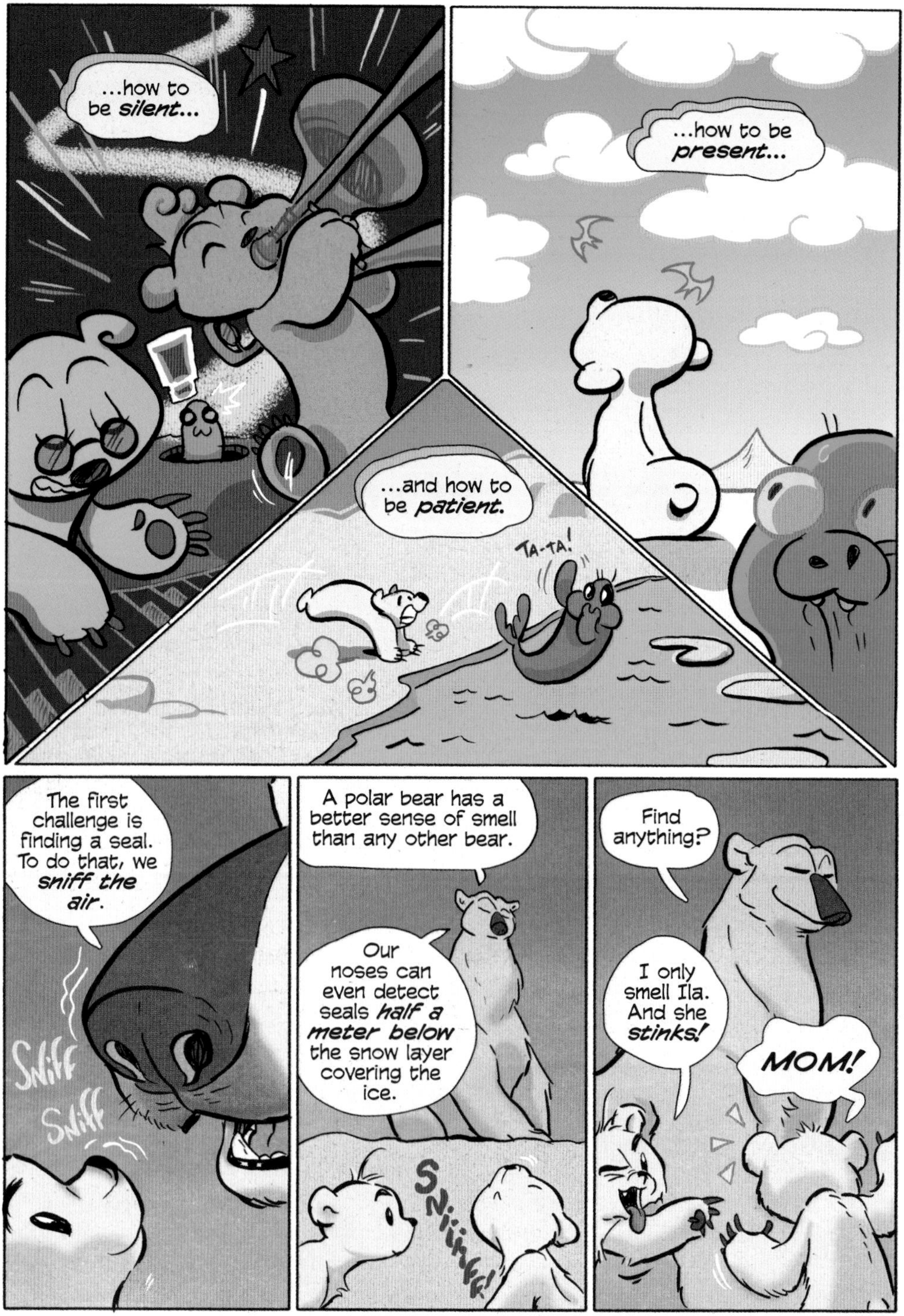
...how to be *silent*...
...how to be *present*...
...and how to be *patient*.
TA-TA!
The first challenge is finding a seal. To do that, we ***sniff the air***.
SNIFF
SNIFF
A polar bear has a better sense of smell than any other bear.
Our noses can even detect seals ***half a meter below*** the snow layer covering the ice.
SNIIIFF!
Find anything?
I only smell Ila. And she ***stinks!***
MOM!

Once you discover a seal, there are *two main strategies* to choose between, and some variations and techniques within those strategies.

OFFICIAL STRATEGY 1
STALKING

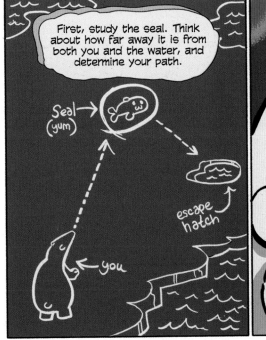

First, study the seal. Think about how far away it is from both you and the water, and determine your path.

Seal (yum) →

escape hatch →

← you

You want to get as close as you possibly can without alerting the seal.

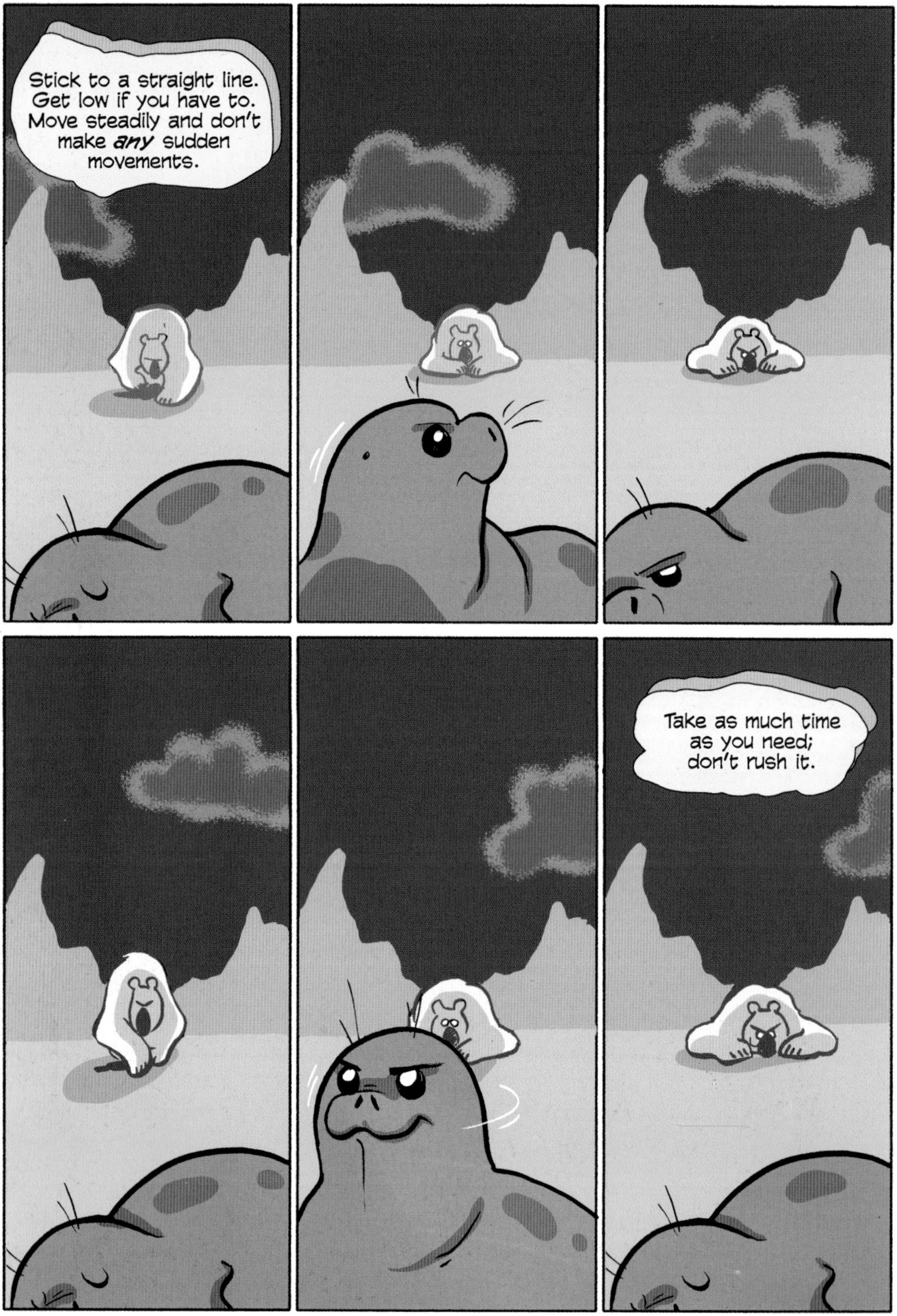
Stick to a straight line. Get low if you have to. Move steadily and don't make *any* sudden movements.
Take as much time as you need; don't rush it.

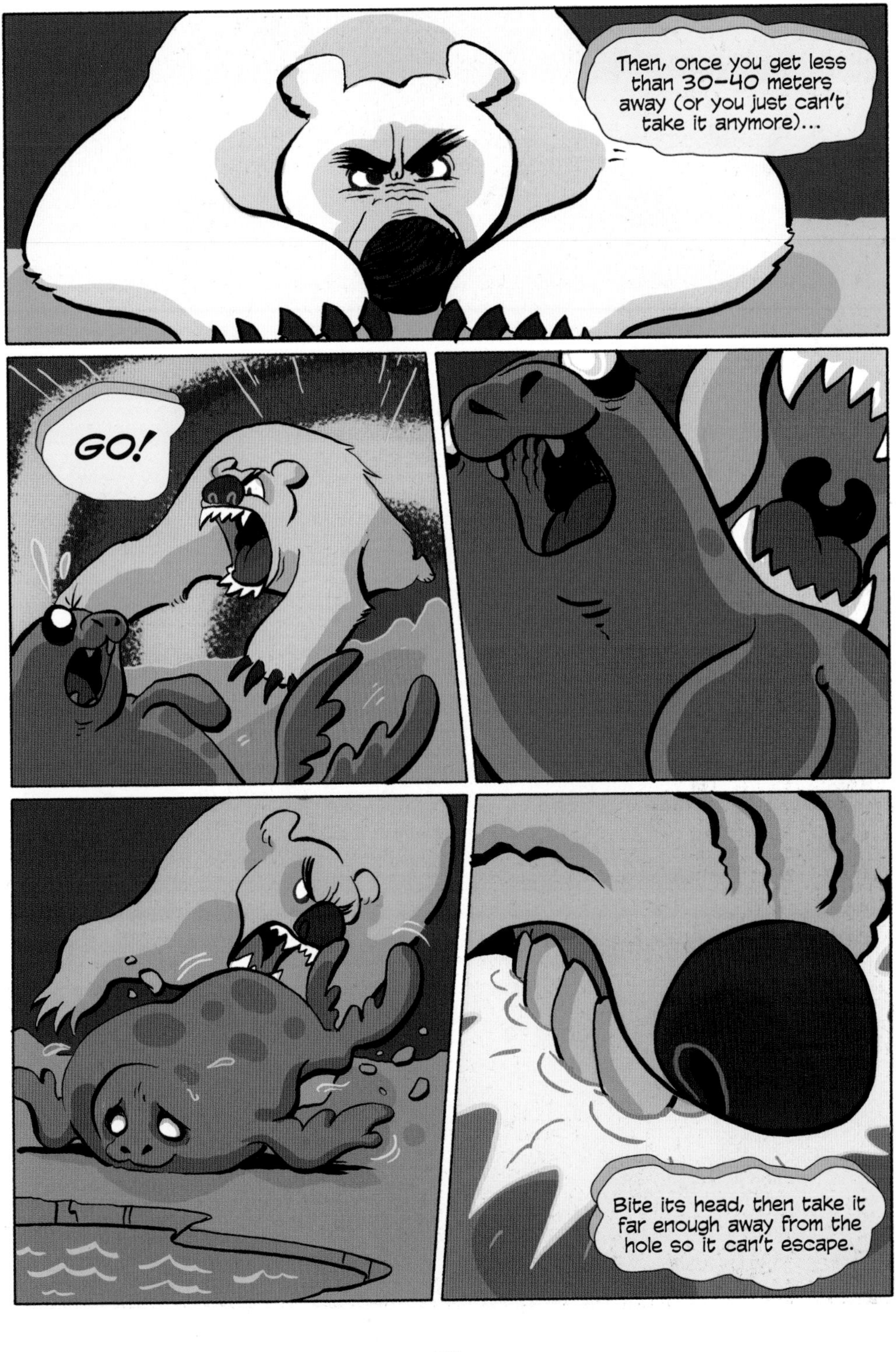
Then, once you get less than 30–40 meters away (or you just can't take it anymore)...
GO!
Bite its head, then take it far enough away from the hole so it can't escape.

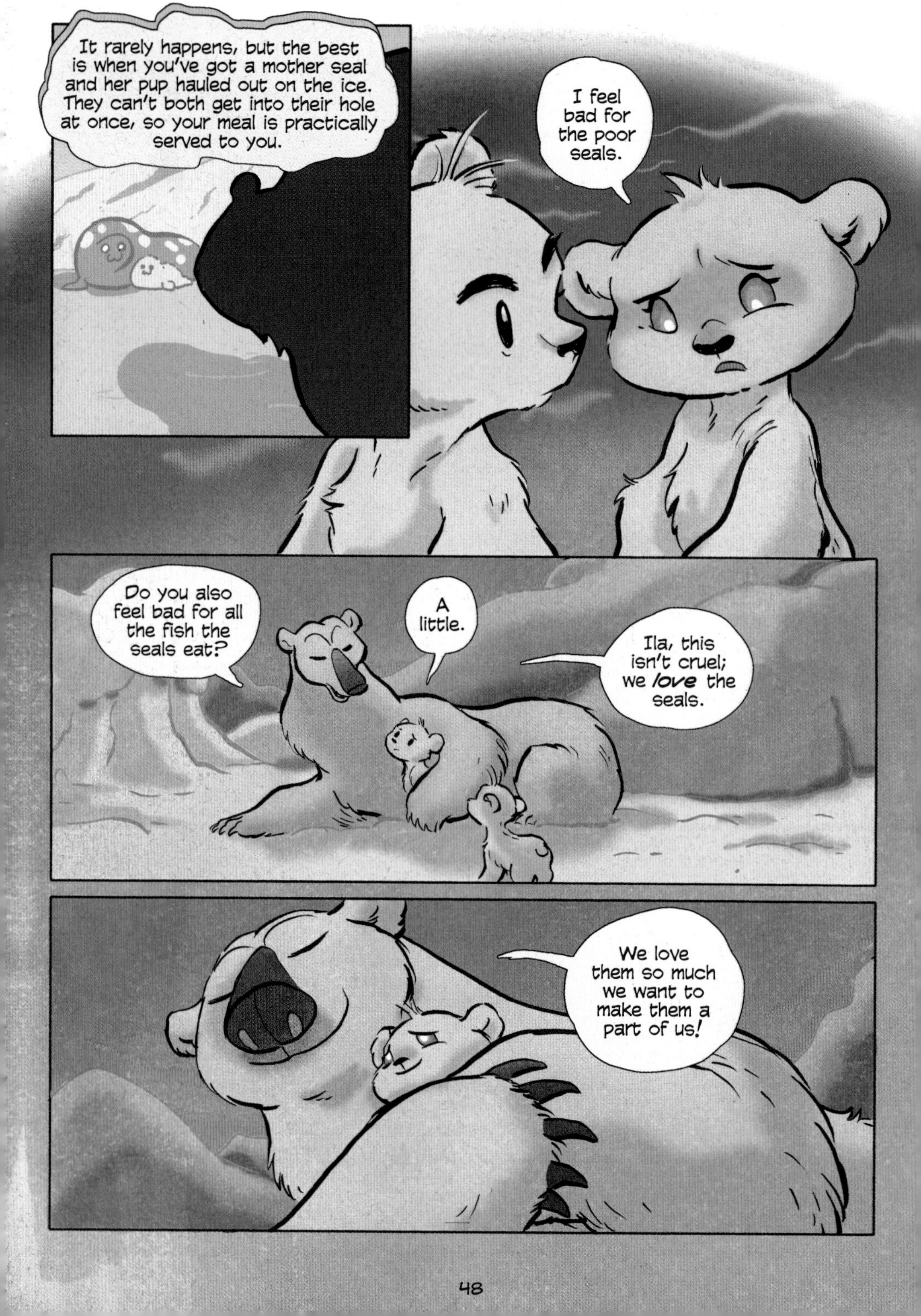
It rarely happens, but the best is when you've got a mother seal and her pup hauled out on the ice. They can't both get into their hole at once, so your meal is practically served to you.
I feel bad for the poor seals.
Do you also feel bad for all the fish the seals eat?
A little.
Ila, this isn't cruel; we *love* the seals.
We love them so much we want to make them a part of us!

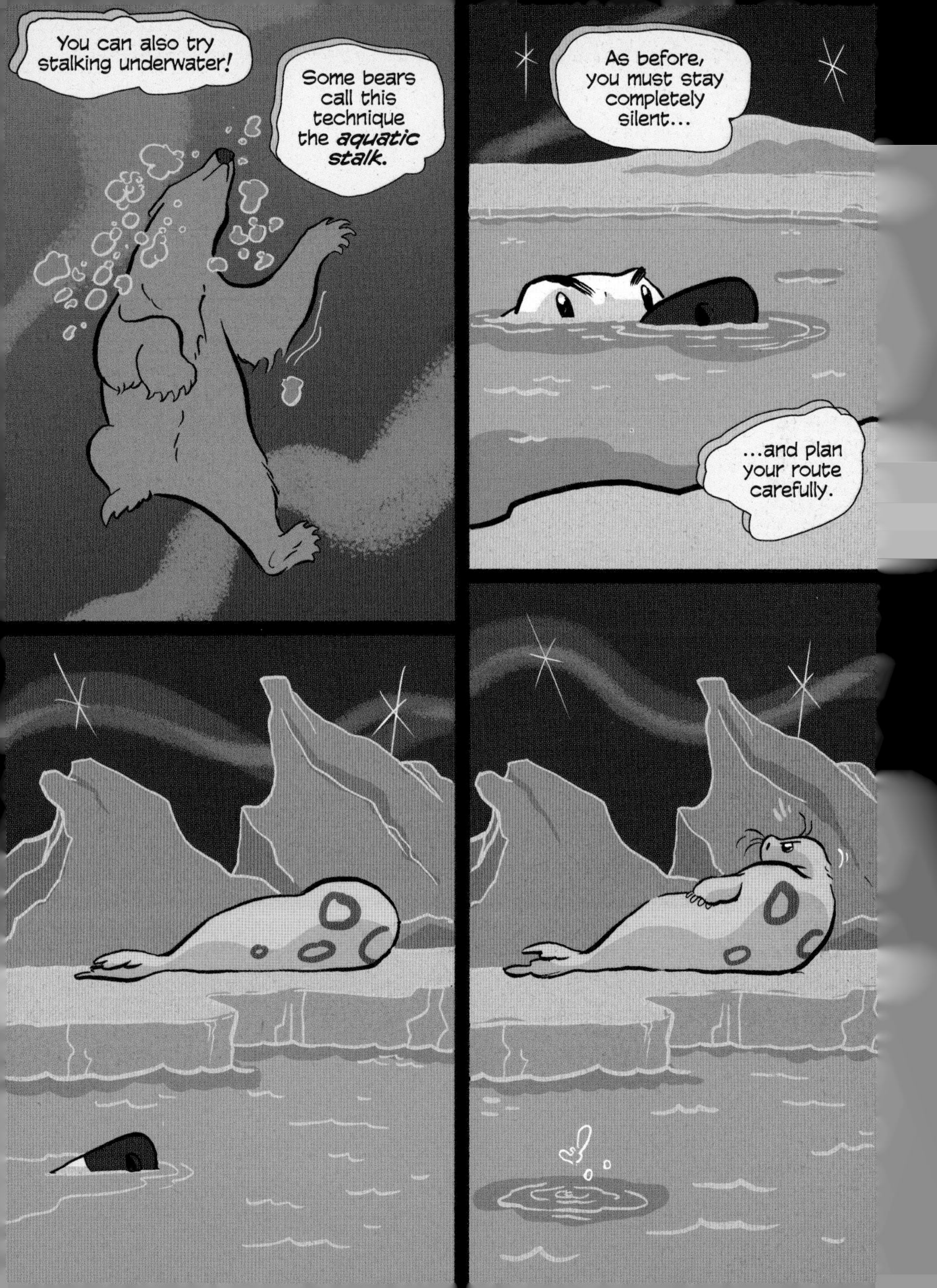
You can also try stalking underwater!
Some bears call this technique the *aquatic stalk.*
As before, you must stay completely silent...
...and plan your route carefully.

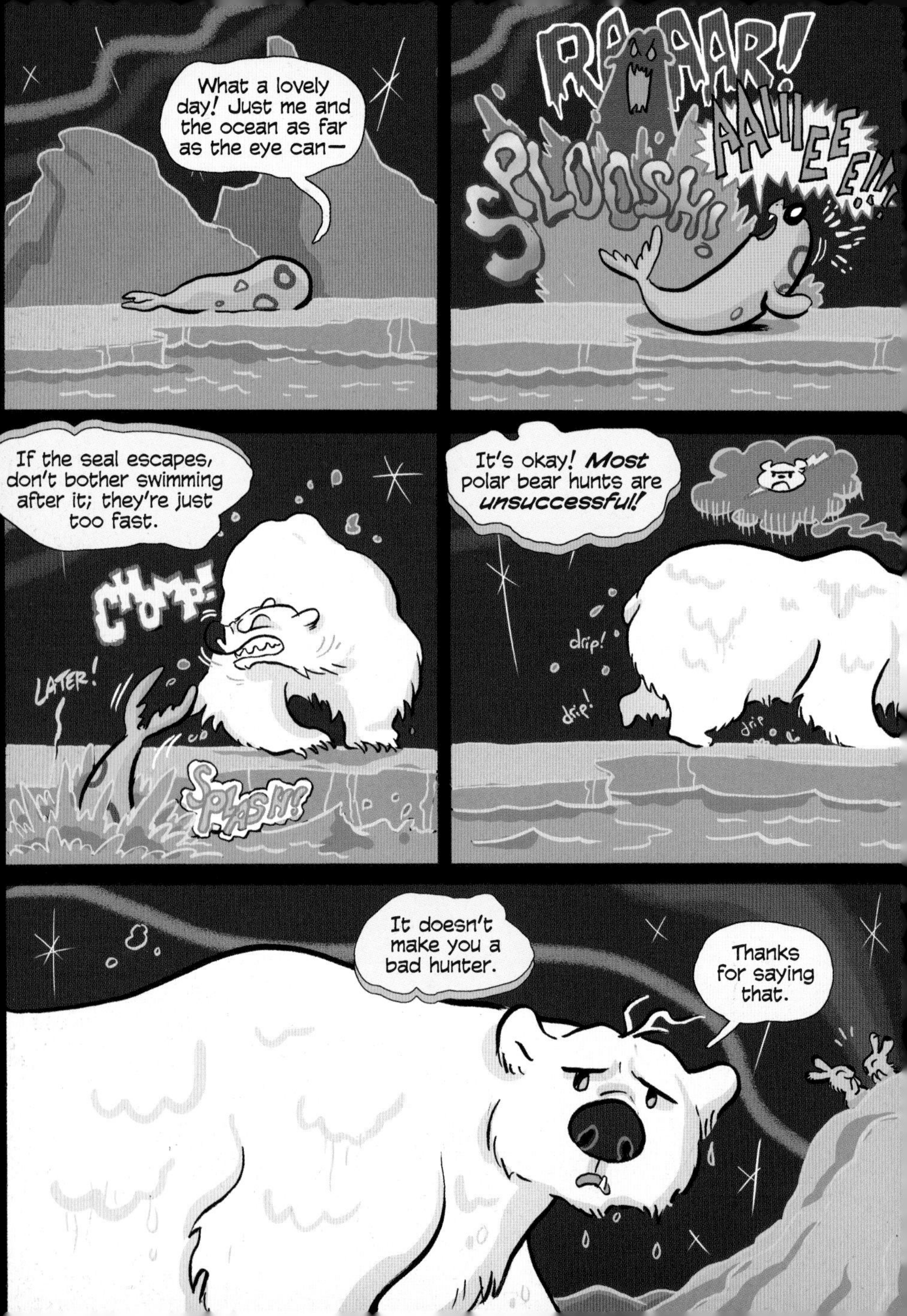
What a lovely day! Just me and the ocean as far as the eye can—
RAAAR!
SPLOOSH!!
AAIIIEEE!!!
If the seal escapes, don't bother swimming after it; they're just too fast.
CHOMP!
LATER!
SPLASH!!
It's okay! Most polar bear hunts are unsuccessful!
drip!
drip!
drip
It doesn't make you a bad hunter.
Thanks for saying that.

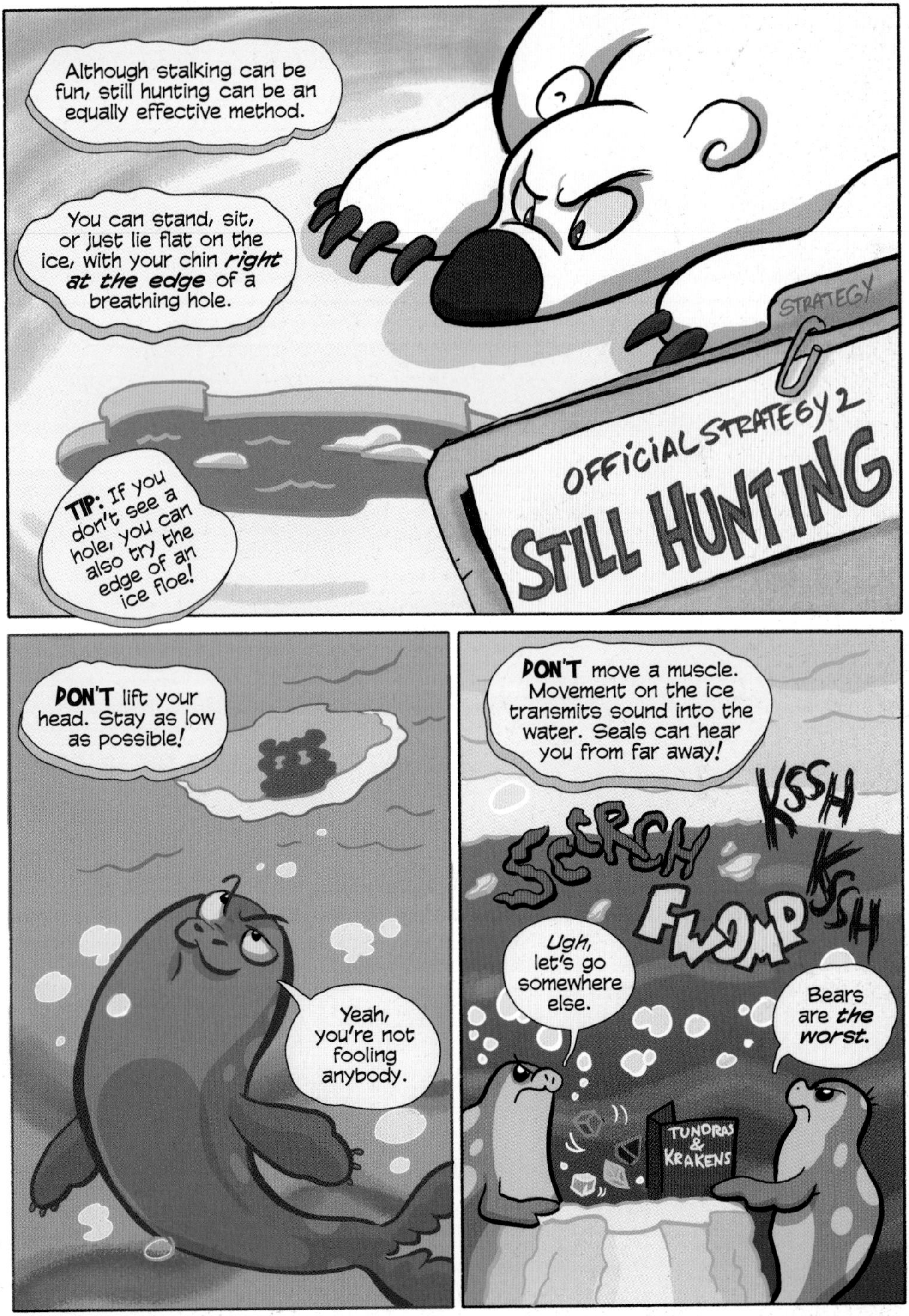

Although stalking can be fun, still hunting can be an equally effective method.
You can stand, sit, or just lie flat on the ice, with your chin *right at the edge* of a breathing hole.
STRATEGY
OFFICIAL STRATEGY 2
STILL HUNTING
TIP: If you don't see a hole, you can also try the edge of an ice floe!
DON'T lift your head. Stay as low as possible!
Yeah, you're not fooling anybody.
DON'T move a muscle. Movement on the ice transmits sound into the water. Seals can hear you from far away!
SCRCH
KSSH
KSSH
FLOMP
KSSH
Ugh, let's go somewhere else.
Bears are *the worst.*
TUNDRAS & KRAKENS

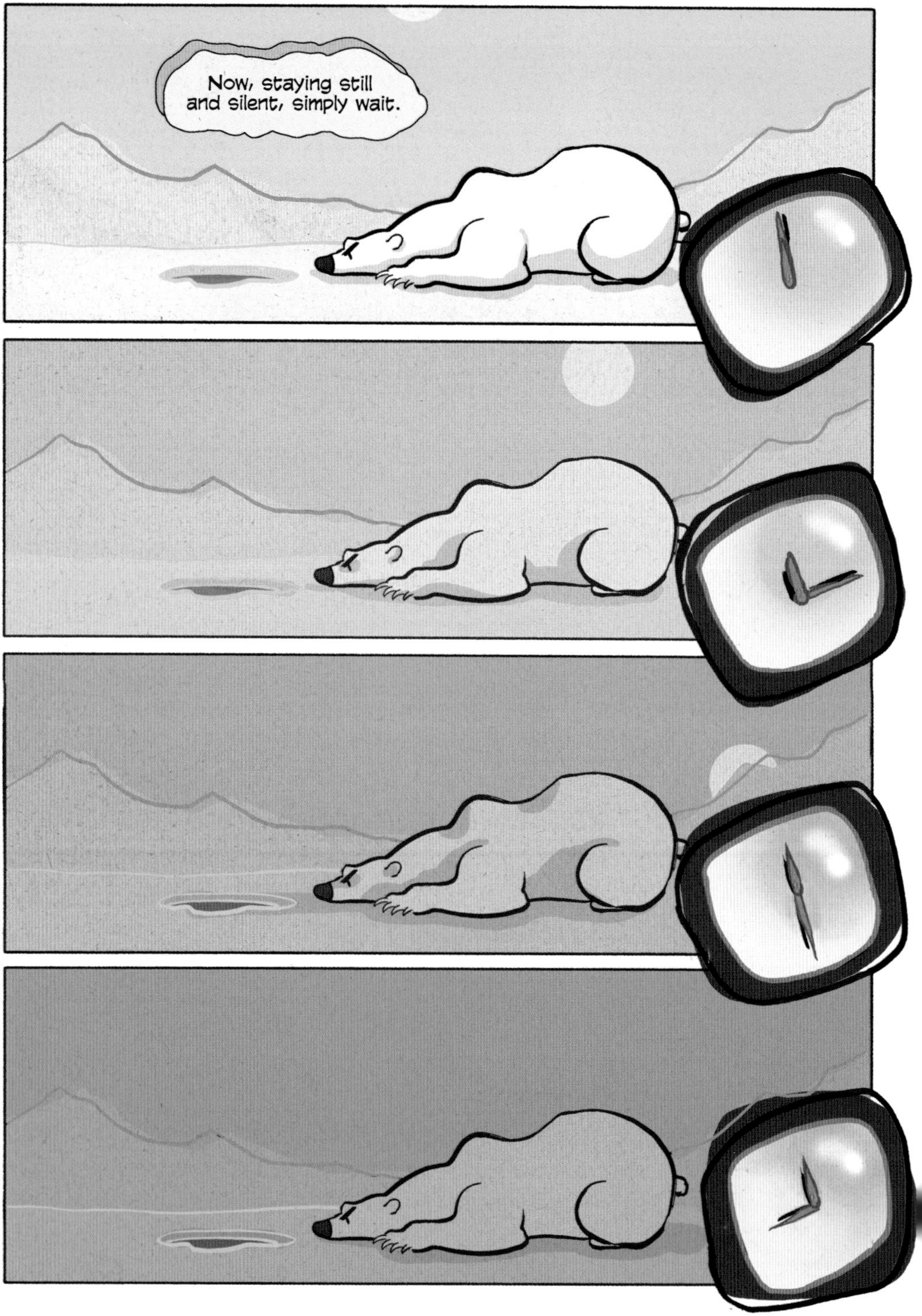
Now, staying still and silent, simply wait.

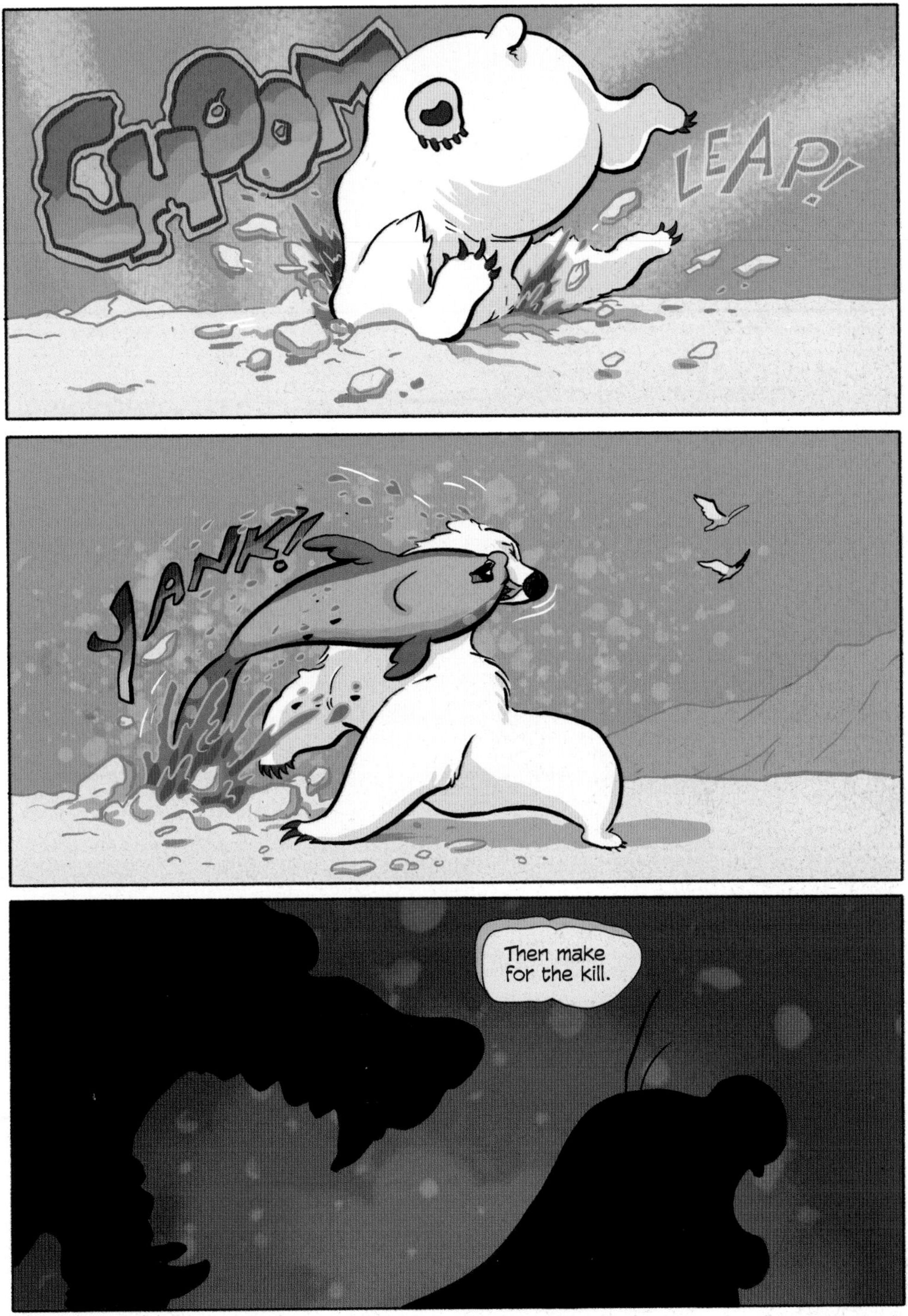
CHOOM
LEAP!
YANK!
Then make for the kill.

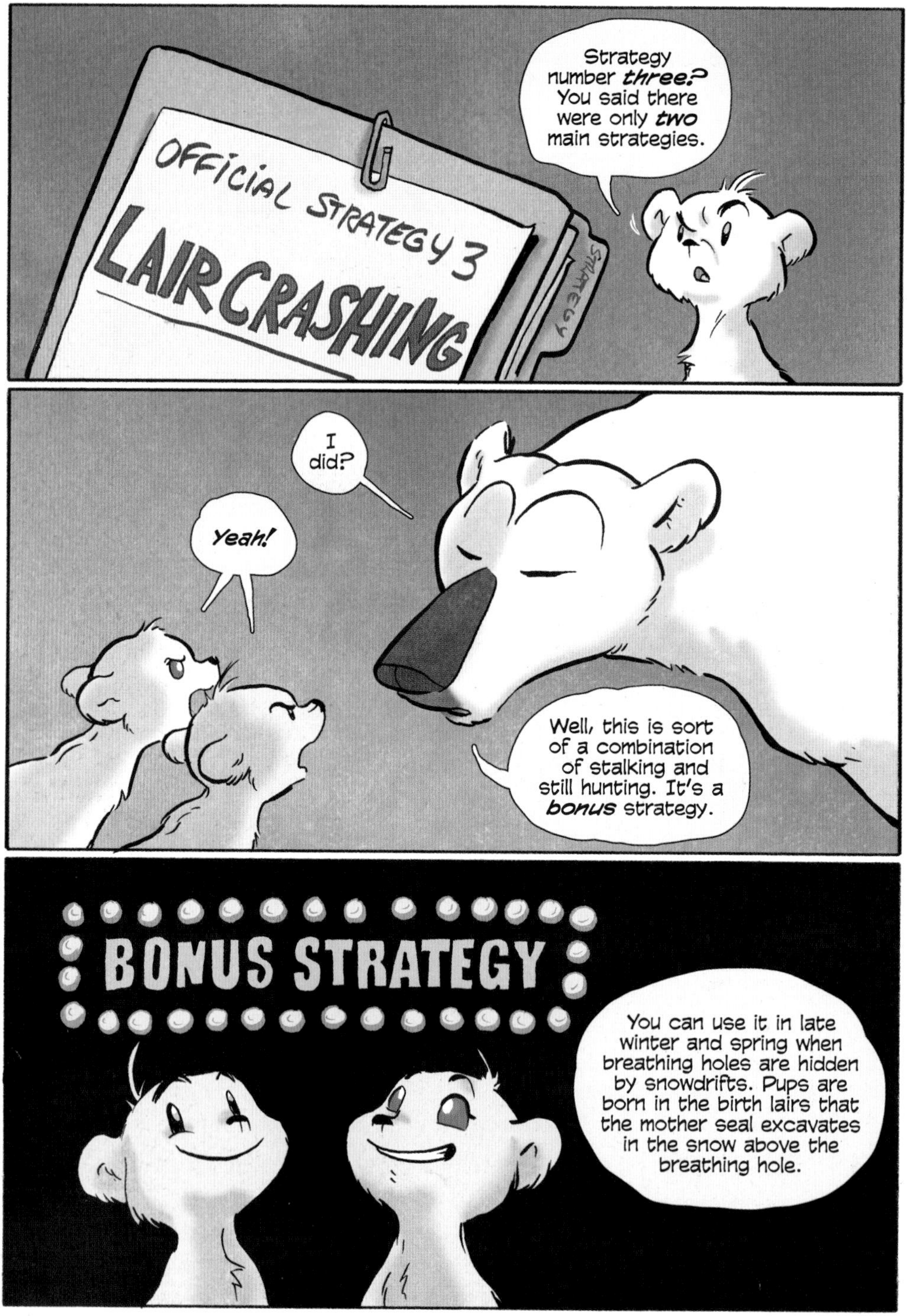
OFFICIAL STRATEGY 3
LAIR CRASHING
STRATEGY
Strategy number *three?* You said there were only *two* main strategies.
I did?
Yeah!
Well, this is sort of a combination of stalking and still hunting. It's a *bonus* strategy.
BONUS STRATEGY
You can use it in late winter and spring when breathing holes are hidden by snowdrifts. Pups are born in the birth lairs that the mother seal excavates in the snow above the breathing hole.

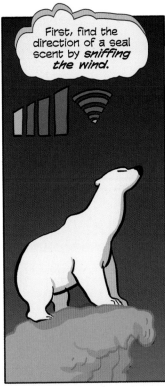

First, find the direction of a seal scent by *sniffing the wind.*

Use your nose to quietly follow the target.

The moment you've identified the source, *stay absolutely still.* Remember, walking on cold snow makes a crunching sound through the ice and into the water.

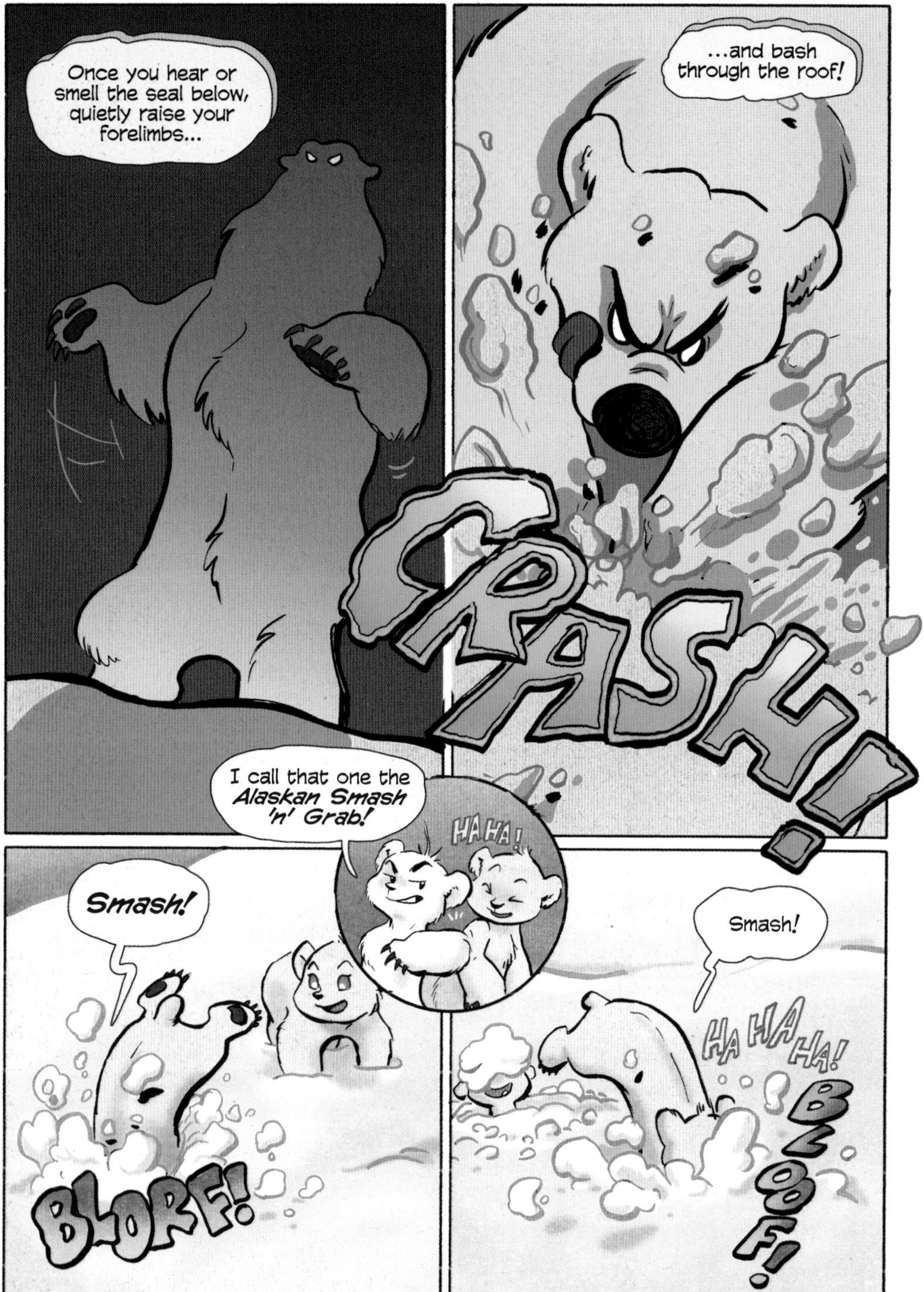
Once you hear or smell the seal below, quietly raise your forelimbs...
...and bash through the roof!
CRASH!!
I call that one the *Alaskan Smash 'n' Grab!*
HA HA!
Smash!
BLORF!
Smash!
HA HA HA HA!
BLOOF!

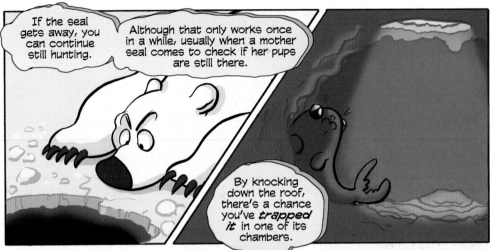

If the seal gets away, you can continue still hunting.

Although that only works once in a while, usually when a mother seal comes to check if her pups are still there.

By knocking down the roof, there's a chance you've *trapped it* in one of its chambers.

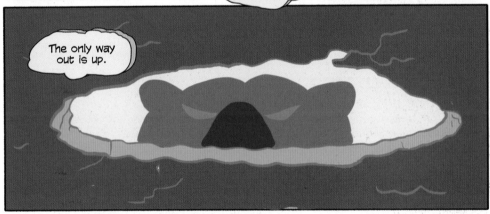

The only way out is up.

I see one, Mama! A big one!

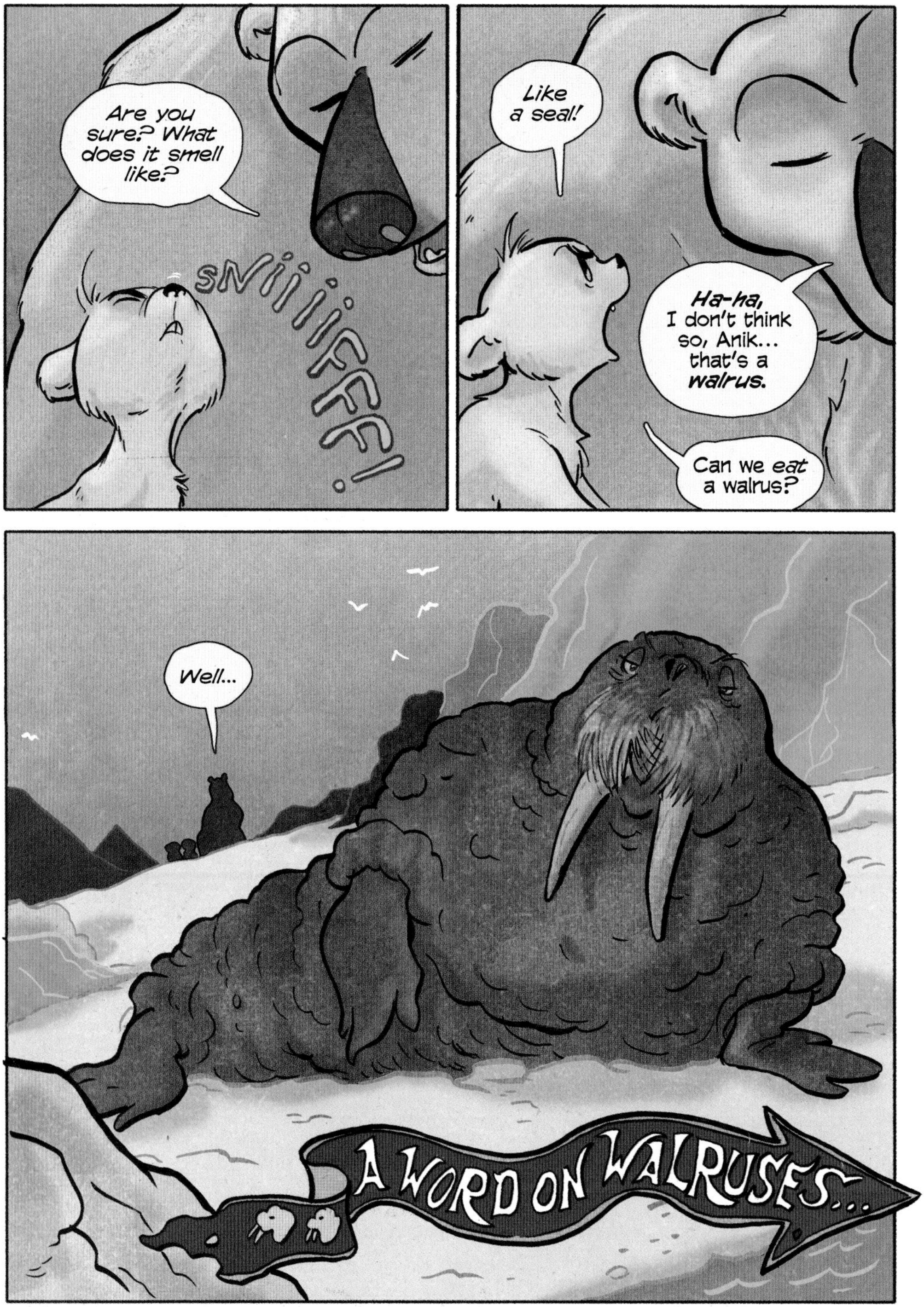
Are you sure? What does it smell like?
SNIIIIIFFF!
Like a seal!
Ha-ha, I don't think so, Anik... that's a ***walrus.***
Can we *eat* a walrus?
Well...
A WORD ON WALRUSES...

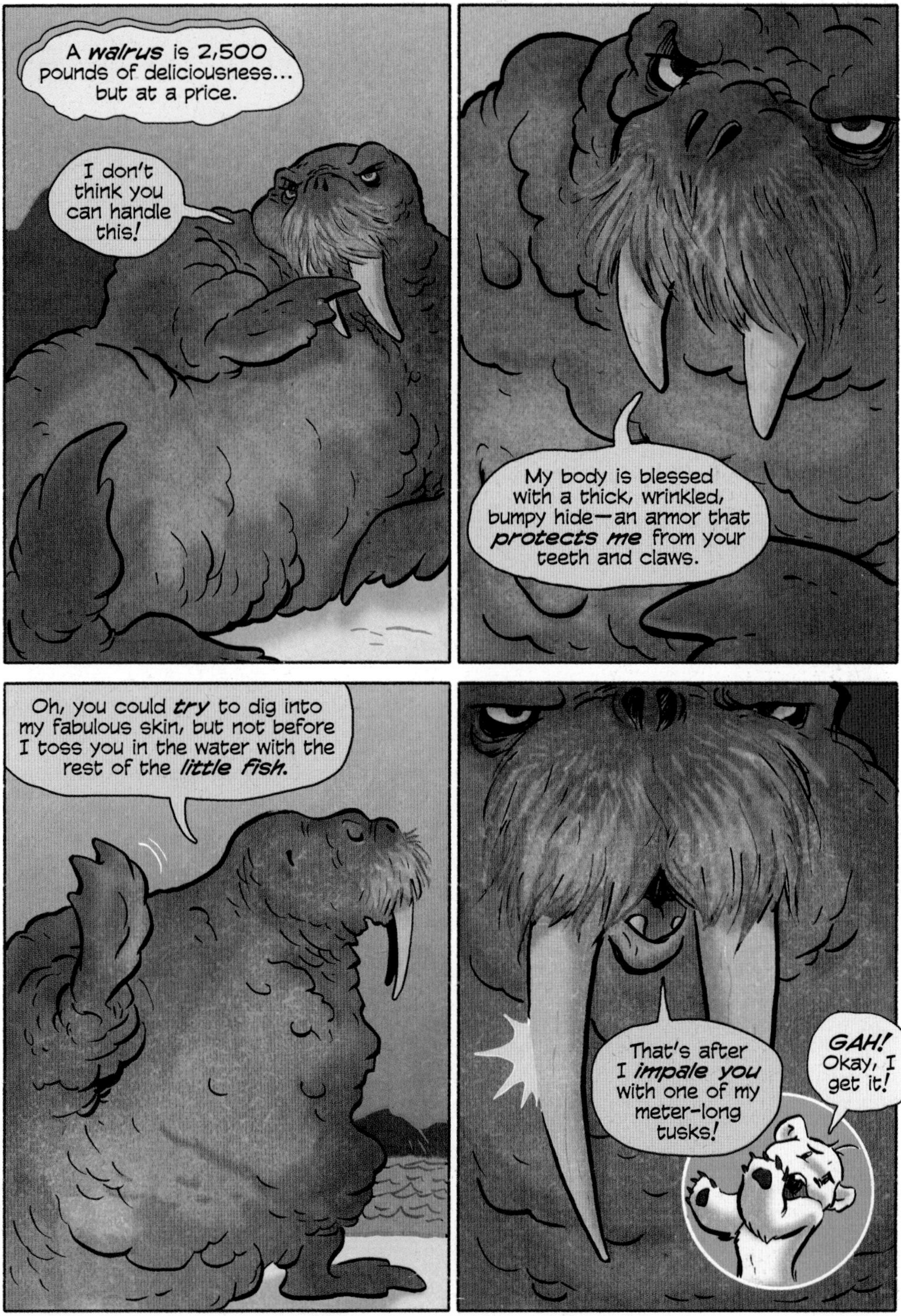

A *walrus* is 2,500 pounds of deliciousness... but at a price.
I don't think you can handle this!
My body is blessed with a thick, wrinkled, bumpy hide—an armor that *protects me* from your teeth and claws.
Oh, you could *try* to dig into my fabulous skin, but not before I toss you in the water with the rest of the *little fish*.
That's after I *impale you* with one of my meter-long tusks!
GAH! Okay, I get it!

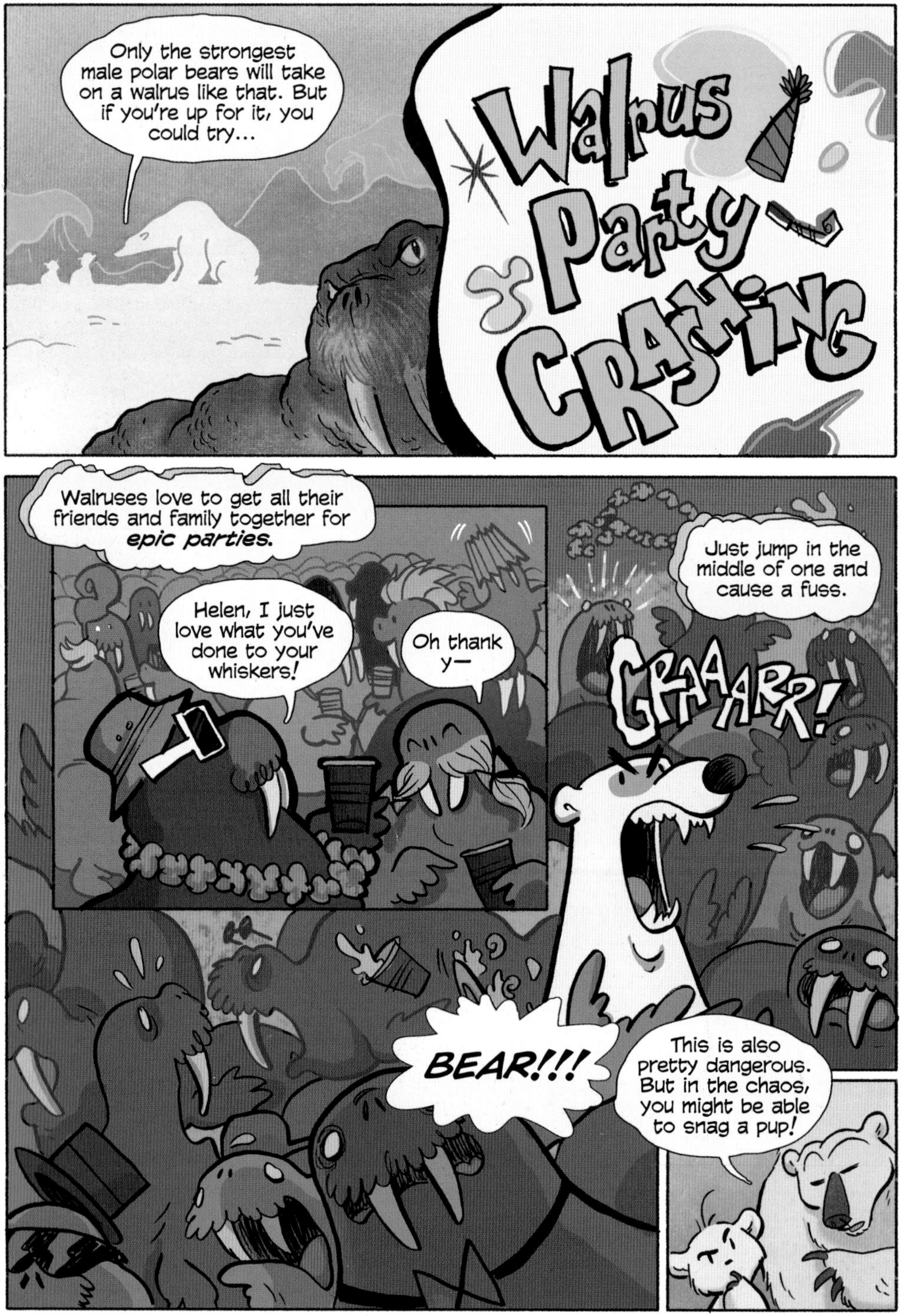
Only the strongest male polar bears will take on a walrus like that. But if you're up for it, you could try...
Walrus Party Crashing
Walruses love to get all their friends and family together for *epic parties.*
Helen, I just love what you've done to your whiskers!
Oh thank y—
Just jump in the middle of one and cause a fuss.
GRAAARRR!
BEAR!!!
This is also pretty dangerous. But in the chaos, you might be able to snag a pup!

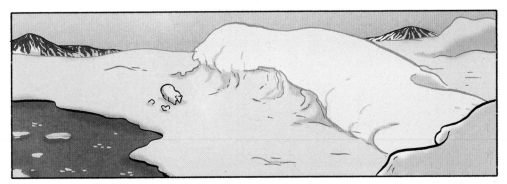

Mama...

Shhh. I smell it too.

SPLOOSH

Oooh... aquatic stalk!

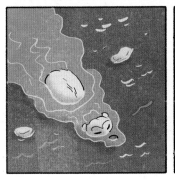

ROLL ROLL ROLL

Can you see her?

She's drying herself off.

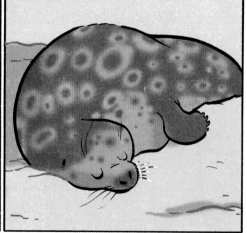

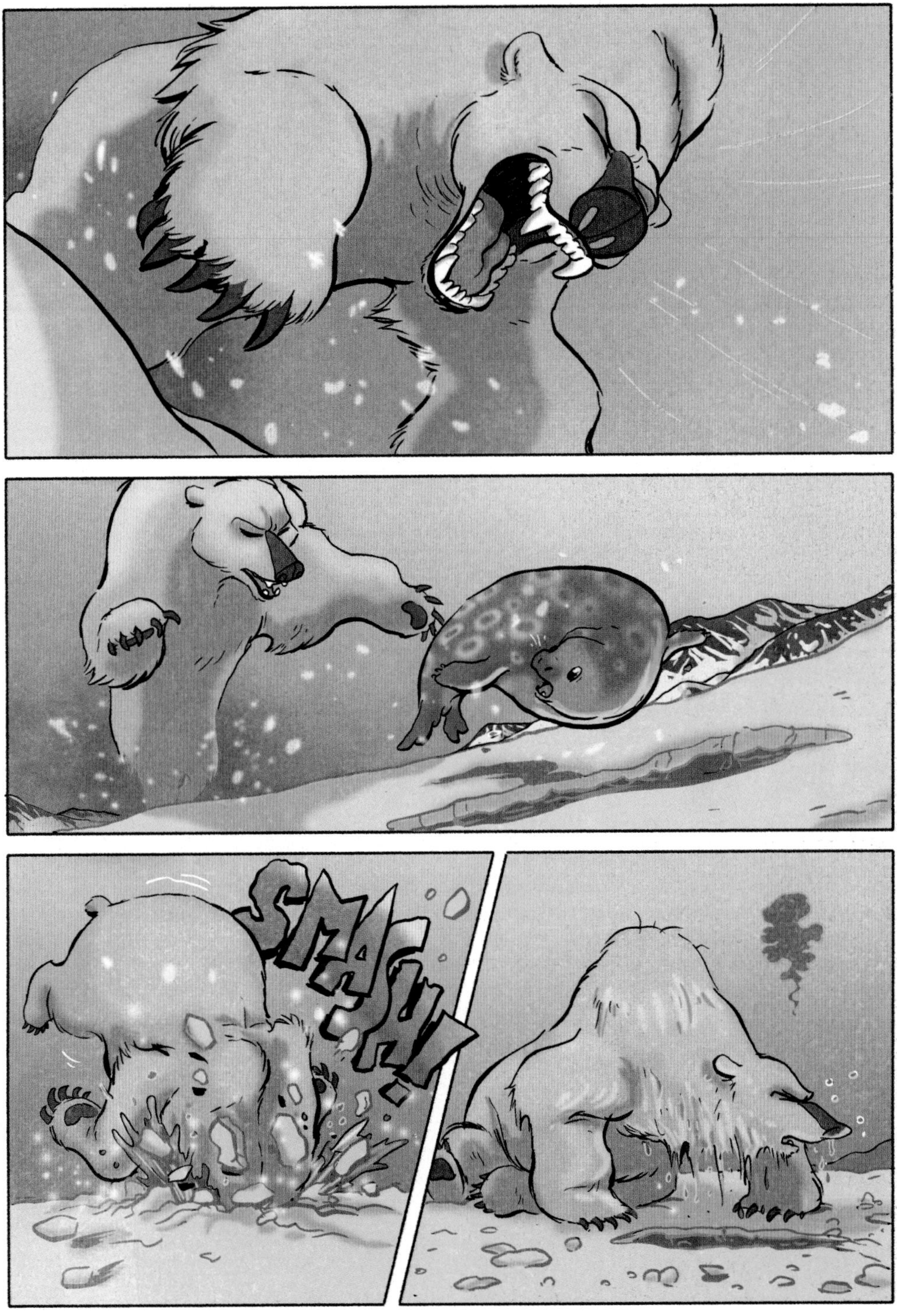
SMASH!

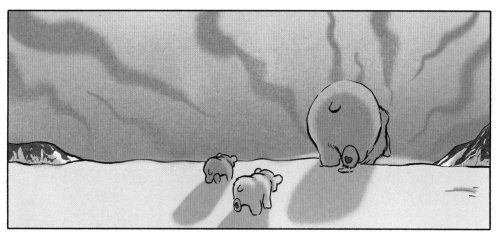

Still hunting is so boring.

You just have to be...

flump

YAWN

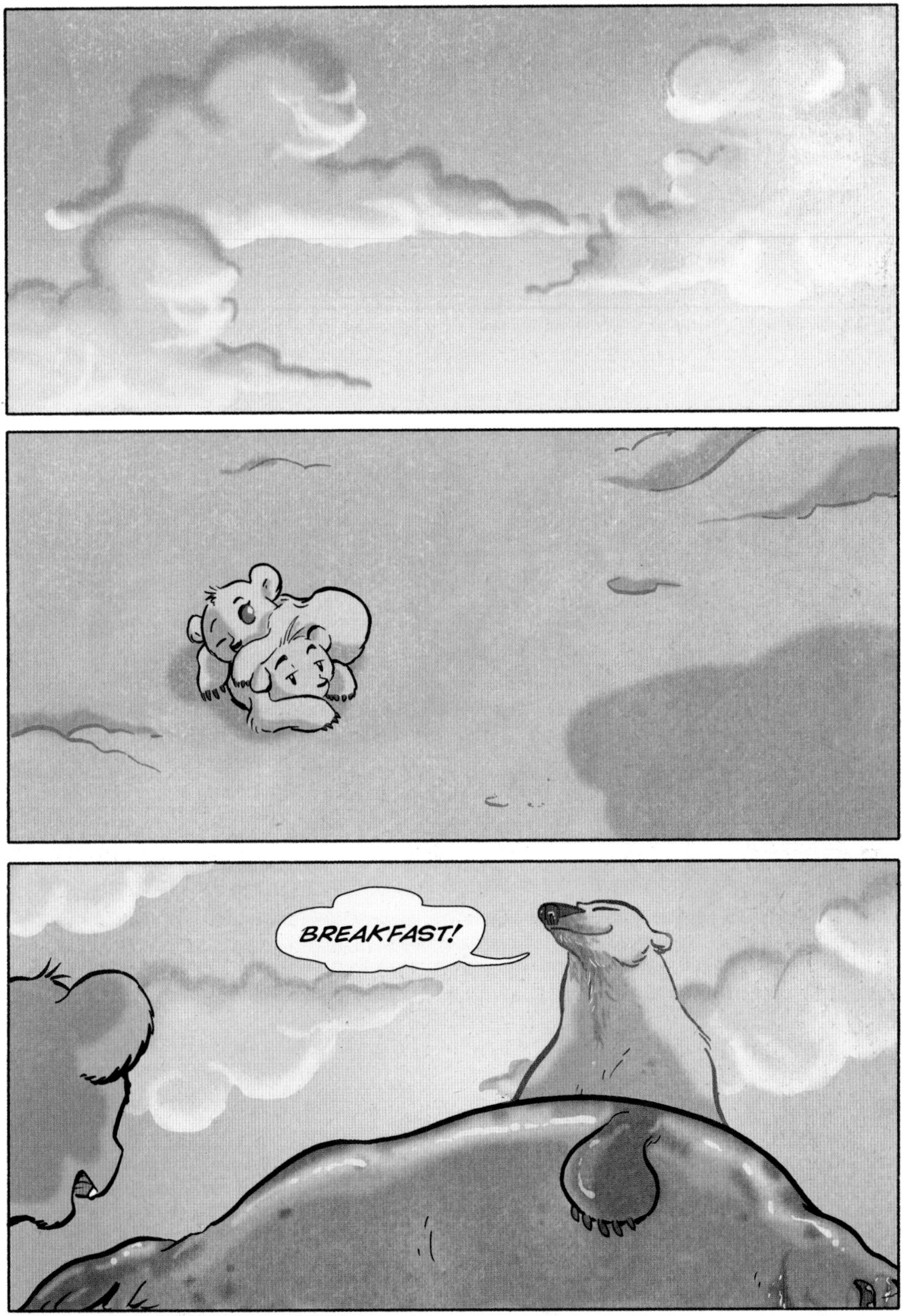
BREAKFAST!

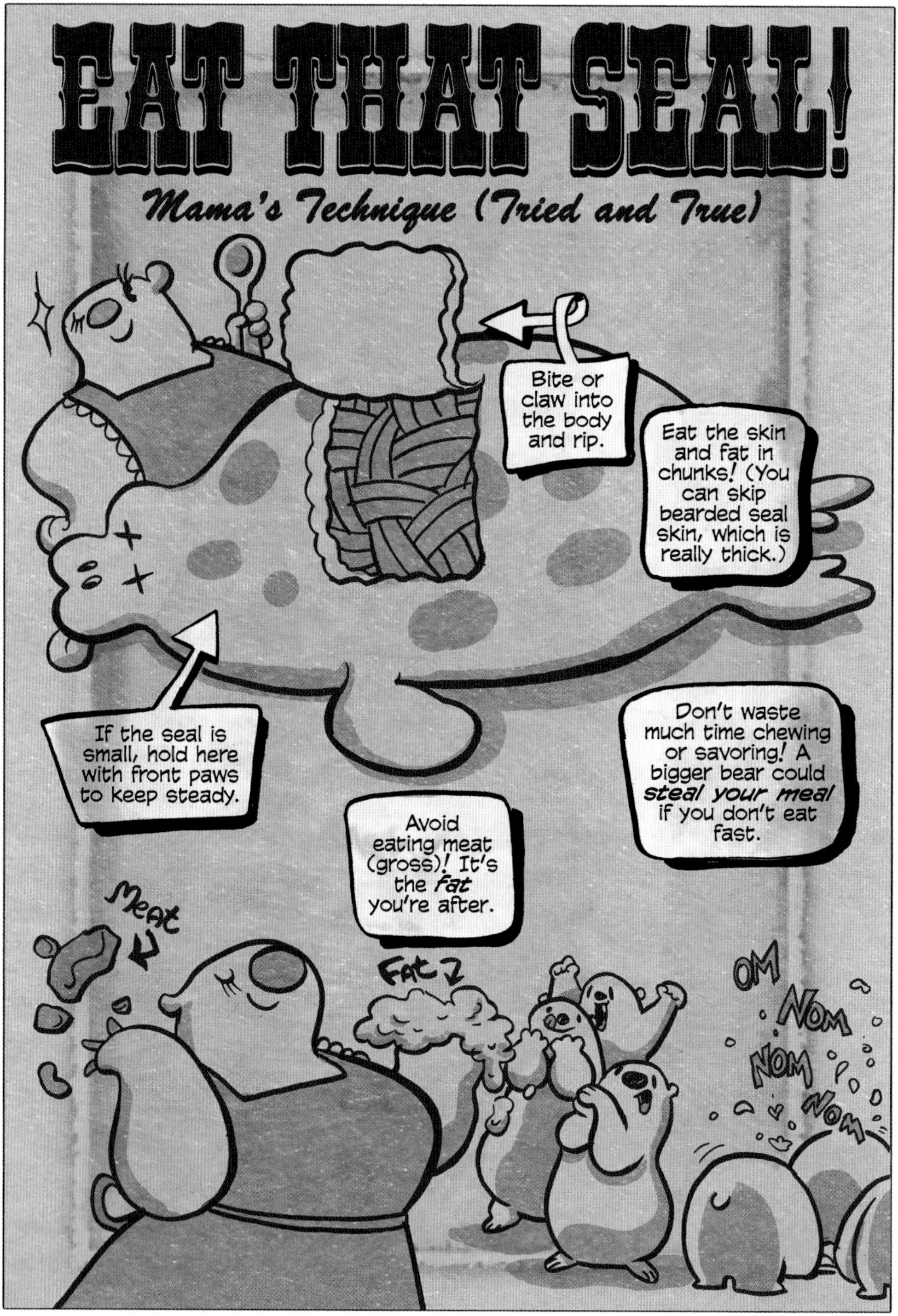
EAT THAT SEAL!
Mama's Technique (Tried and True)
Bite or claw into the body and rip.
Eat the skin and fat in chunks! (You can skip bearded seal skin, which is really thick.)
If the seal is small, hold here with front paws to keep steady.
Don't waste much time chewing or savoring! A bigger bear could steal your meal if you don't eat fast.
Avoid eating meat (gross)! It's the fat you're after.
Meat
Fat
OM NOM NOM NOM

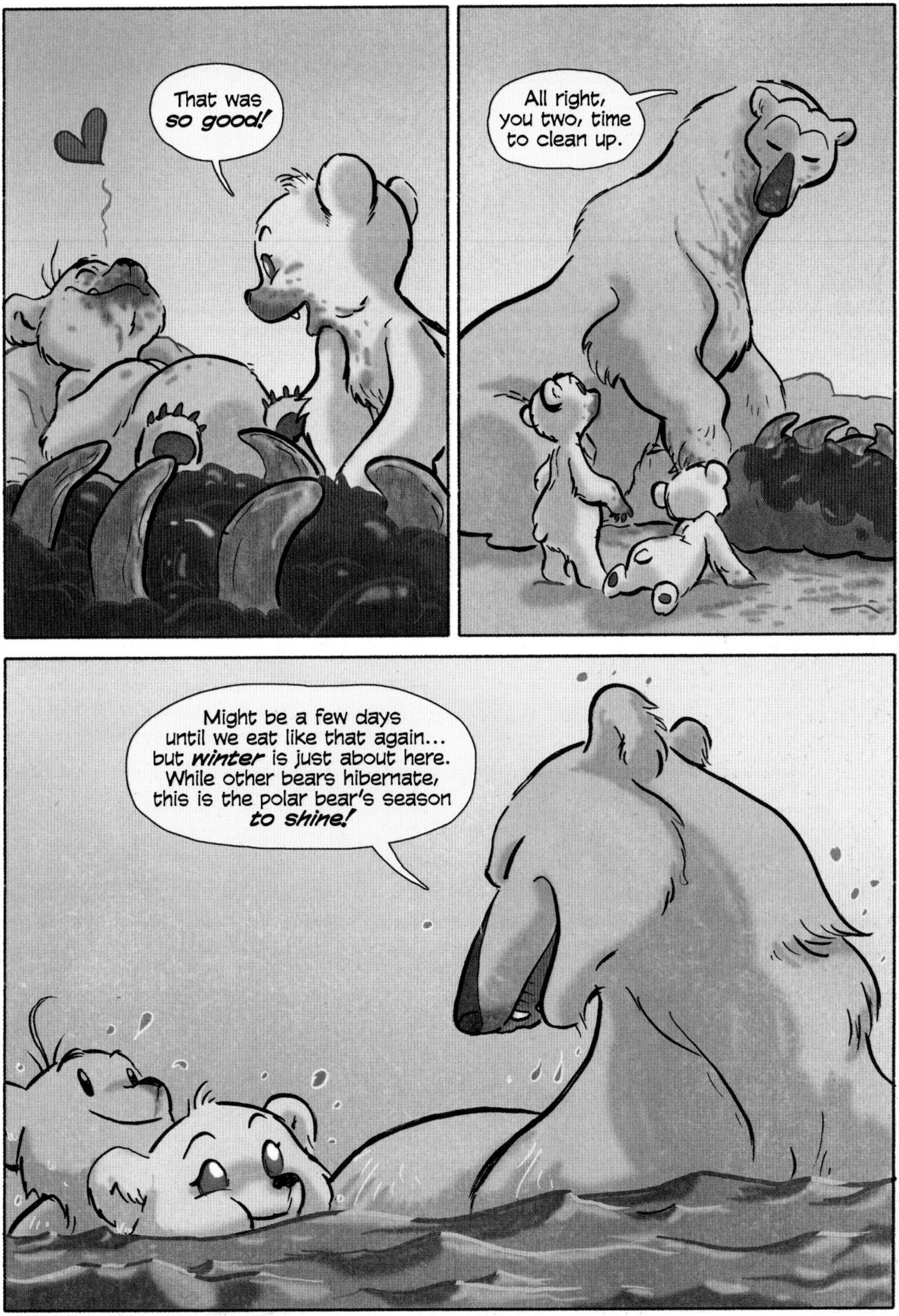
That was *so good!*
All right, you two, time to clean up.
Might be a few days until we eat like that again... but *winter* is just about here. While other bears hibernate, this is the polar bear's season *to shine!*

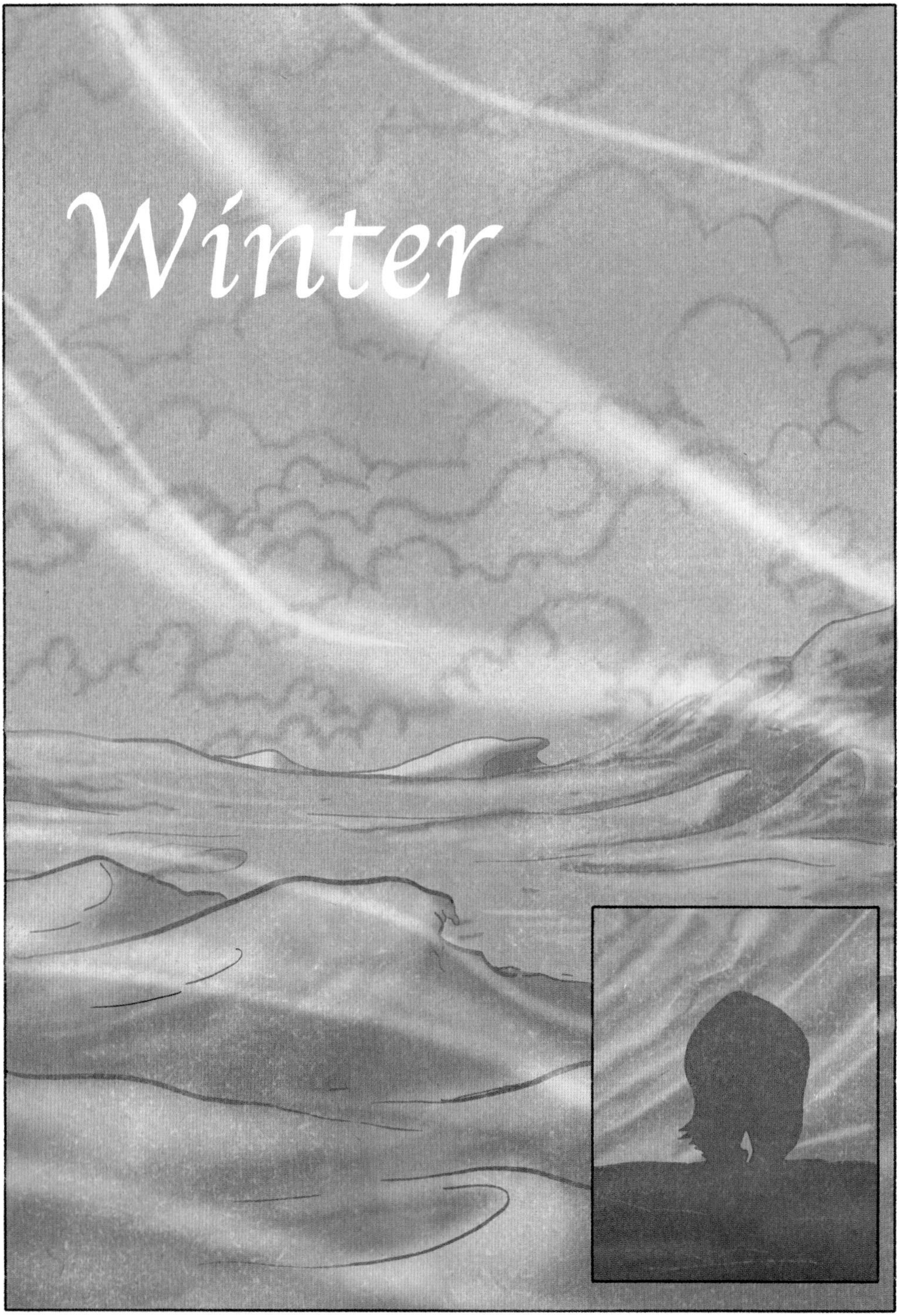
Winter

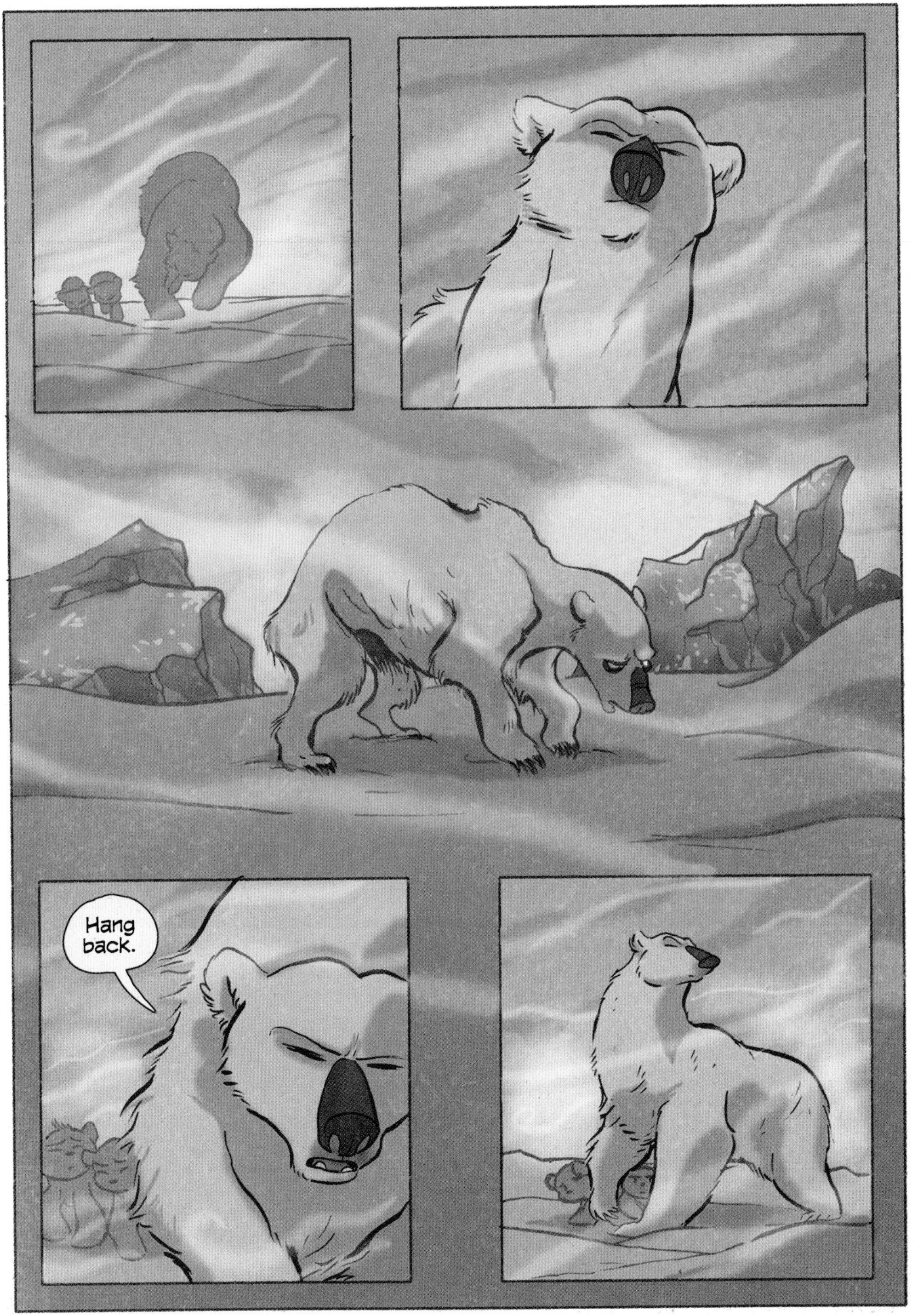
Hang back.

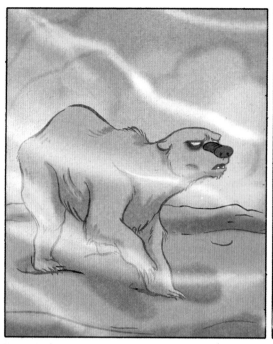

He doesn't have the energy to bother us. He's starving.

Where's his mom?

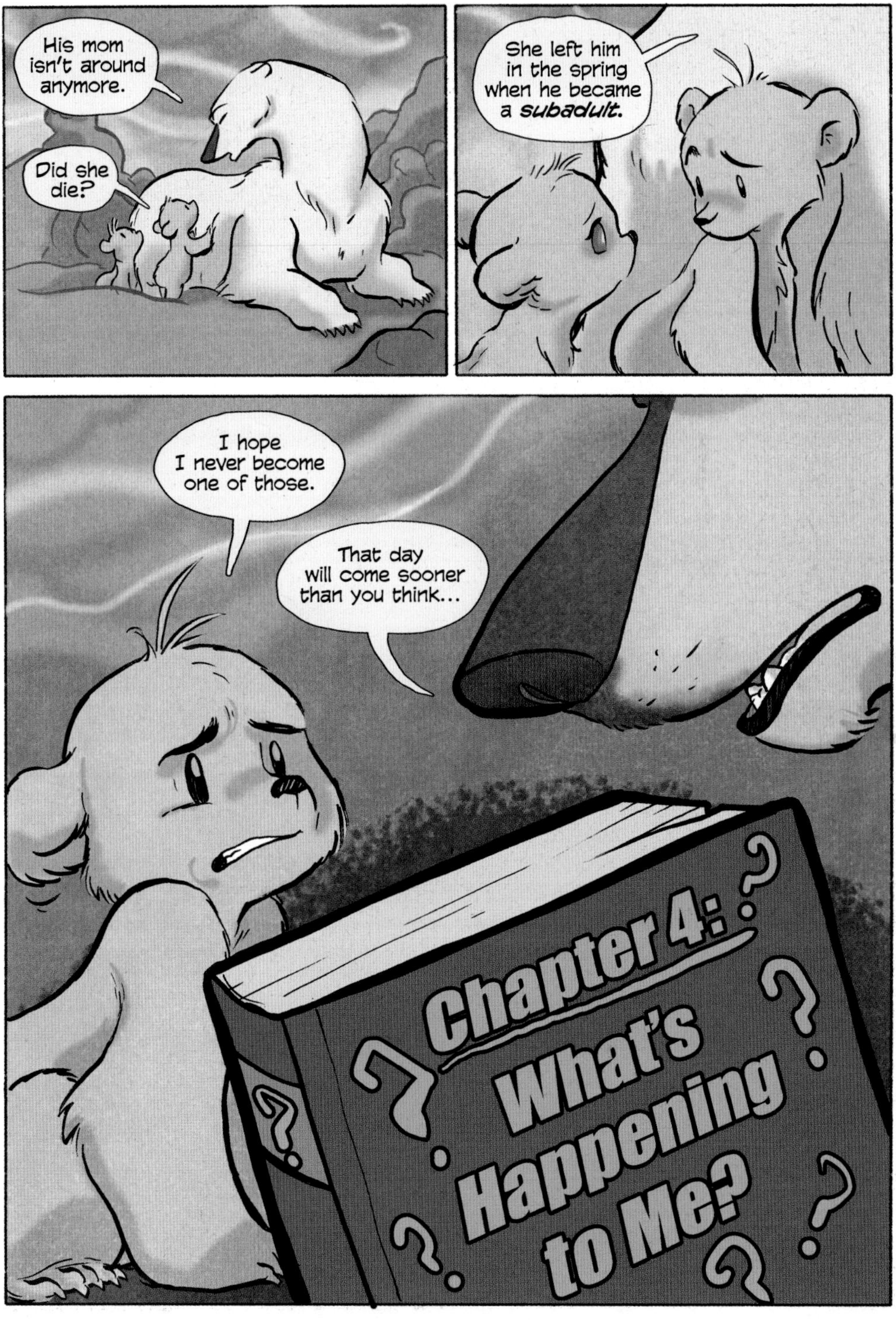
His mom isn't around anymore.
Did she die?
She left him in the spring when he became a ***subadult.***
I hope I never become one of those.
That day will come sooner than you think...
Chapter 4: What's Happening to Me?

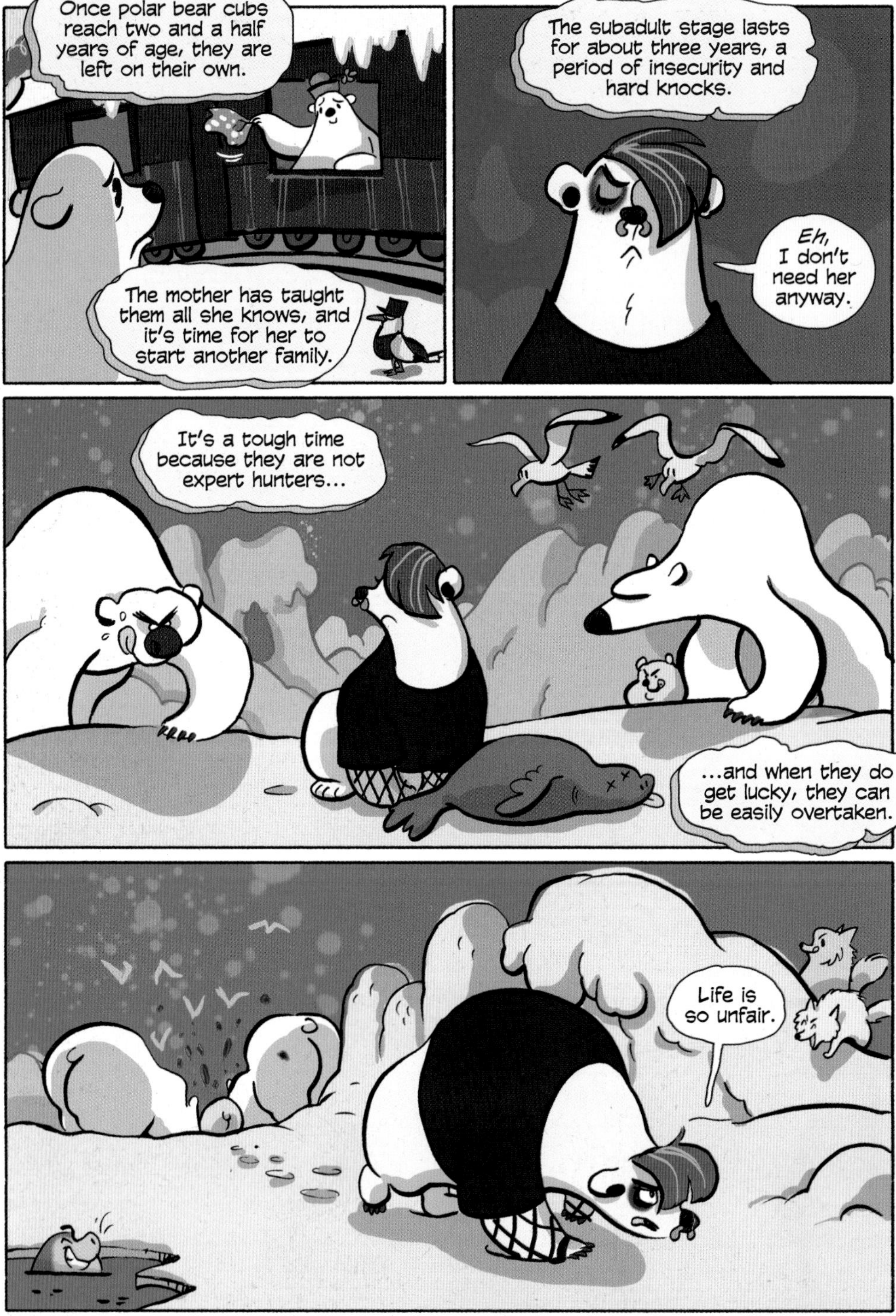
Once polar bear cubs reach two and a half years of age, they are left on their own.
The mother has taught them all she knows, and it's time for her to start another family.
The subadult stage lasts for about three years, a period of insecurity and hard knocks.
Eh, I don't need her anyway.
It's a tough time because they are not expert hunters...
...and when they do get lucky, they can be easily overtaken.
Life is so unfair.

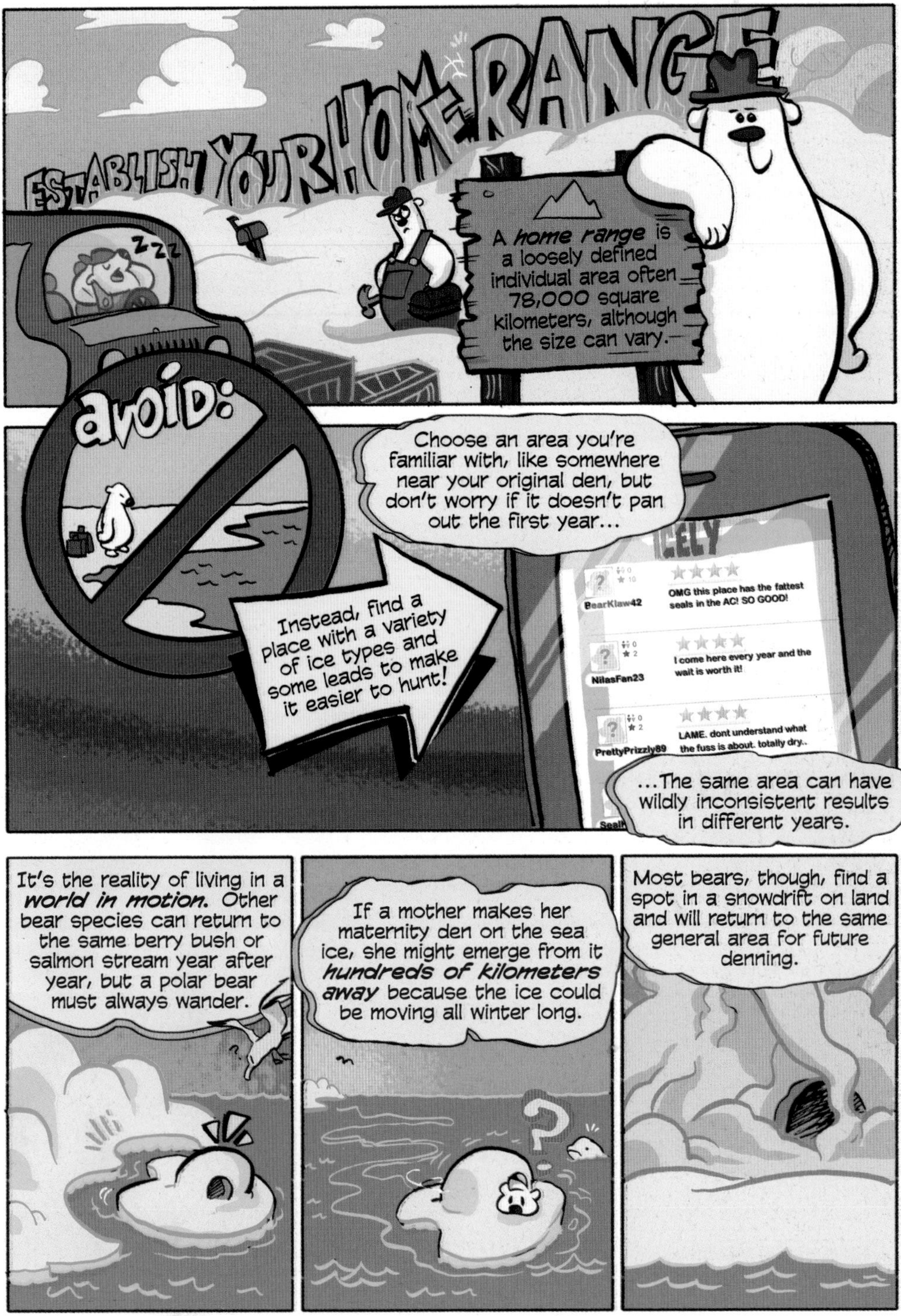
ESTABLISH YOUR HOME RANGE
Z Z Z
A *home range* is a loosely defined individual area often 78,000 square kilometers, although the size can vary.
avoid:
Choose an area you're familiar with, like somewhere near your original den, but don't worry if it doesn't pan out the first year...
Instead, find a place with a variety of ice types and some leads to make it easier to hunt!
ICELY
BearKlaw42
OMG this place has the fattest seals in the AC! SO GOOD!
NilasFan23
I come here every year and the wait is worth it!
PrettyPrizzly89
LAME. dont understand what the fuss is about. totally dry..
...The same area can have wildly inconsistent results in different years.
It's the reality of living in a *world in motion.* Other bear species can return to the same berry bush or salmon stream year after year, but a polar bear must always wander.
If a mother makes her maternity den on the sea ice, she might emerge from it *hundreds of kilometers away* because the ice could be moving all winter long.
Most bears, though, find a spot in a snowdrift on land and will return to the same general area for future denning.

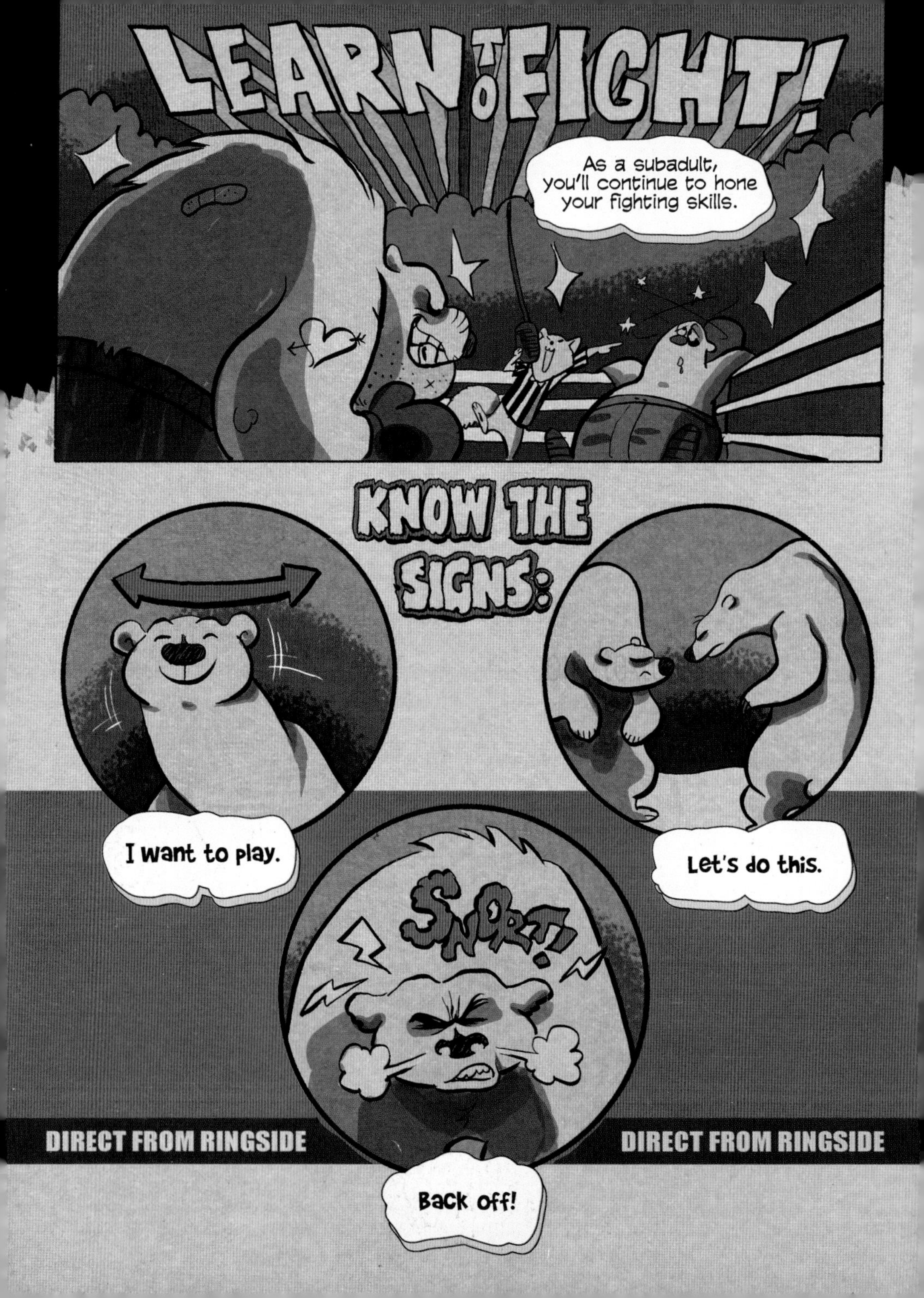
LEARN TO FIGHT!
As a subadult, you'll continue to hone your fighting skills.
KNOW THE SIGNS:
I want to play.
Let's do this.
SNORT!
Back off!
DIRECT FROM RINGSIDE
DIRECT FROM RINGSIDE

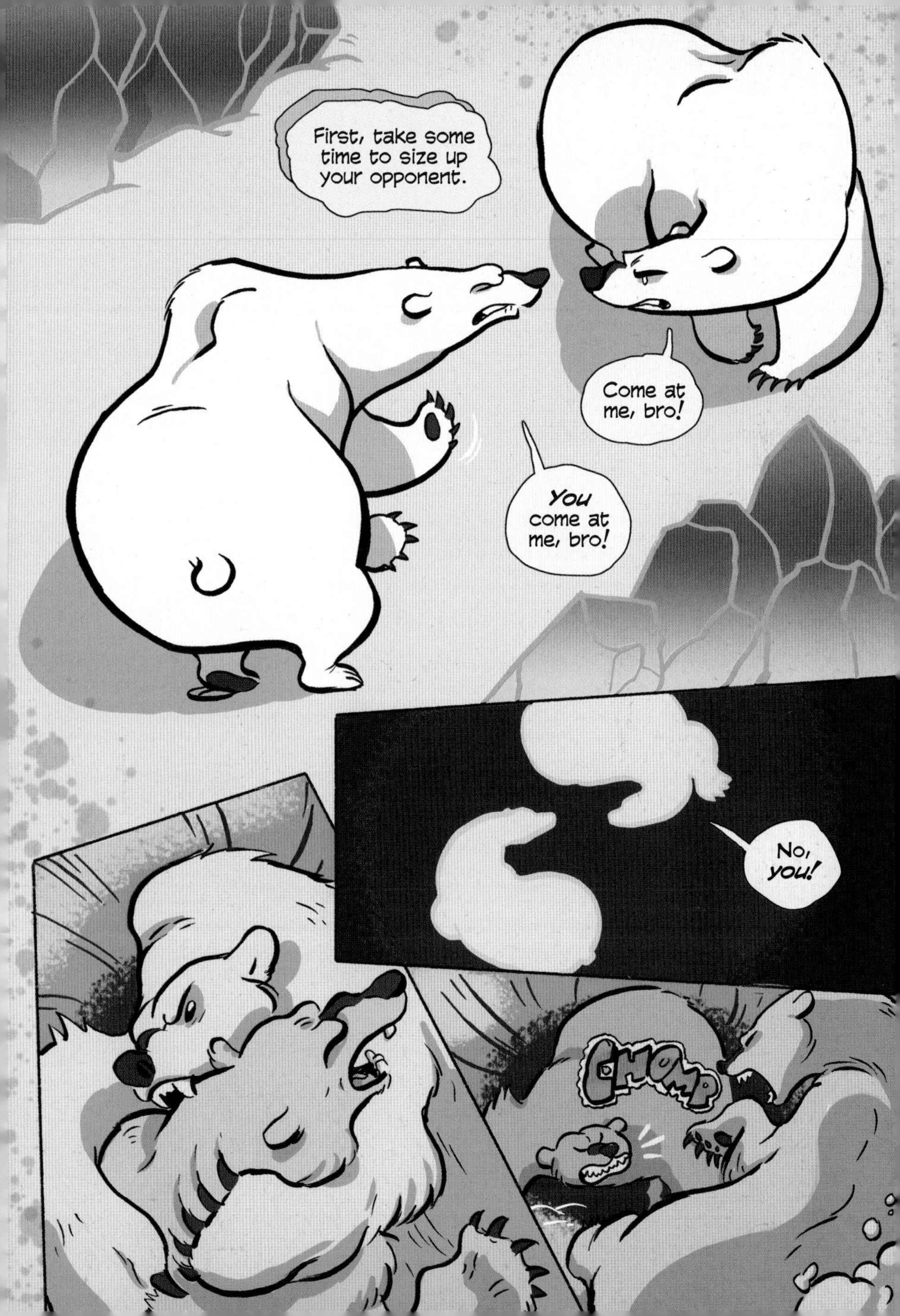
First, take some time to size up your opponent.
Come at me, bro!
You come at me, bro!
No, you!
CHOMP

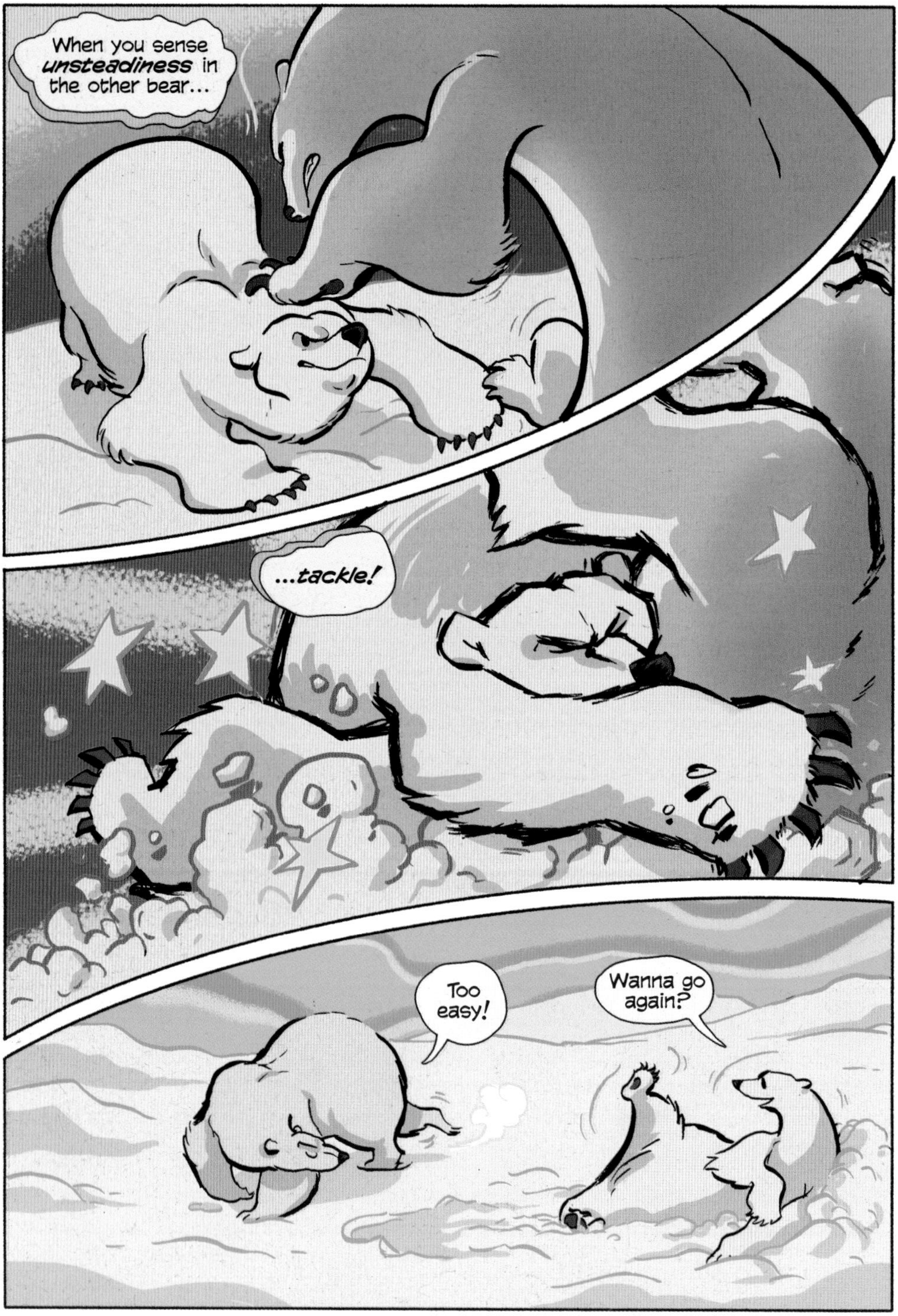
When you sense *unsteadiness* in the other bear...
...*tackle!*
Too easy!
Wanna go again?

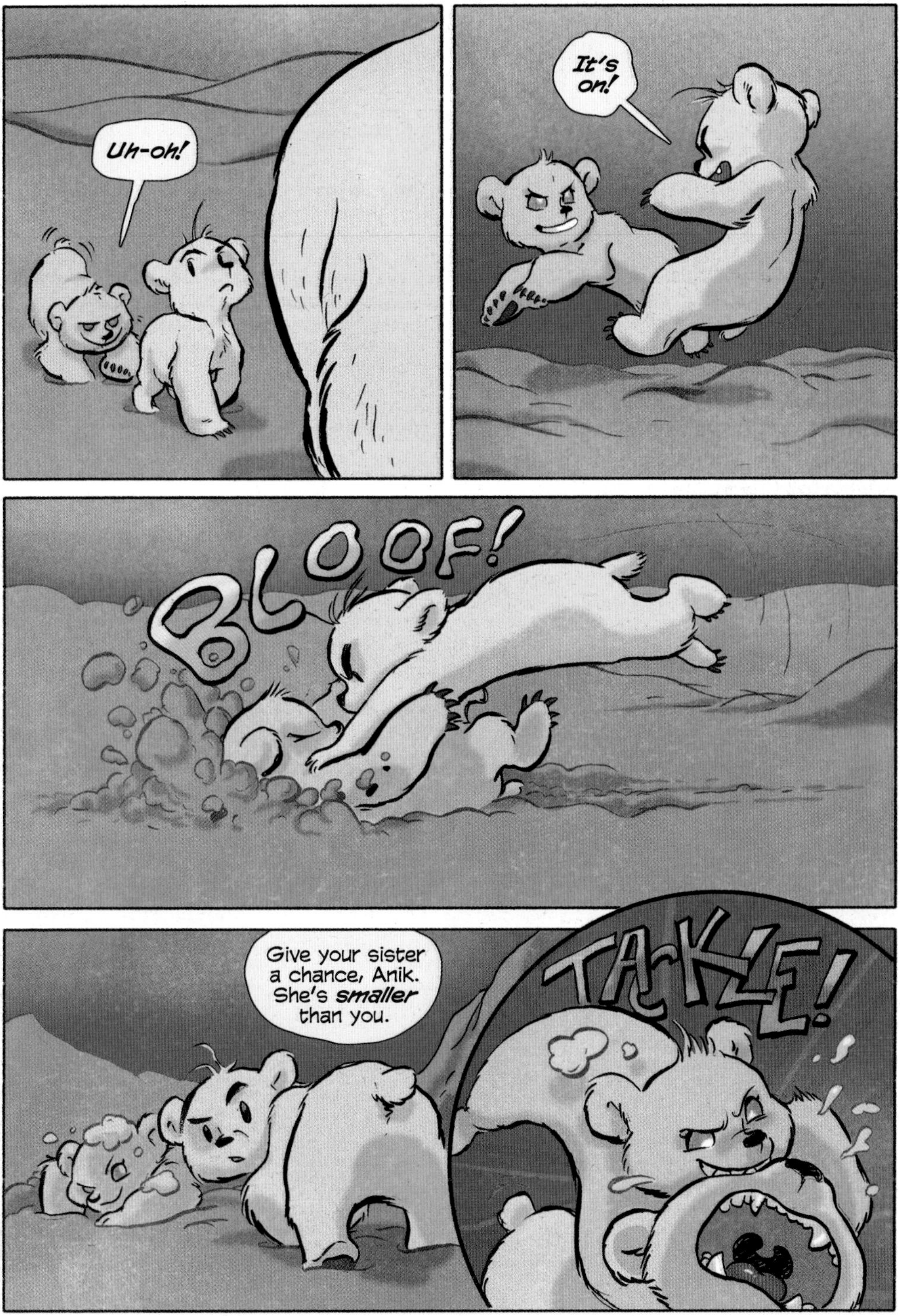
Uh-oh!
It's on!
BLOOF!
Give your sister a chance, Anik. She's *smaller* than you.
TACKLE!

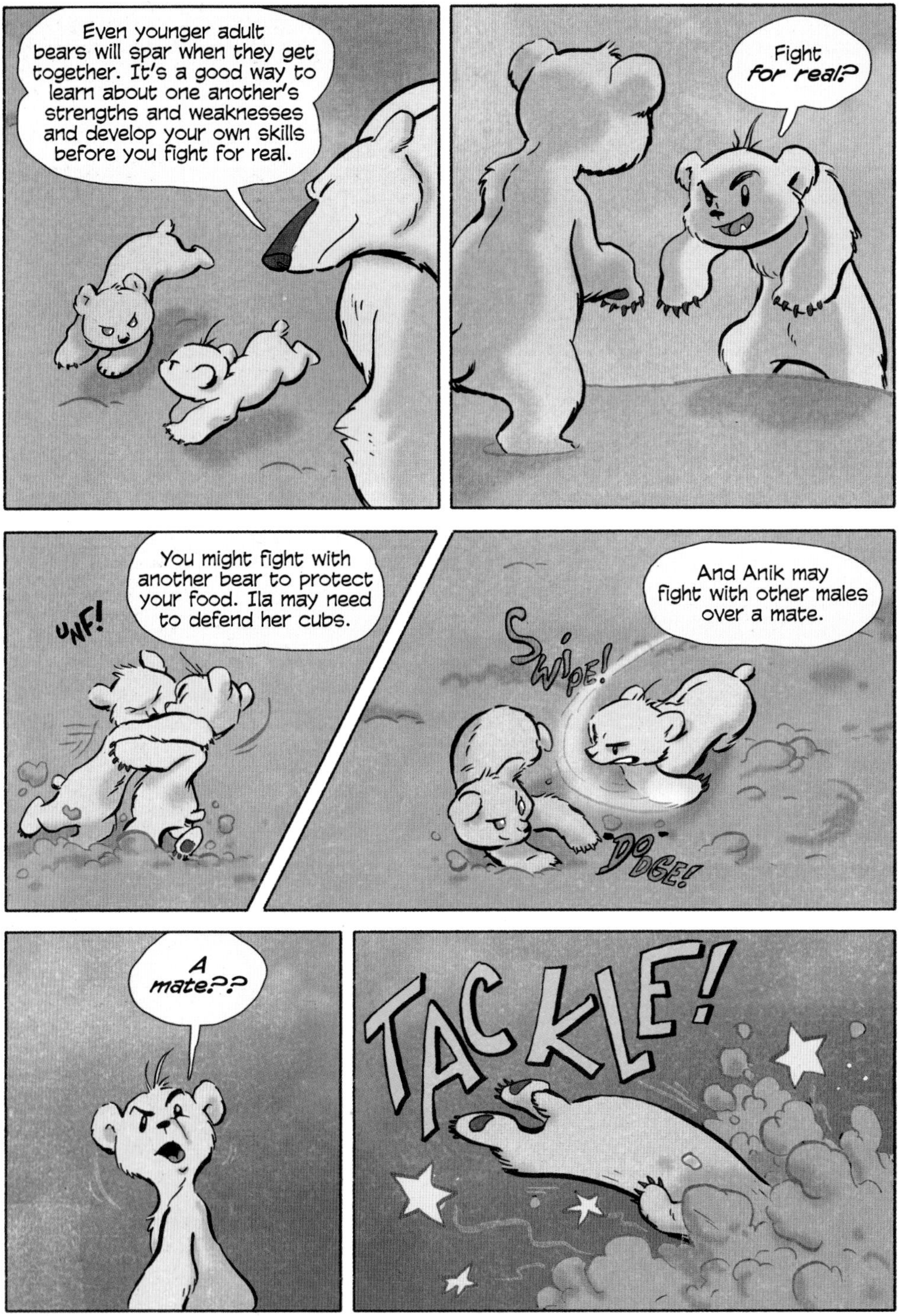
Even younger adult bears will spar when they get together. It's a good way to learn about one another's strengths and weaknesses and develop your own skills before you fight for real.
Fight *for real?*
UNF!
You might fight with another bear to protect your food. Ila may need to defend her cubs.
And Anik may fight with other males over a mate.
SWIPE!
DODGE!
A mate?!?
TACKLE!

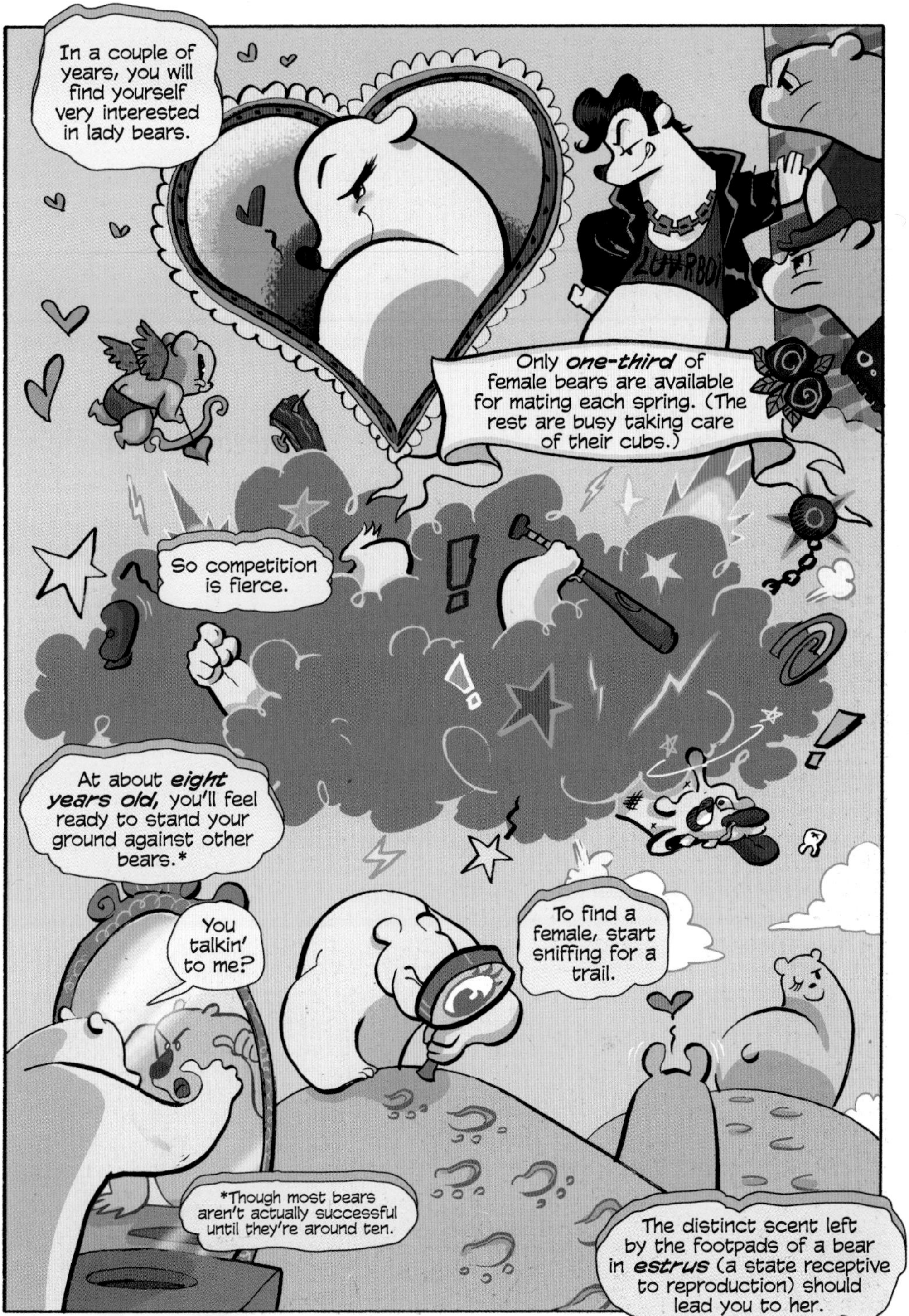
In a couple of years, you will find yourself very interested in lady bears.
LUVRBOI
Only one-third of female bears are available for mating each spring. (The rest are busy taking care of their cubs.)
So competition is fierce.
At about eight years old, you'll feel ready to stand your ground against other bears.*
You talkin' to me?
To find a female, start sniffing for a trail.
*Though most bears aren't actually successful until they're around ten.
The distinct scent left by the footpads of a bear in estrus (a state receptive to reproduction) should lead you to her.

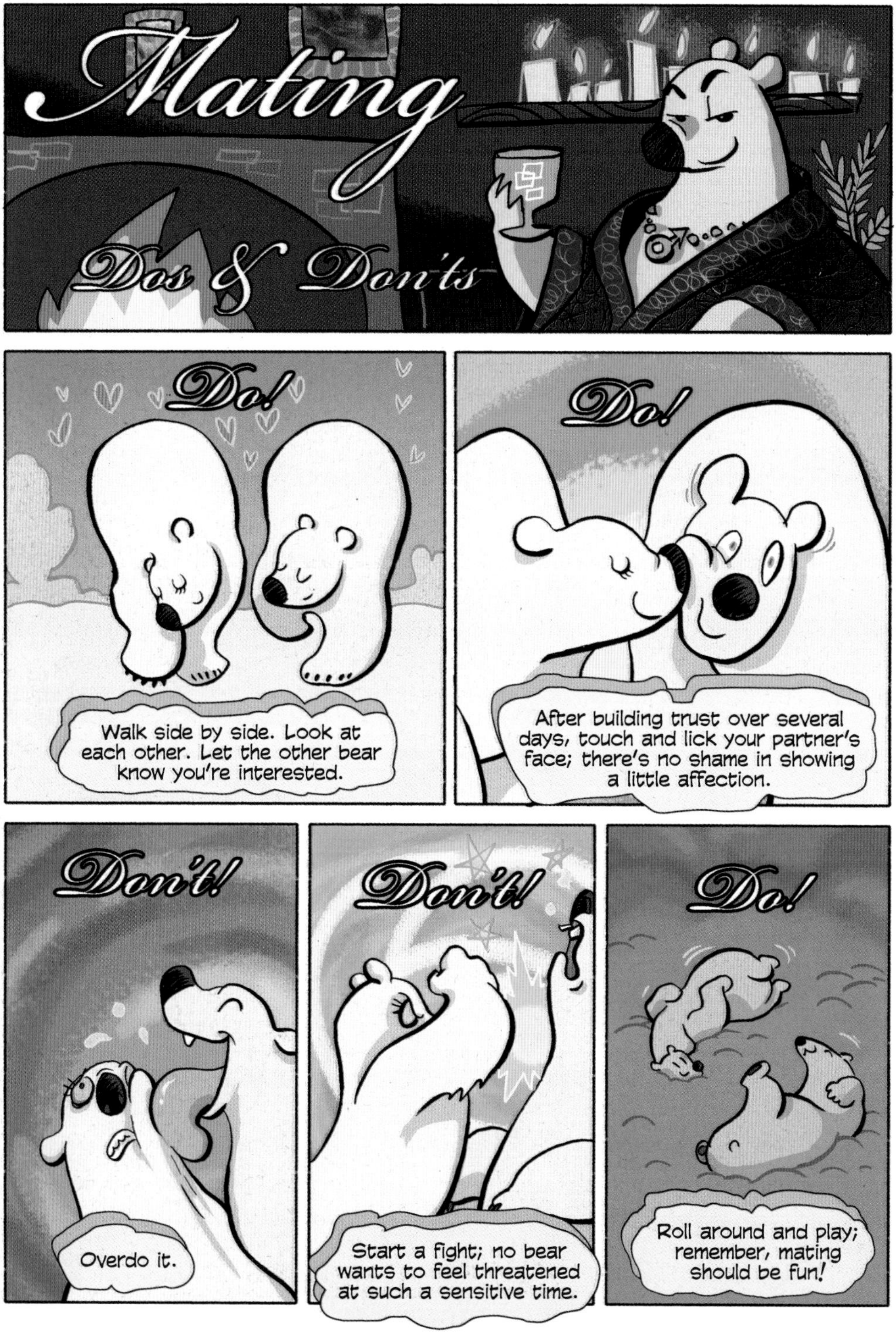
Mating
Dos & Don'ts
Do!
Walk side by side. Look at each other. Let the other bear know you're interested.
Do!
After building trust over several days, touch and lick your partner's face; there's no shame in showing a little affection.
Don't!
Overdo it.
Don't!
Start a fight; no bear wants to feel threatened at such a sensitive time.
Do!
Roll around and play; remember, mating should be fun!

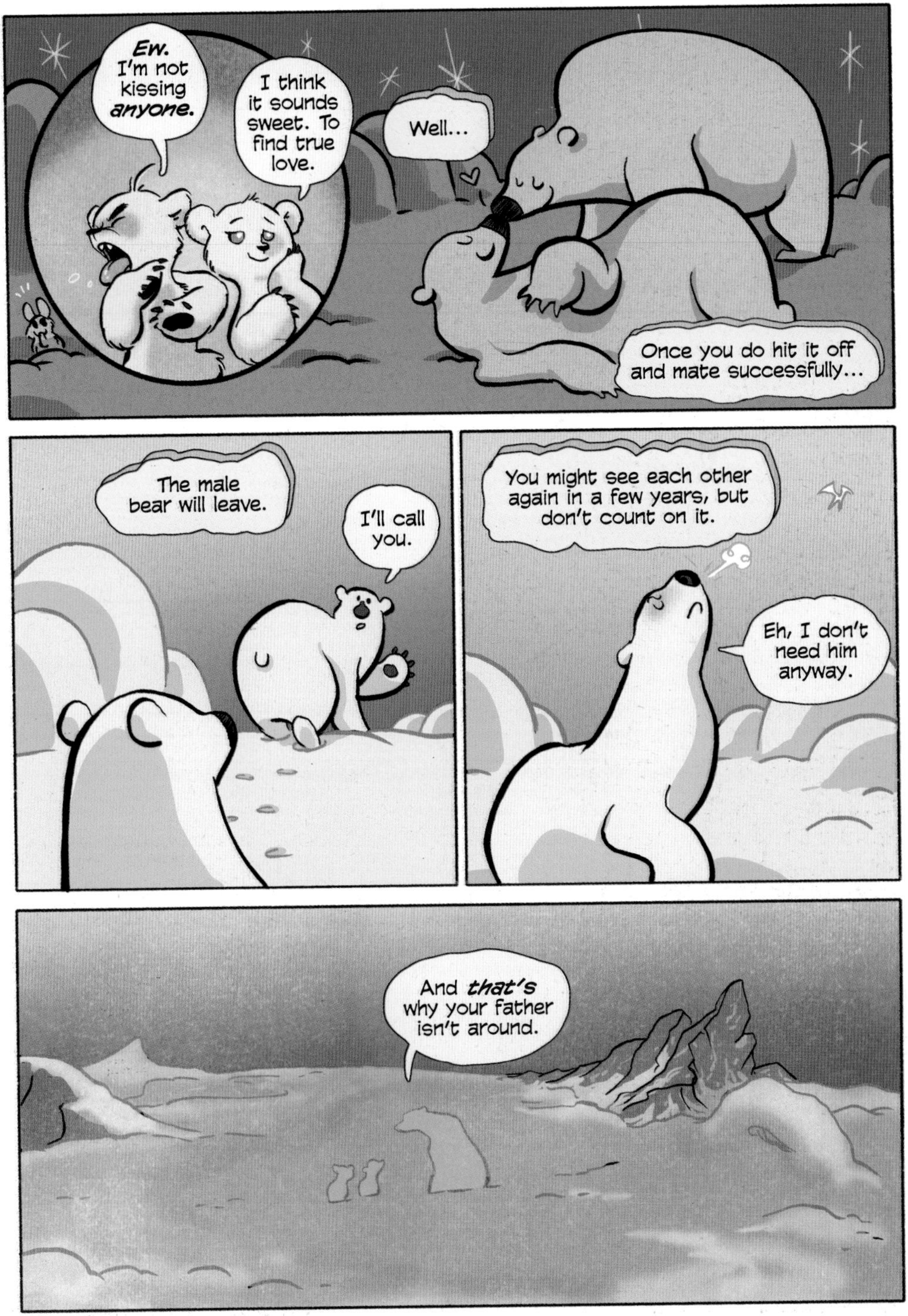
Ew. I'm not kissing anyone.
I think it sounds sweet. To find true love.
Well...
Once you do hit it off and mate successfully...
The male bear will leave.
I'll call you.
You might see each other again in a few years, but don't count on it.
Eh, I don't need him anyway.
And that's why your father isn't around.

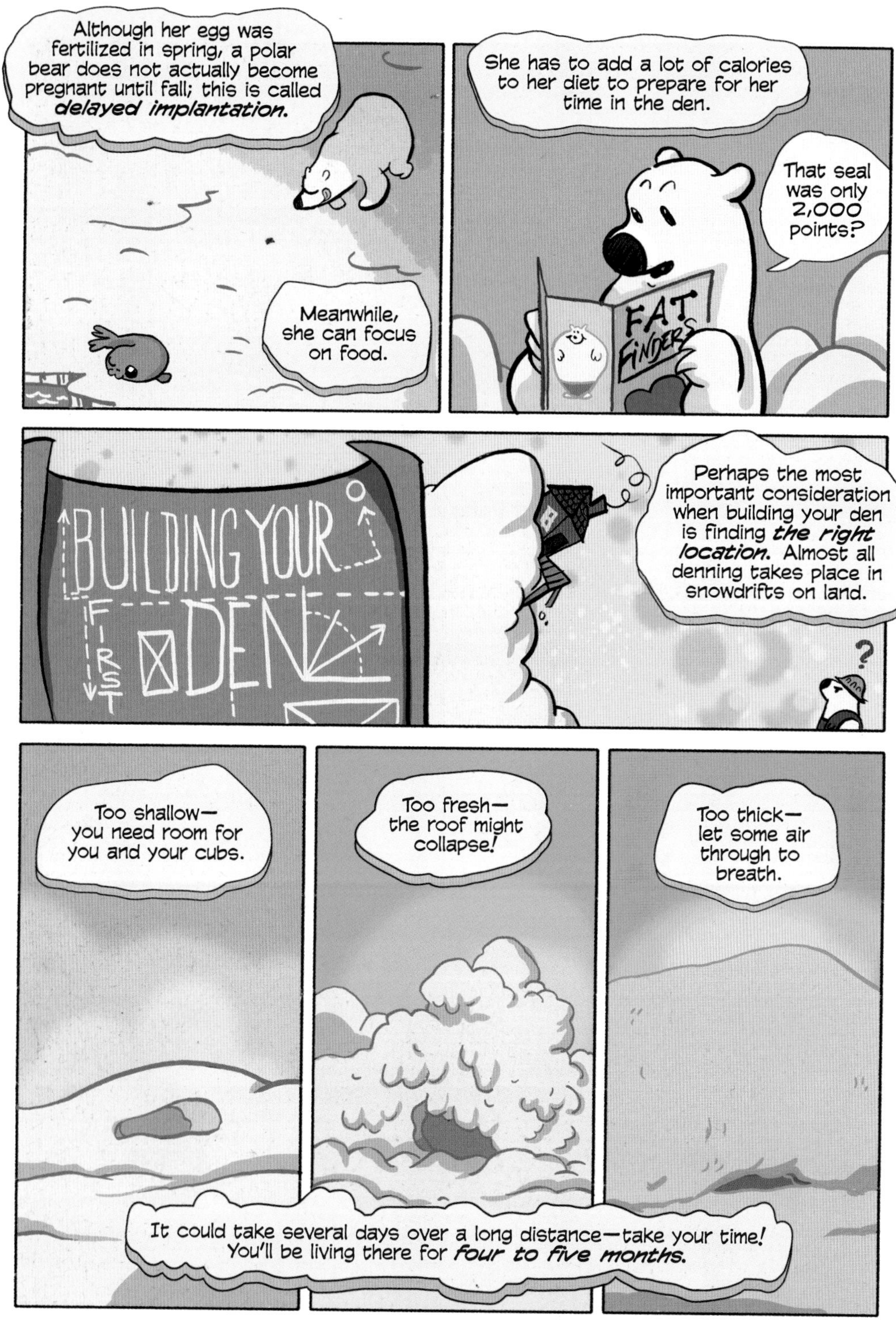
Although her egg was fertilized in spring, a polar bear does not actually become pregnant until fall; this is called ***delayed implantation.***
Meanwhile, she can focus on food.
She has to add a lot of calories to her diet to prepare for her time in the den.
That seal was only 2,000 points?
FAT FINDERS
BUILDING YOUR DEN
FIRST
Perhaps the most important consideration when building your den is finding ***the right location.*** Almost all denning takes place in snowdrifts on land.
?
Too shallow—you need room for you and your cubs.
Too fresh—the roof might collapse!
Too thick—let some air through to breath.
It could take several days over a long distance—take your time! You'll be living there for ***four to five months.***

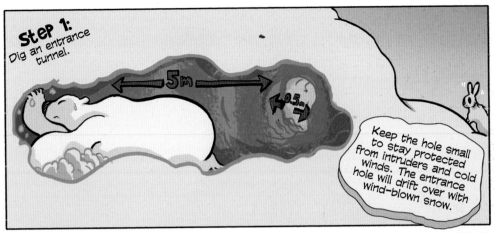

Step 1: Dig an entrance tunnel.

5m

0.5m

Keep the hole small to stay protected from intruders and cold winds. The entrance hole will drift over with wind-blown snow.

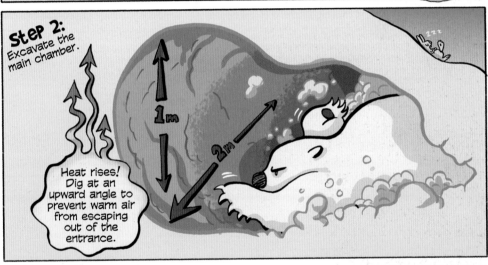

Step 2: Excavate the main chamber.

1m

2m

Heat rises! Dig at an upward angle to prevent warm air from escaping out of the entrance.

zzz

Step 3: Add some personal touches (optional).

boing!

Almost all dens have a *single chamber!* But every once in a while a creative bear might make a three-room complex. Sometimes cubs will dig their own alcove!

Ventilation shafts and back entrances are cool but pretty uncommon.

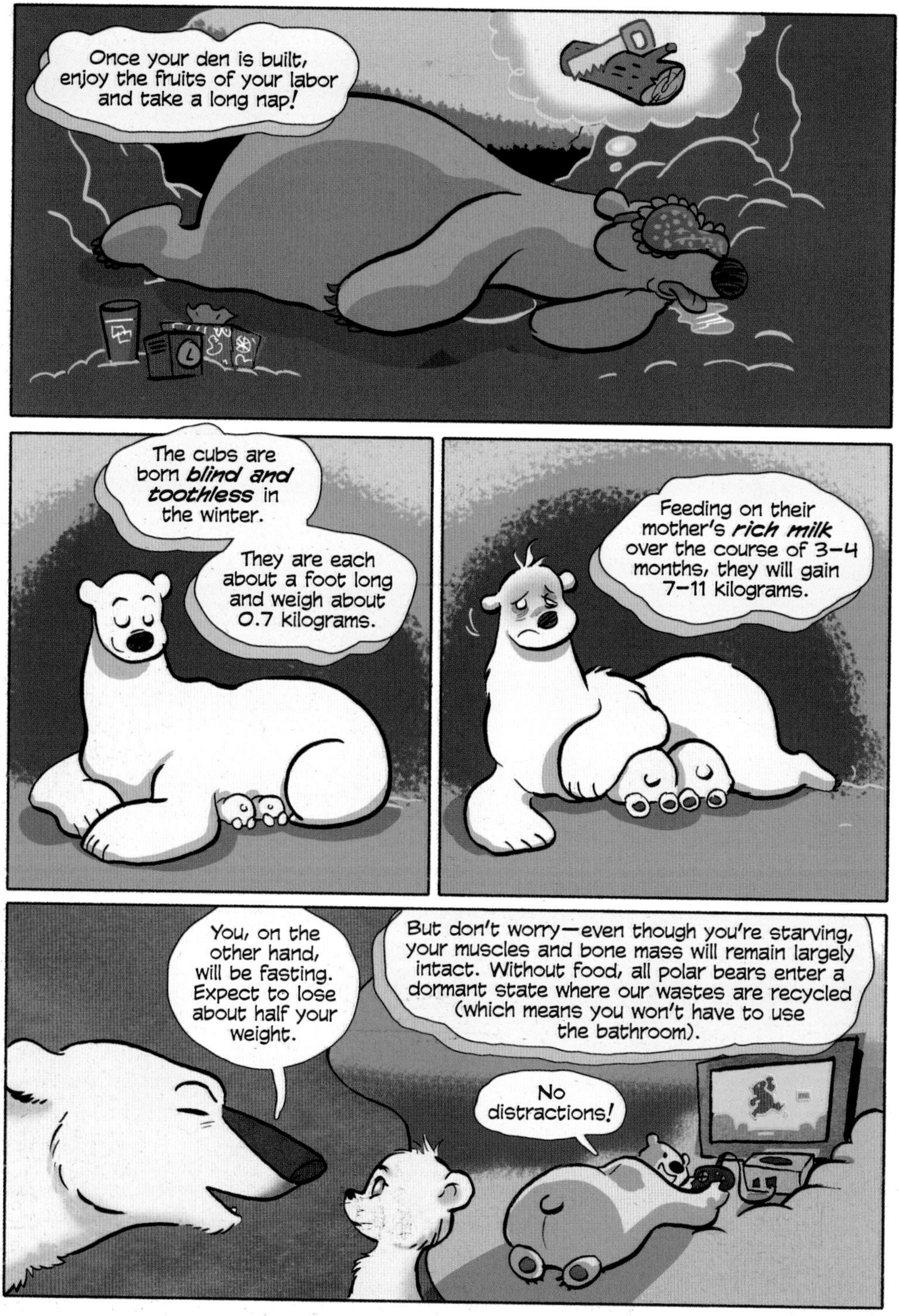
Once your den is built, enjoy the fruits of your labor and take a long nap!
The cubs are born *blind and toothless* in the winter.
They are each about a foot long and weigh about 0.7 kilograms.
Feeding on their mother's *rich milk* over the course of 3–4 months, they will gain 7–11 kilograms.
You, on the other hand, will be fasting. Expect to lose about half your weight.
But don't worry—even though you're starving, your muscles and bone mass will remain largely intact. Without food, all polar bears enter a dormant state where our wastes are recycled (which means you won't have to use the bathroom).
No distractions!

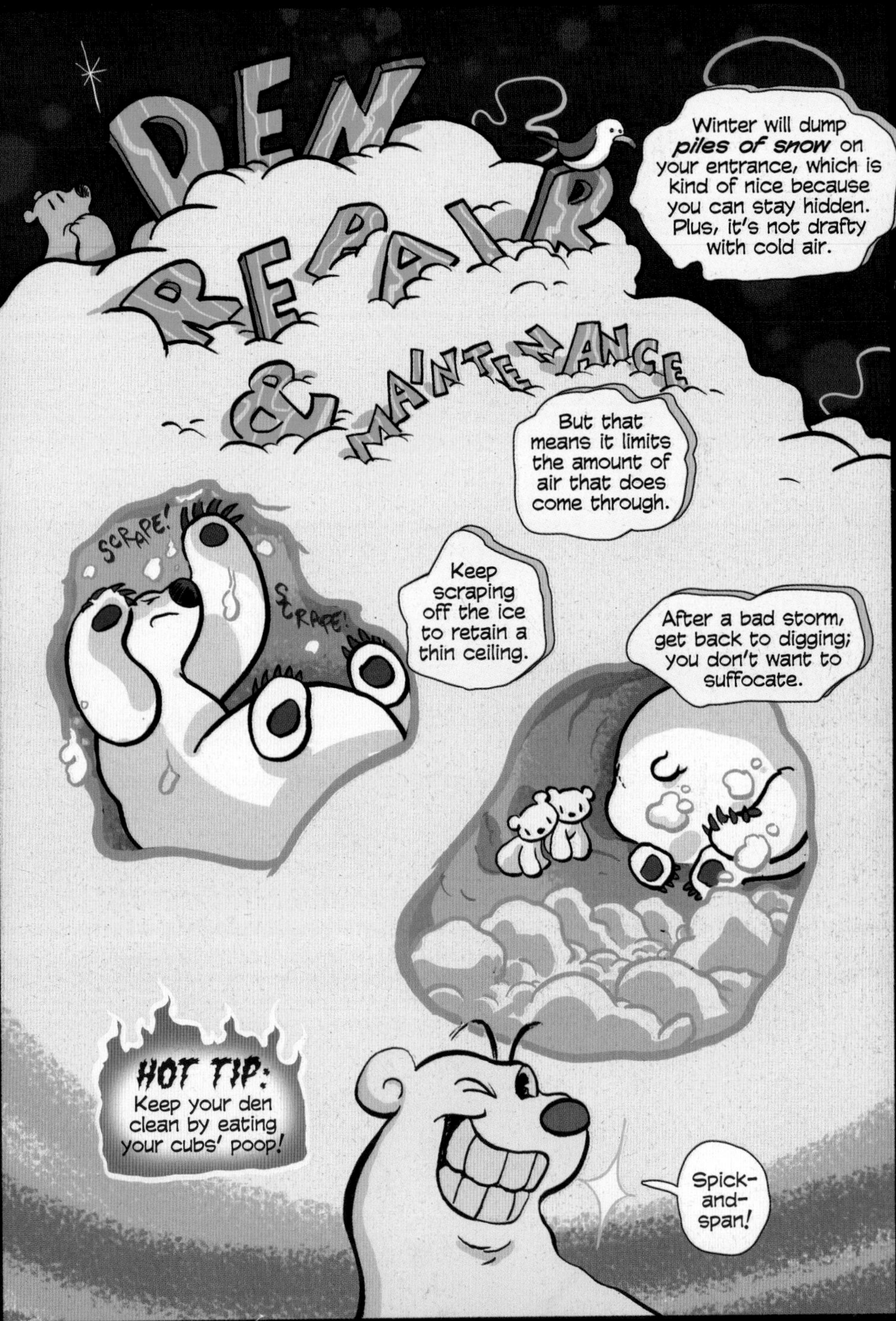
DEN REPAIR & MAINTENANCE
Winter will dump *piles of snow* on your entrance, which is kind of nice because you can stay hidden. Plus, it's not drafty with cold air.
But that means it limits the amount of air that does come through.
SCRAPE!
SCRAPE!
Keep scraping off the ice to retain a thin ceiling.
After a bad storm, get back to digging; you don't want to suffocate.
HOT TIP:
Keep your den clean by eating your cubs' poop!
Spick-and-span!

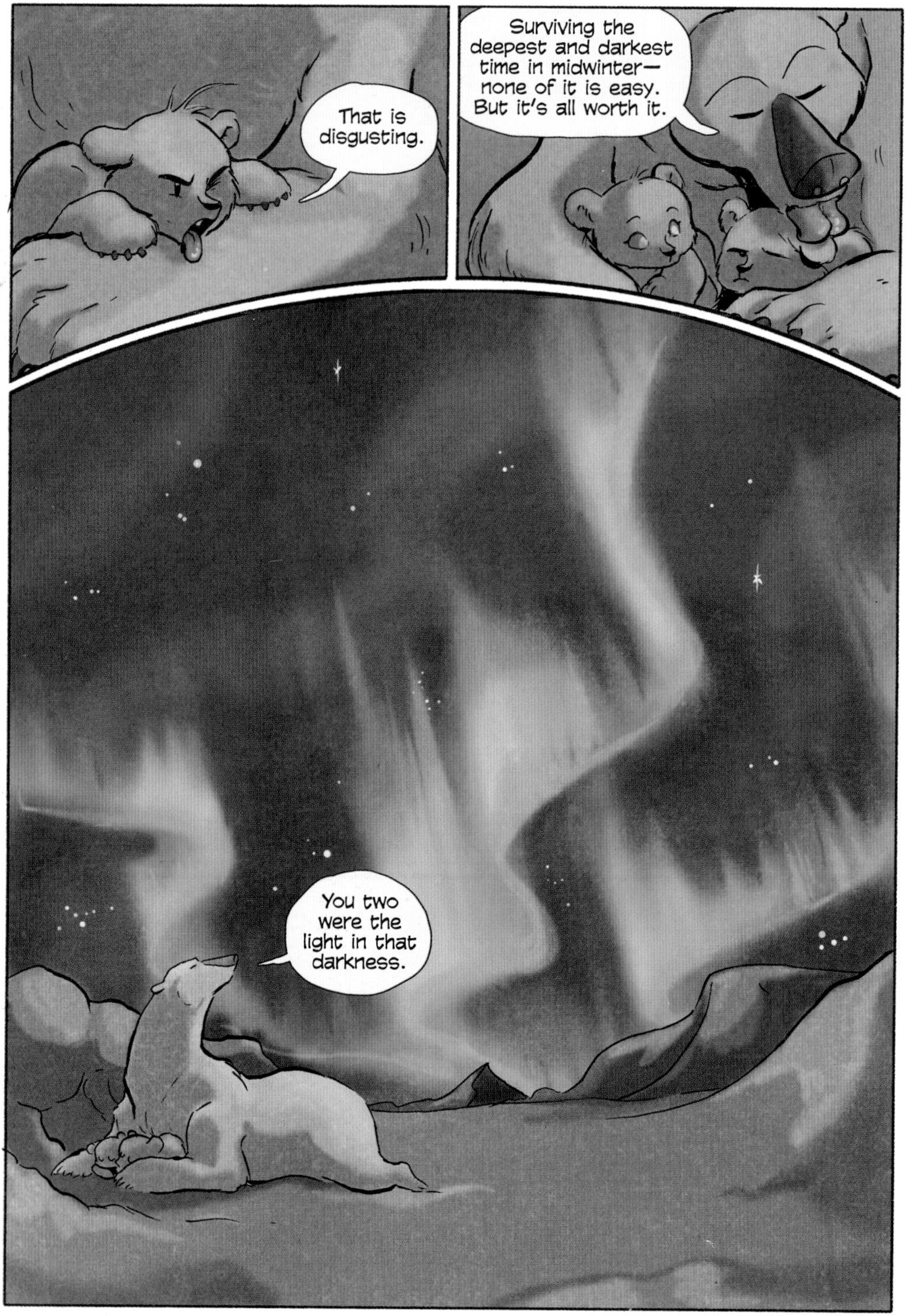
That is disgusting.
Surviving the deepest and darkest time in midwinter— none of it is easy. But it's all worth it.
You two were the light in that darkness.

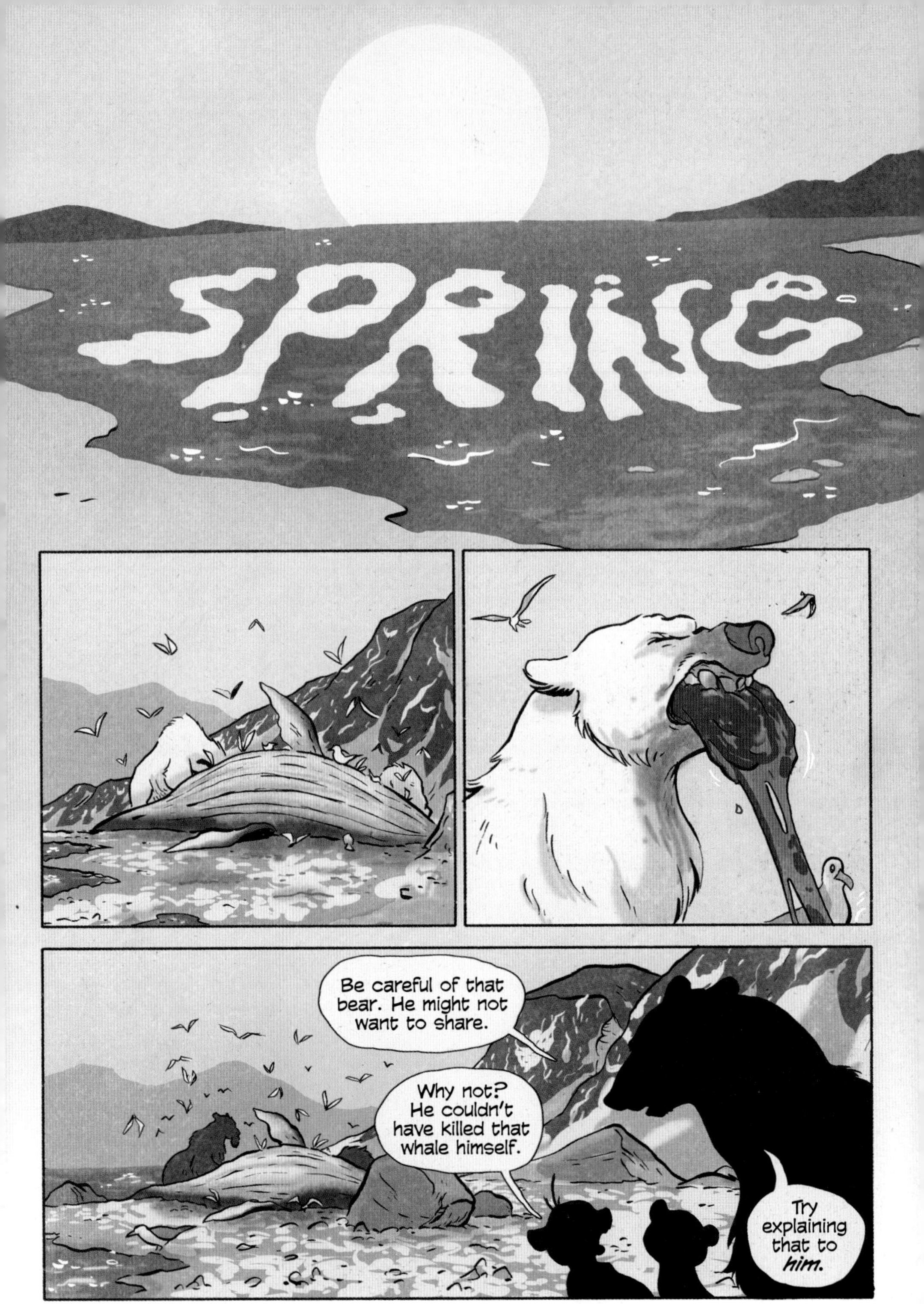
SPRING
Be careful of that bear. He might not want to share.
Why not? He couldn't have killed that whale himself.
Try explaining that to *him*.

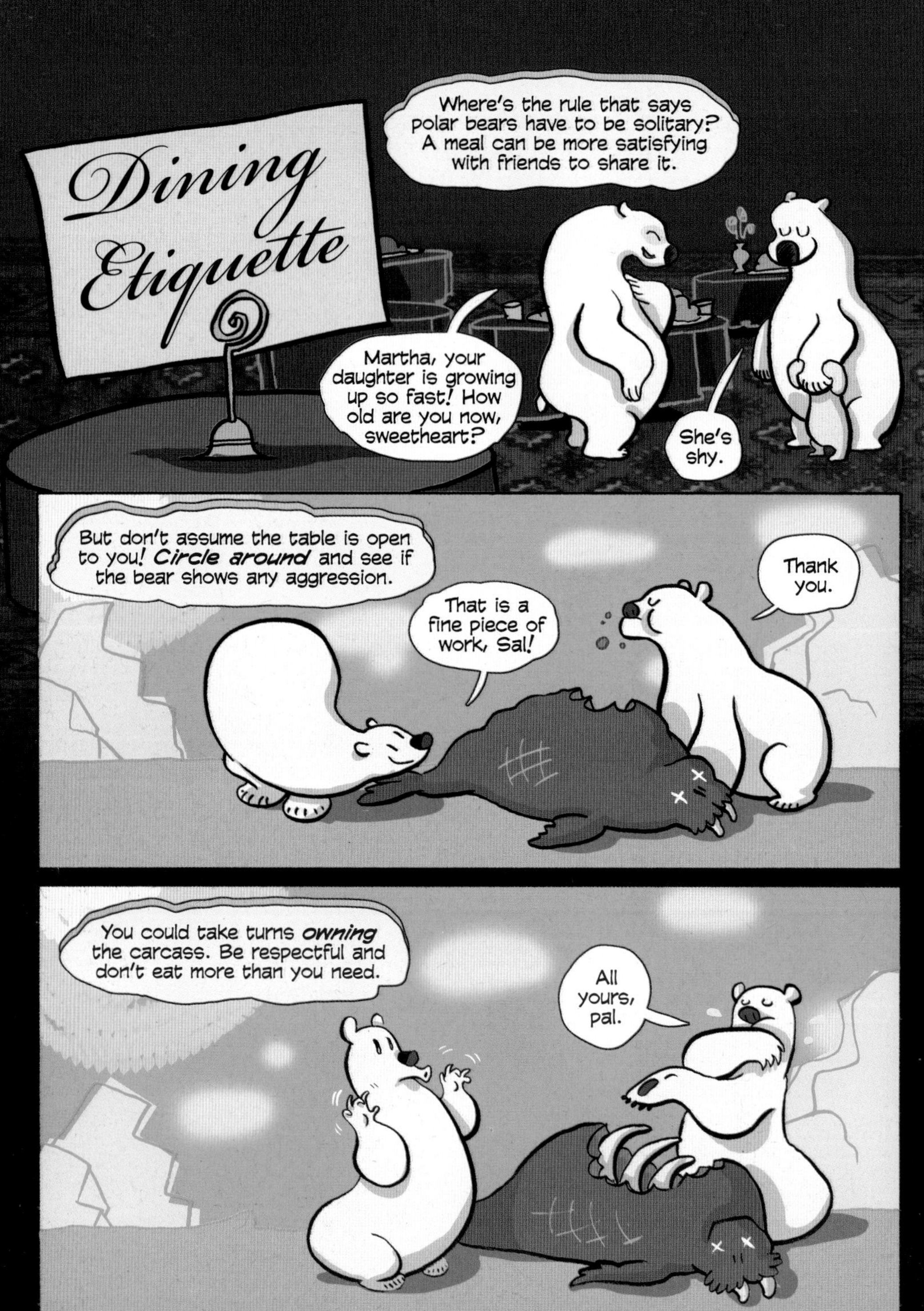
Dining Etiquette
Where's the rule that says polar bears have to be solitary? A meal can be more satisfying with friends to share it.
Martha, your daughter is growing up so fast! How old are you now, sweetheart?
She's shy.
But don't assume the table is open to you! *Circle around* and see if the bear shows any aggression.
That is a fine piece of work, Sal!
Thank you.
You could take turns *owning* the carcass. Be respectful and don't eat more than you need.
All yours, pal.

STARE

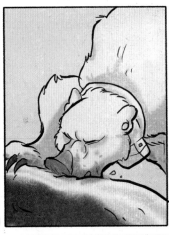

Okay, he says it's fine! Just find a spot and start eating.

Mama, what happened to that bear?

They came from the sky!

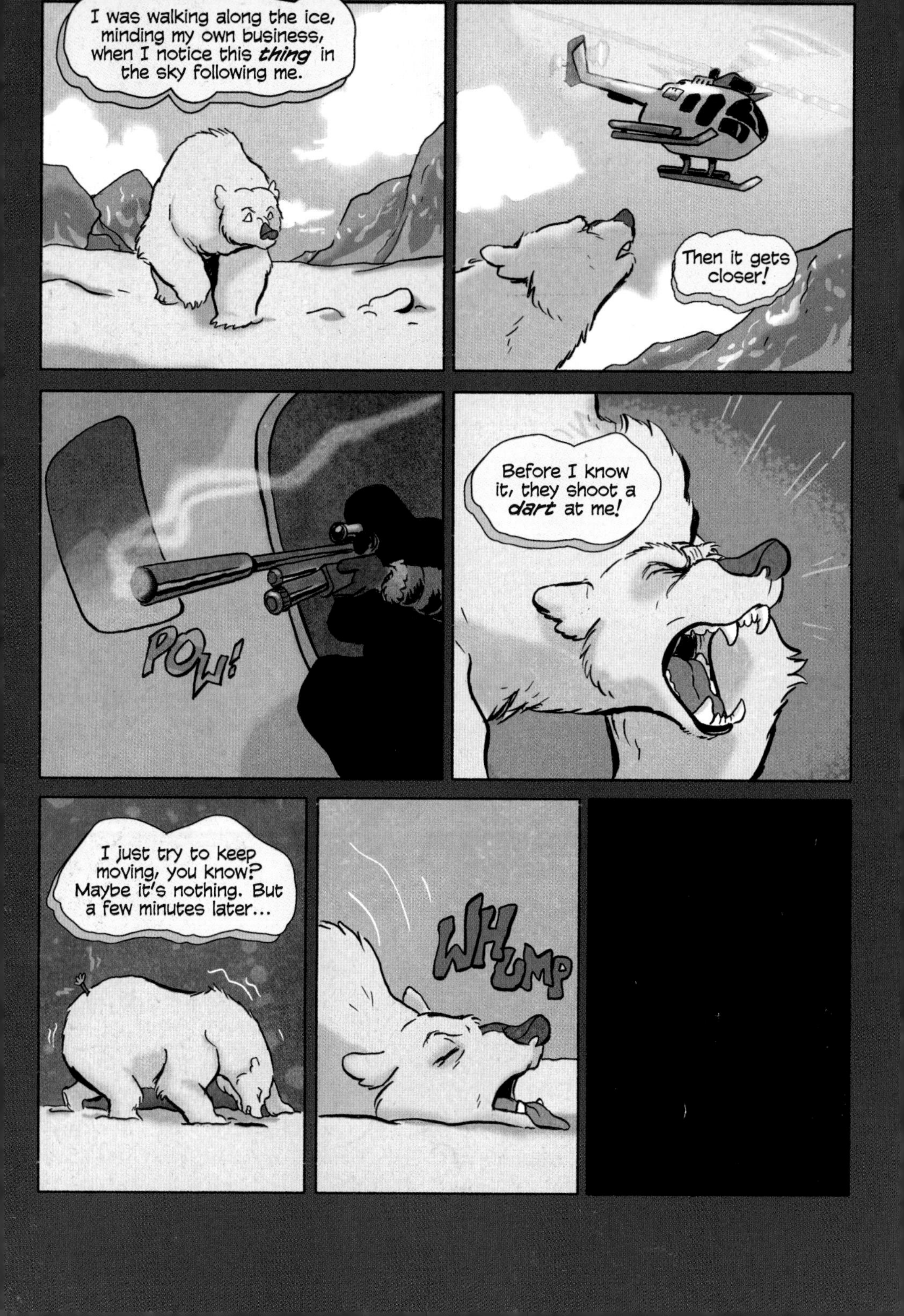
I was walking along the ice, minding my own business, when I notice this *thing* in the sky following me.
Then it gets closer!
POW!
Before I know it, they shoot a *dart* at me!
I just try to keep moving, you know? Maybe it's nothing. But a few minutes later...
WHUMP

Why don't you two leave that nice bear alone and have a taste?

I'm out for thirty minutes, and I wake up with this *collar* around my neck and something punched through *my ear!*

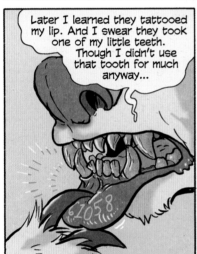

Later I learned they tattooed my lip. And I swear they took one of my little teeth. Though I didn't use that tooth for much anyway...

They're *tracking me.* My every move. Do you understand?

No, they *don't* understand. They're too young.

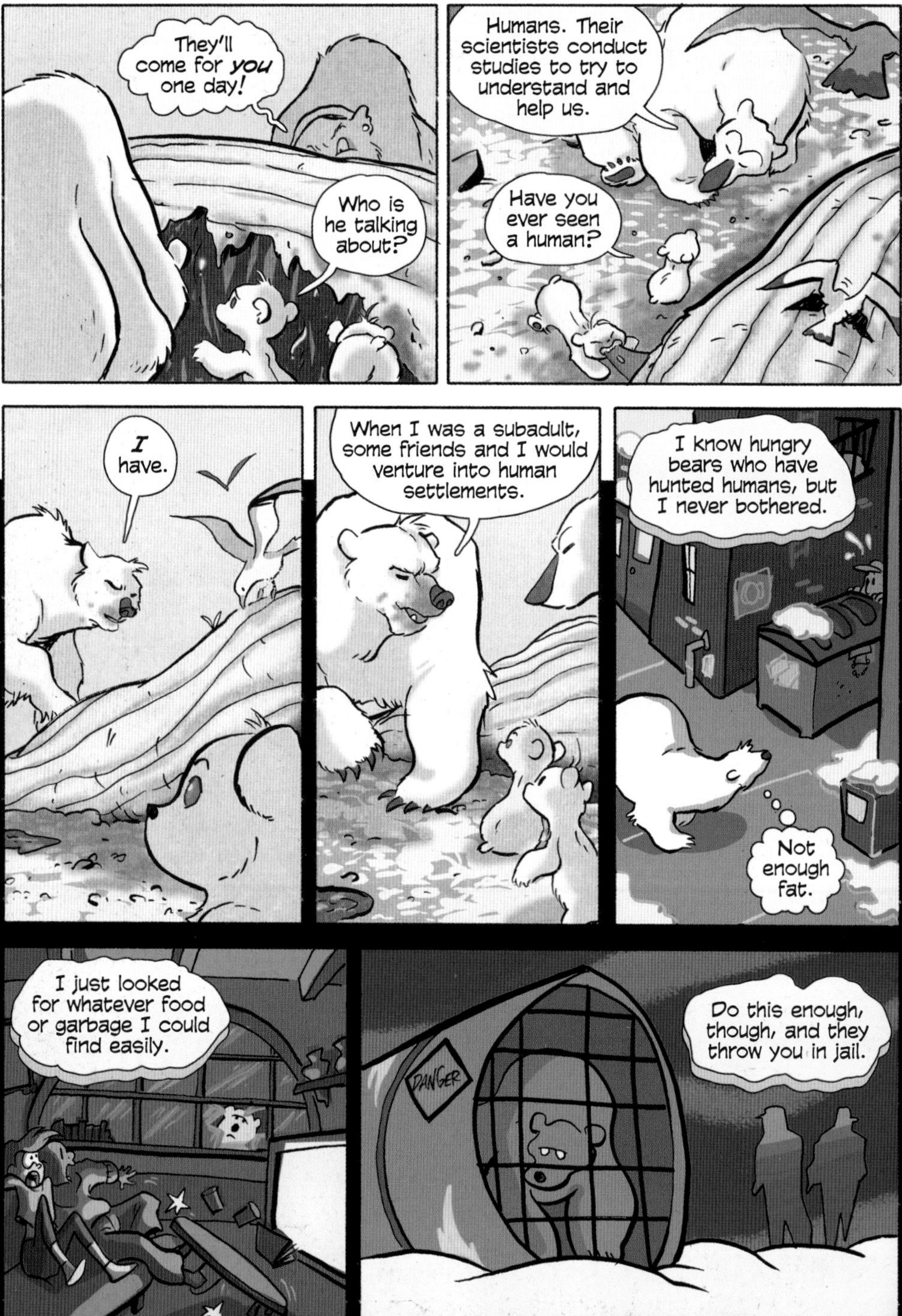
They'll come for *you* one day!
Who is he talking about?
Humans. Their scientists conduct studies to try to understand and help us.
Have you ever seen a human?
I have.
When I was a subadult, some friends and I would venture into human settlements.
I know hungry bears who have hunted humans, but I never bothered.
Not enough fat.
I just looked for whatever food or garbage I could find easily.
DANGER
Do this enough, though, and they throw you in jail.

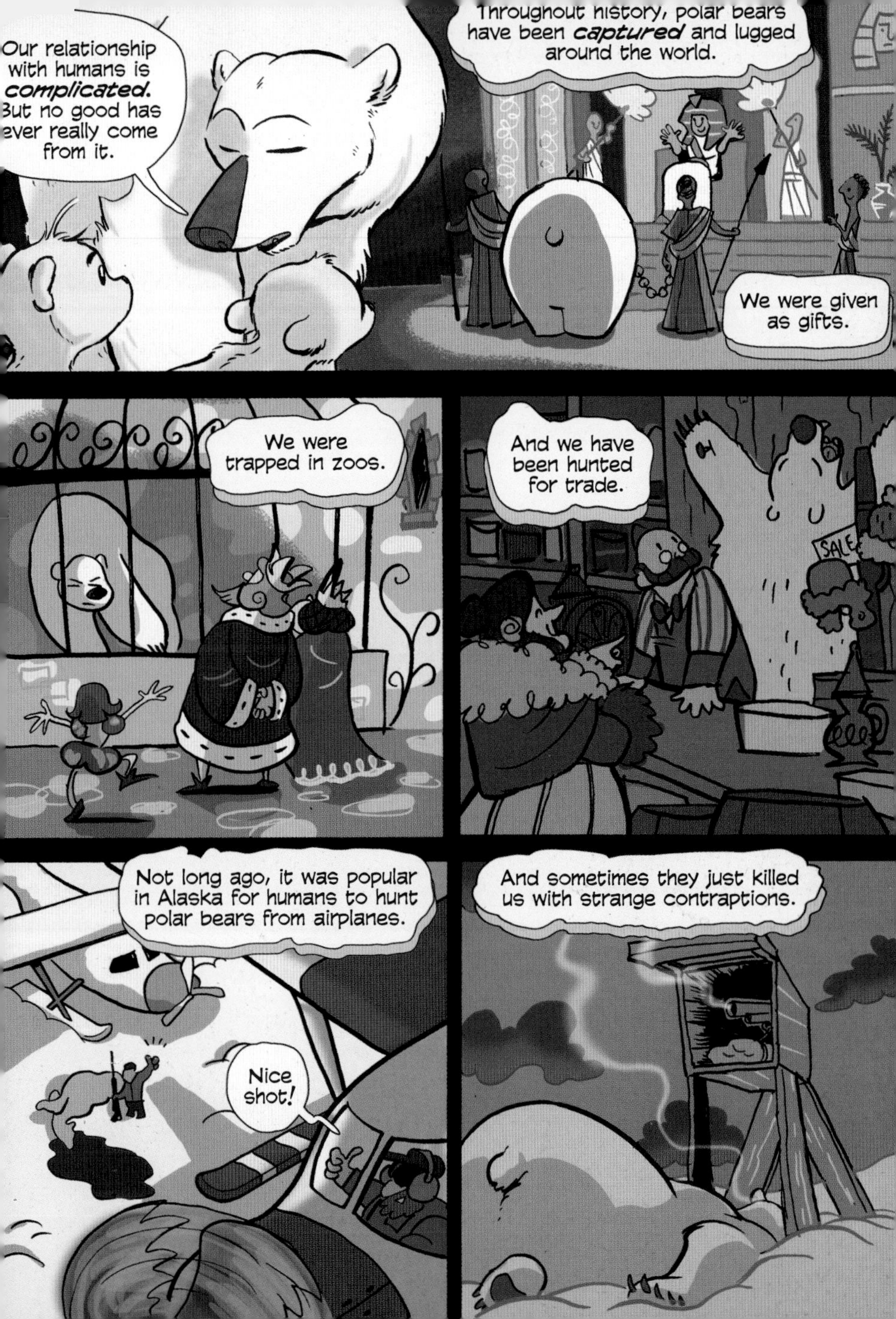
Our relationship with humans is *complicated.* But no good has ever really come from it.
Throughout history, polar bears have been *captured* and lugged around the world.
We were given as gifts.
We were trapped in zoos.
And we have been hunted for trade.
SALE
Not long ago, it was popular in Alaska for humans to hunt polar bears from airplanes.
Nice shot!
And sometimes they just killed us with strange contraptions.

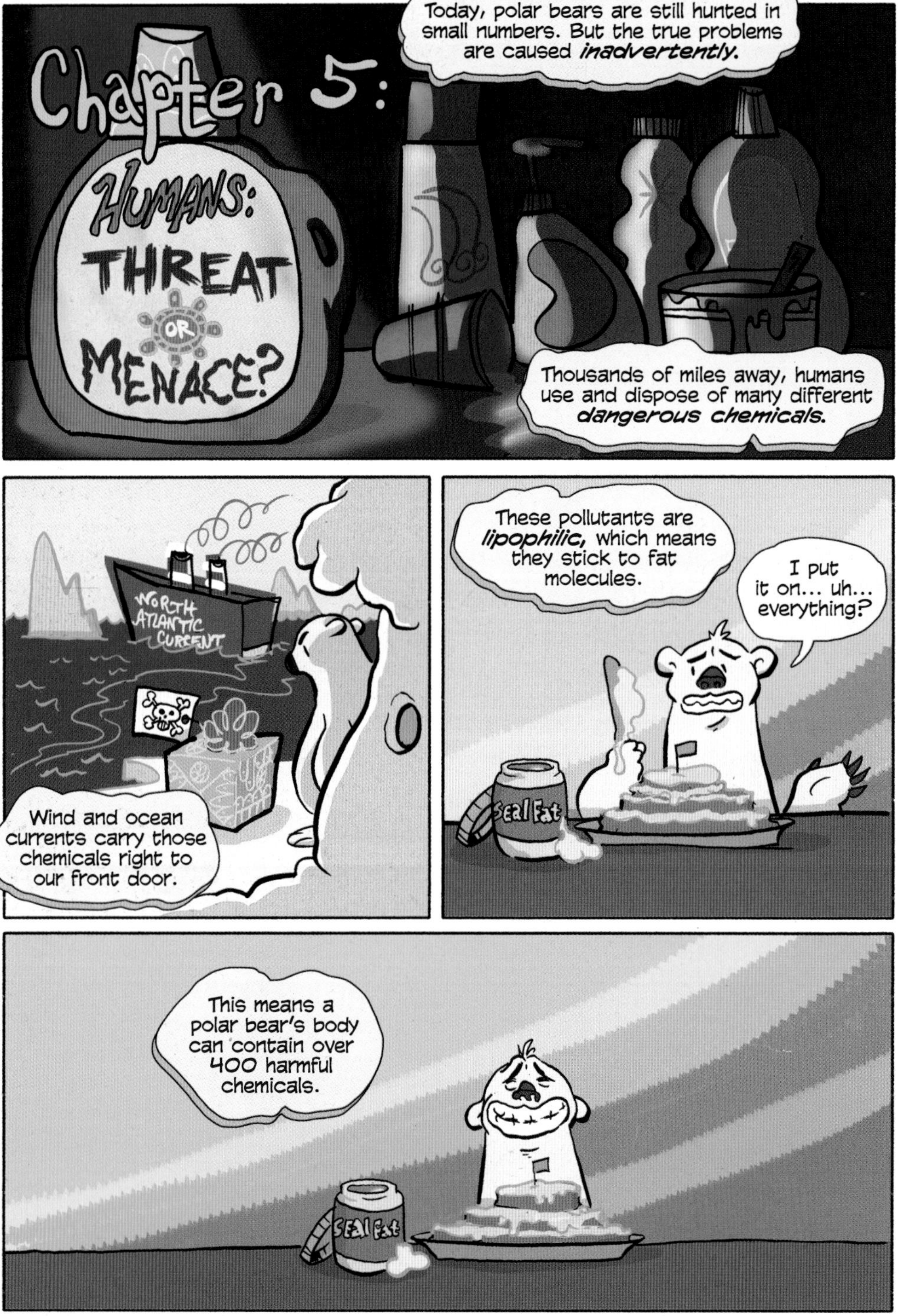
Chapter 5:
Humans:
THREAT
OR
MENACE?
Today, polar bears are still hunted in small numbers. But the true problems are caused *inadvertently.*
Thousands of miles away, humans use and dispose of many different ***dangerous chemicals.***
WORTH ATLANTIC CURRENT
Wind and ocean currents carry those chemicals right to our front door.
These pollutants are ***lipophilic,*** which means they stick to fat molecules.
I put it on... uh... everything?
SEAL FAT
This means a polar bear's body can contain over 400 harmful chemicals.
SEAL FAT

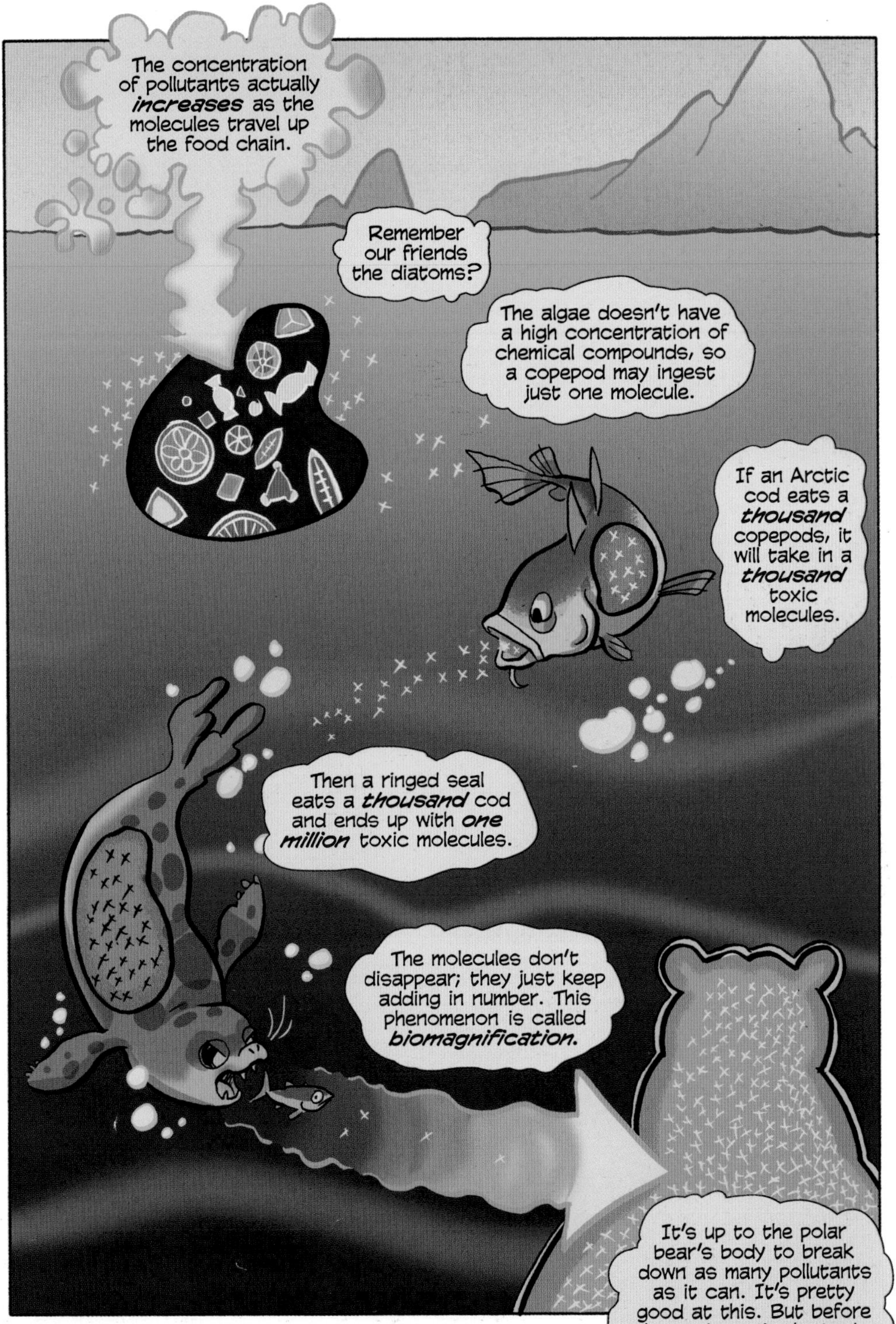

The concentration of pollutants actually *increases* as the molecules travel up the food chain.
Remember our friends the diatoms?
The algae doesn't have a high concentration of chemical compounds, so a copepod may ingest just one molecule.
If an Arctic cod eats a *thousand* copepods, it will take in a *thousand* toxic molecules.
Then a ringed seal eats a *thousand* cod and ends up with *one million* toxic molecules.
The molecules don't disappear; they just keep adding in number. This phenomenon is called *biomagnification.*
It's up to the polar bear's body to break down as many pollutants as it can. It's pretty good at this. But before the toxins exit the body, they are very active.

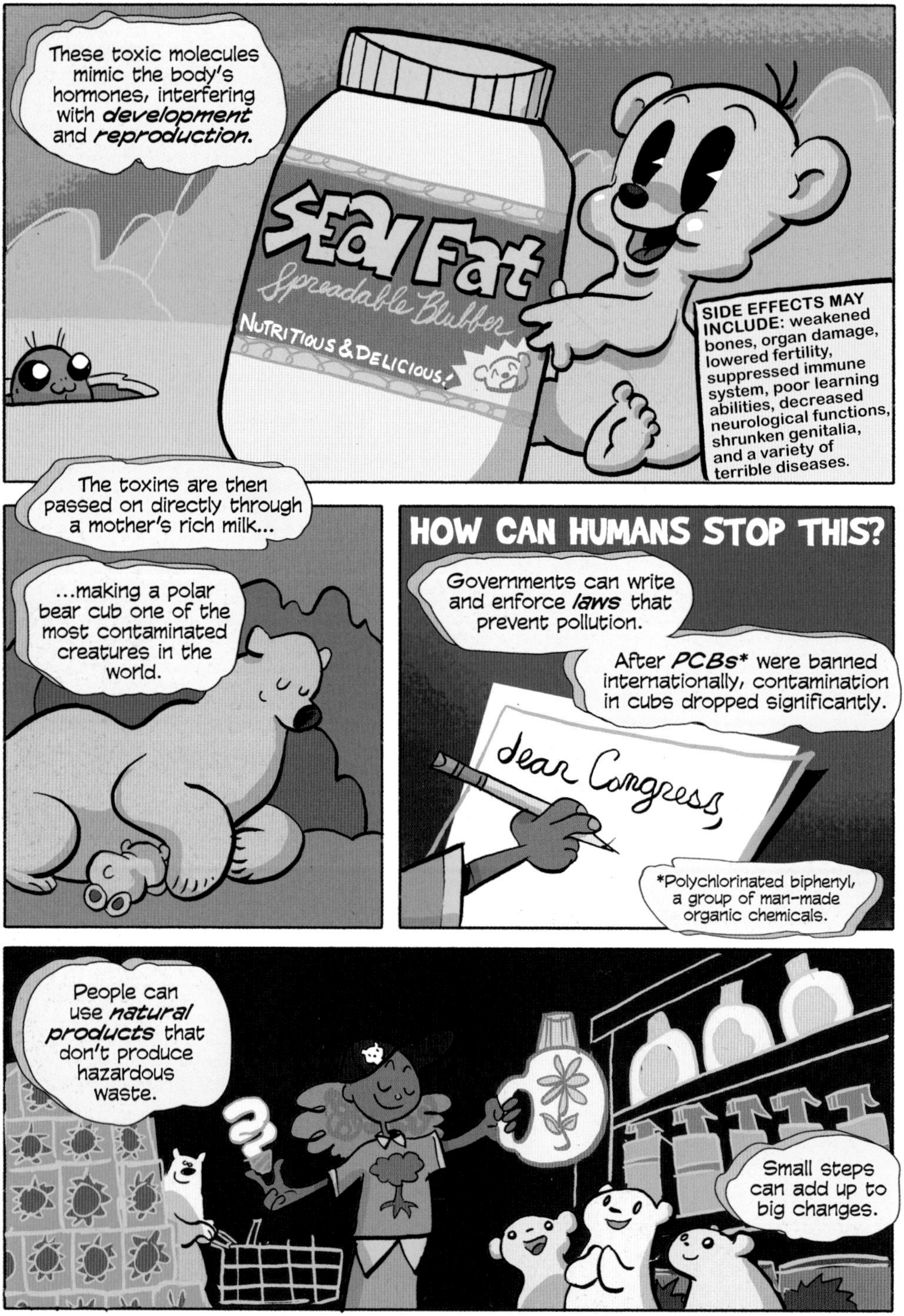

These toxic molecules mimic the body's hormones, interfering with *development* and *reproduction*.
SEAL Fat
Spreadable Blubber
NUTRITIOUS & DELICIOUS!
SIDE EFFECTS MAY INCLUDE: weakened bones, organ damage, lowered fertility, suppressed immune system, poor learning abilities, decreased neurological functions, shrunken genitalia, and a variety of terrible diseases.
The toxins are then passed on directly through a mother's rich milk...
...making a polar bear cub one of the most contaminated creatures in the world.
HOW CAN HUMANS STOP THIS?
Governments can write and enforce *laws* that prevent pollution.
After *PCBs** were banned internationally, contamination in cubs dropped significantly.
dear Congress,
*Polychlorinated biphenyl, a group of man-made organic chemicals.
People can use *natural products* that don't produce hazardous waste.
Small steps can add up to big changes.

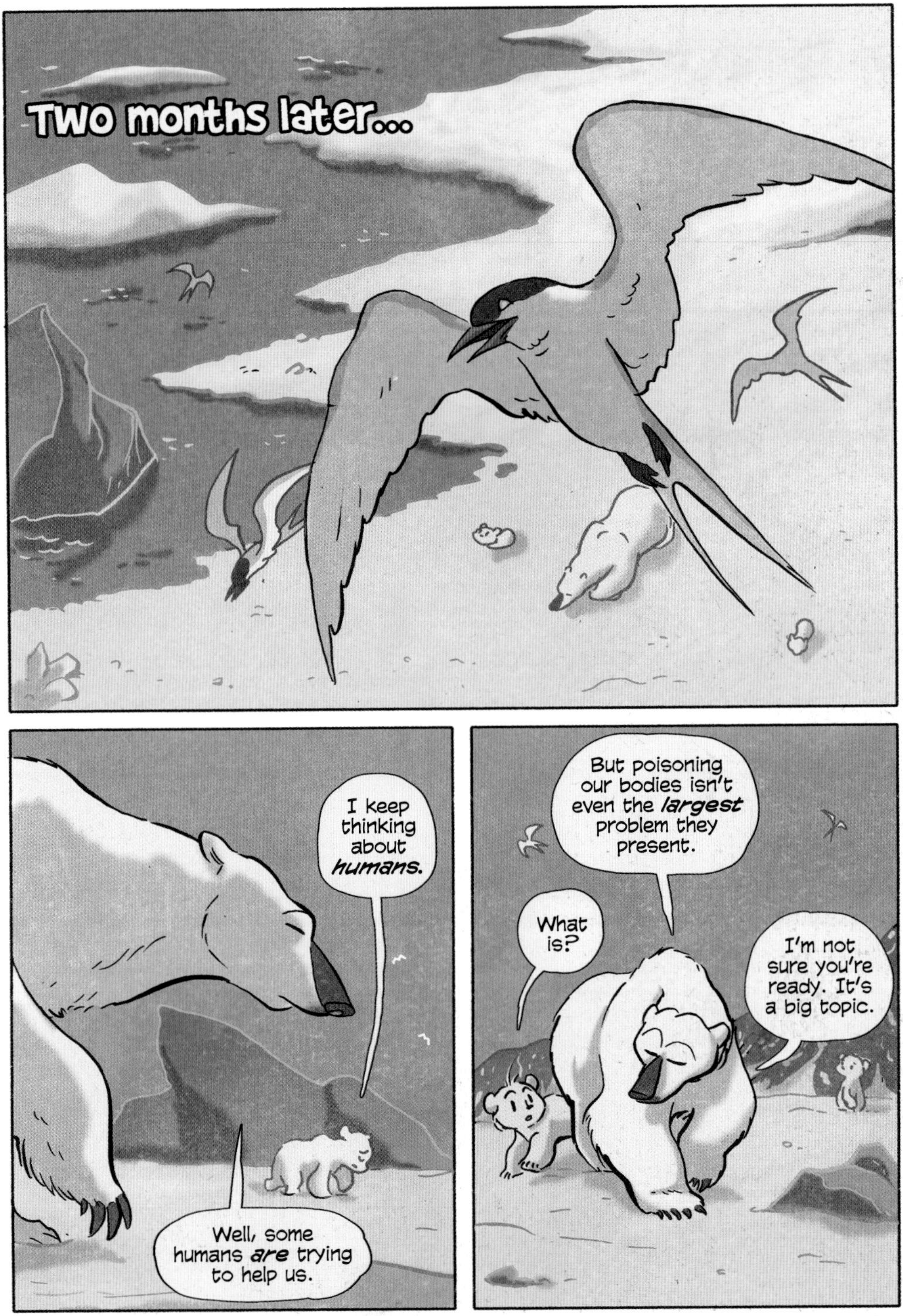
Two months later...
I keep thinking about *humans.*
Well, some humans *are* trying to help us.
But poisoning our bodies isn't even the *largest* problem they present.
What is?
I'm not sure you're ready. It's a big topic.

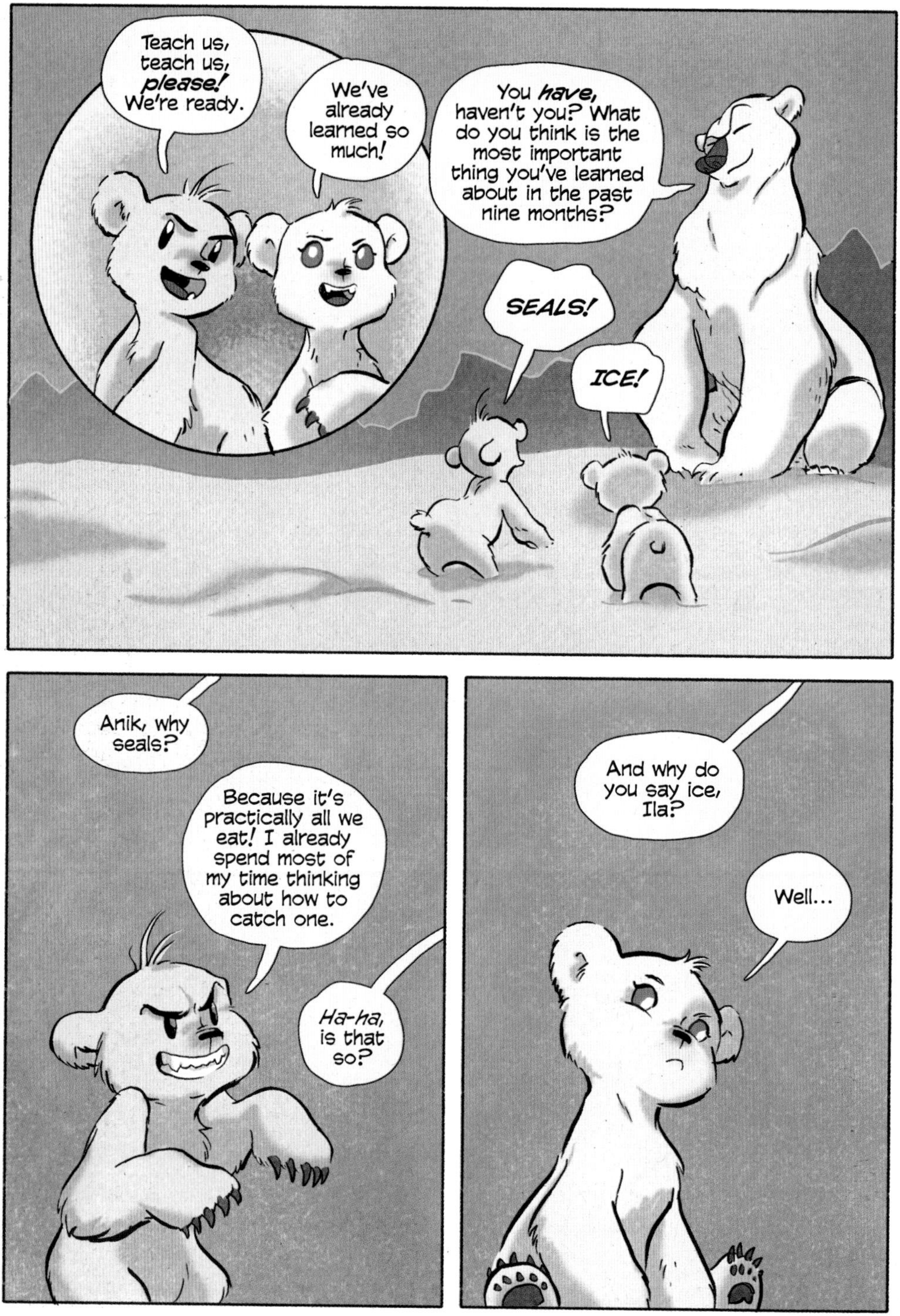
Teach us, teach us, ***please!*** We're ready.
We've already learned so much!
You ***have,*** haven't you? What do you think is the most important thing you've learned about in the past nine months?
SEALS!
ICE!
Anik, why seals?
Because it's practically all we eat! I already spend most of my time thinking about how to catch one.
Ha-ha, is that so?
And why do you say ice, Ila?
Well...

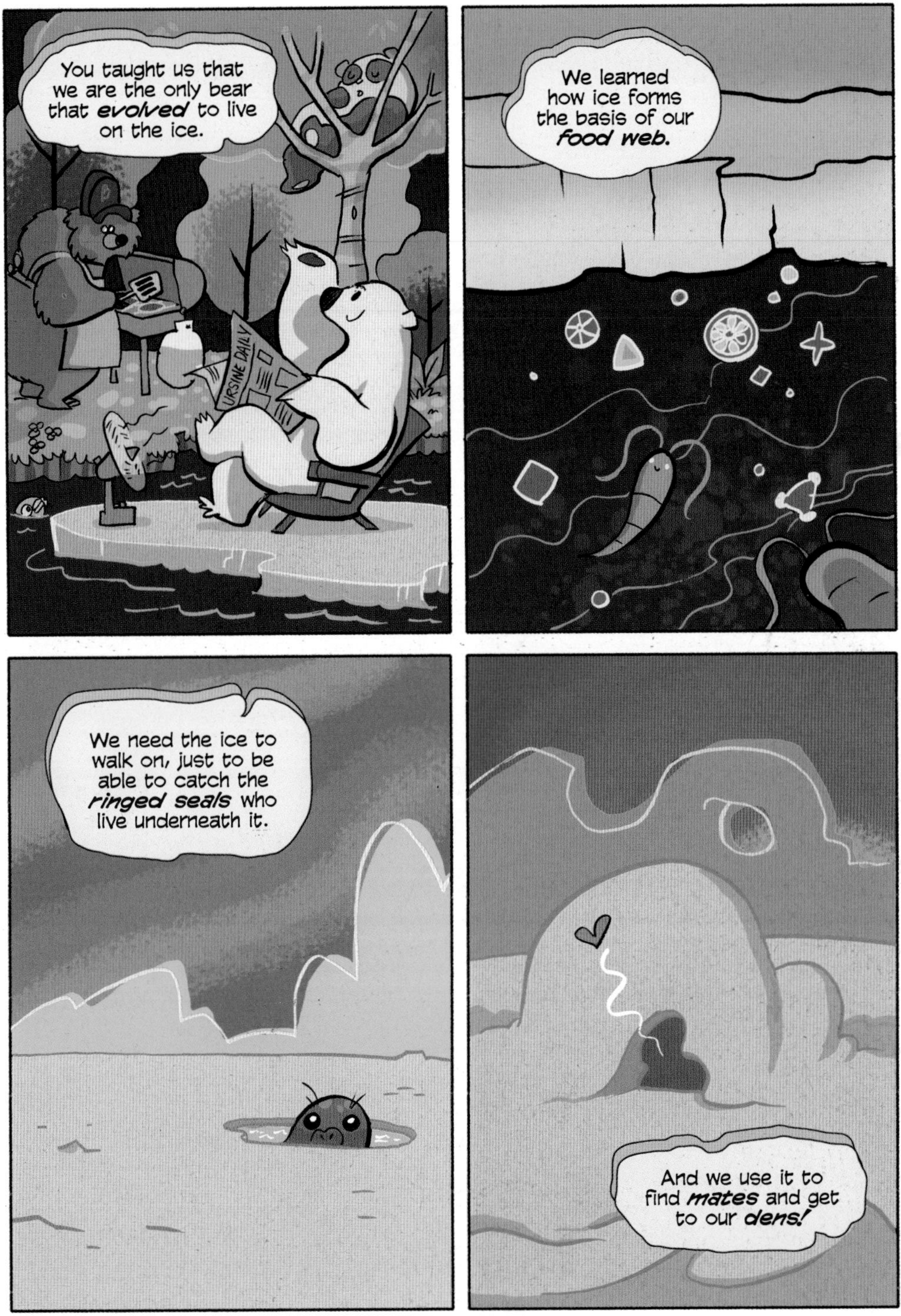
You taught us that we are the only bear that *evolved* to live on the ice.
URSINE DAILY
We learned how ice forms the basis of our *food web.*
We need the ice to walk on, just to be able to catch the *ringed seals* who live underneath it.
And we use it to find *mates* and get to our *dens!*

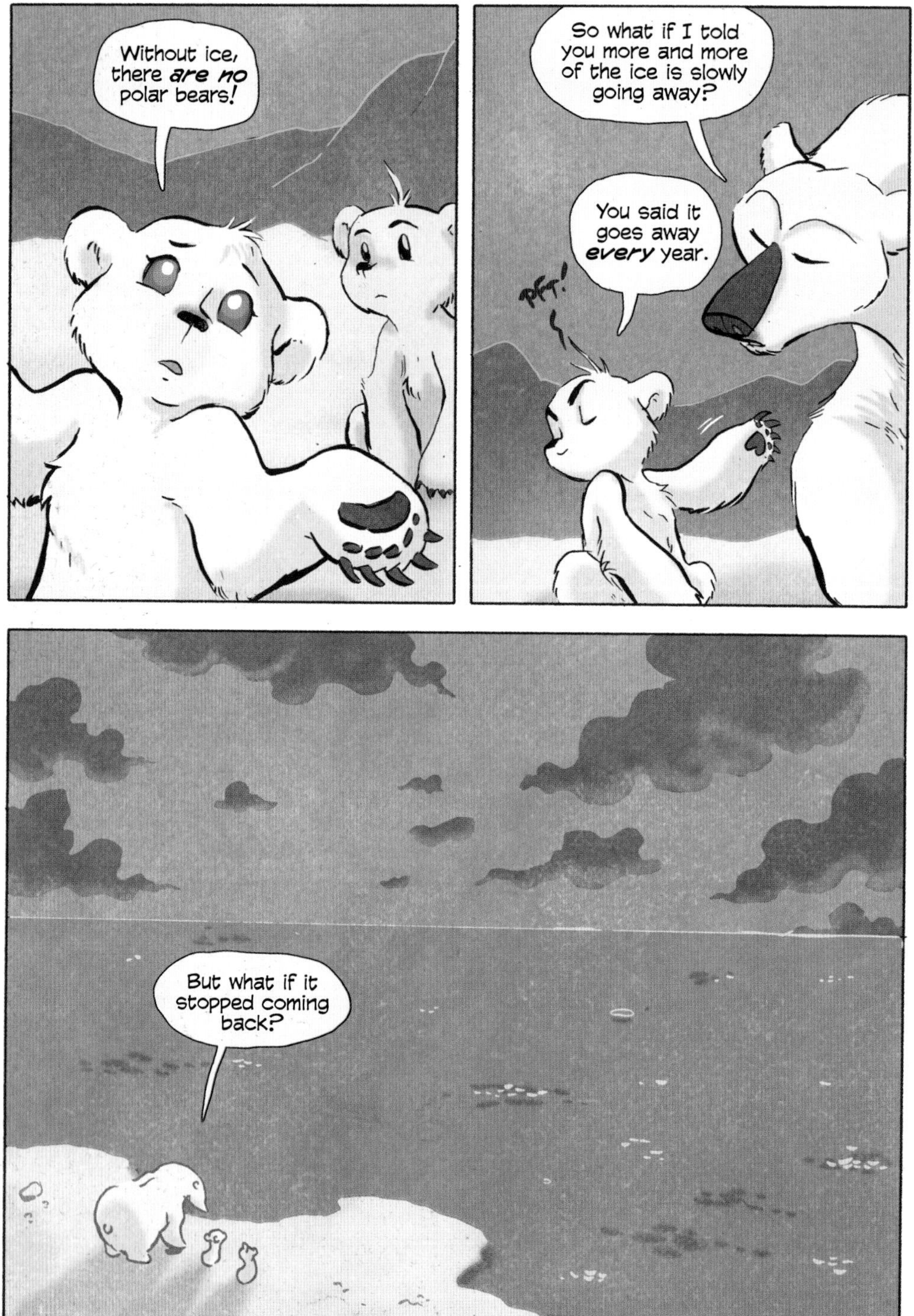
Without ice, there *are no* polar bears!
So what if I told you more and more of the ice is slowly going away?
You said it goes away *every* year.
PFFT!
But what if it stopped coming back?

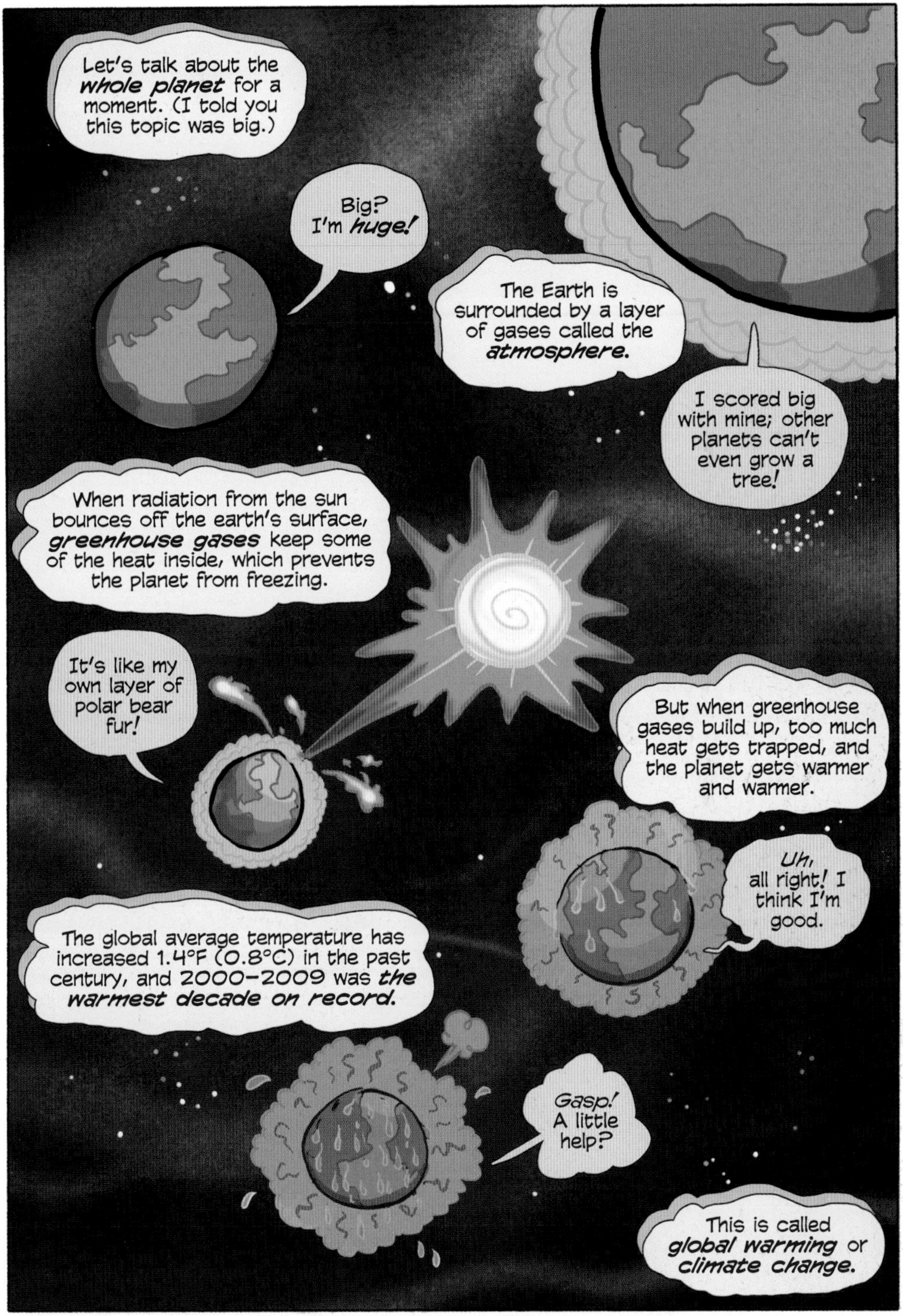
Let's talk about the whole planet for a moment. (I told you this topic was big.)
Big? I'm huge!
The Earth is surrounded by a layer of gases called the atmosphere.
I scored big with mine; other planets can't even grow a tree!
When radiation from the sun bounces off the earth's surface, greenhouse gases keep some of the heat inside, which prevents the planet from freezing.
It's like my own layer of polar bear fur!
But when greenhouse gases build up, too much heat gets trapped, and the planet gets warmer and warmer.
Uh, all right! I think I'm good.
The global average temperature has increased 1.4°F (0.8°C) in the past century, and 2000–2009 was the warmest decade on record.
Gasp! A little help?
This is called global warming or climate change.

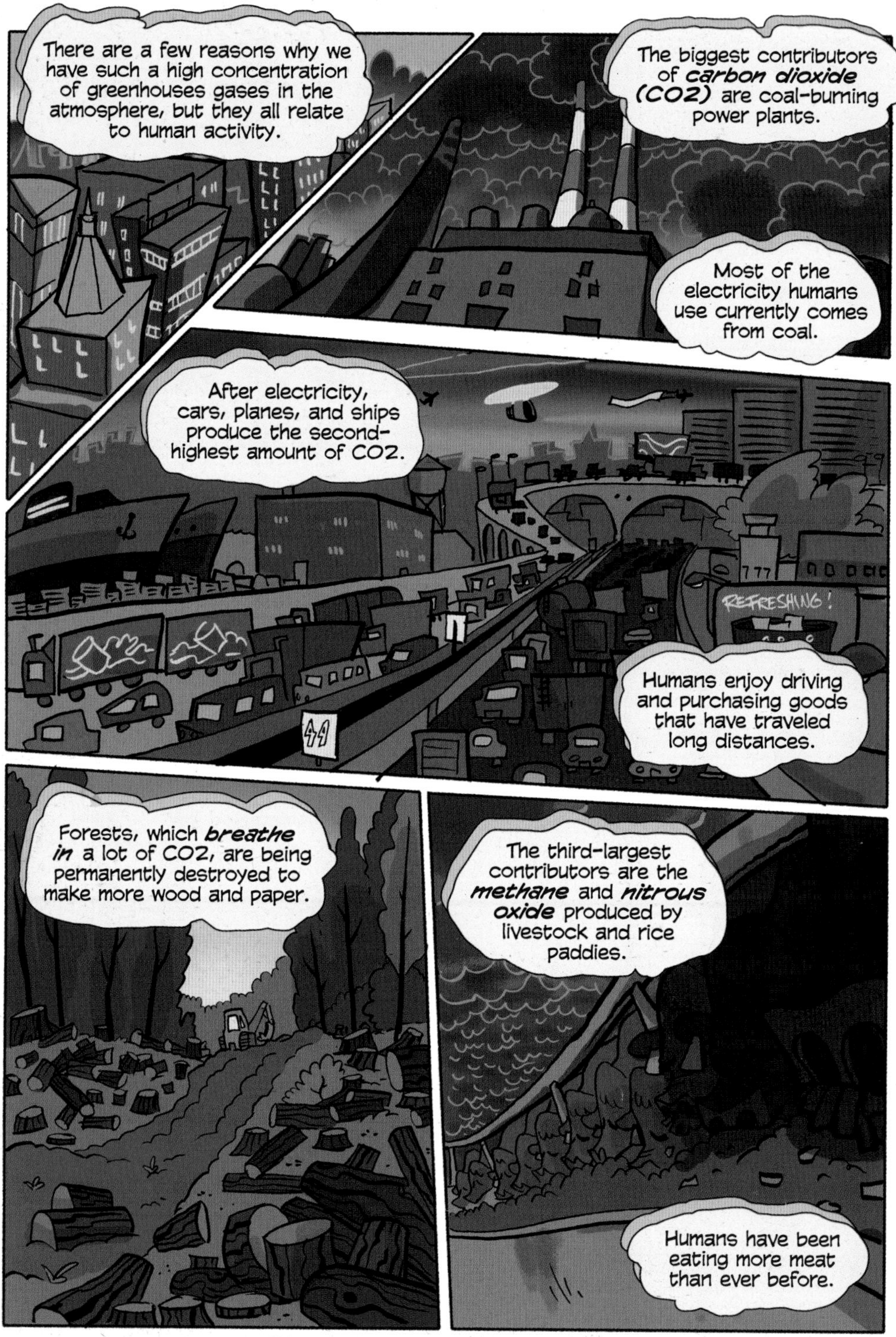
There are a few reasons why we have such a high concentration of greenhouses gases in the atmosphere, but they all relate to human activity.
The biggest contributors of ***carbon dioxide (CO2)*** are coal-burning power plants.
Most of the electricity humans use currently comes from coal.
After electricity, cars, planes, and ships produce the second-highest amount of CO2.
REFRESHING!
Humans enjoy driving and purchasing goods that have traveled long distances.
Forests, which ***breathe in*** a lot of CO2, are being permanently destroyed to make more wood and paper.
The third-largest contributors are the ***methane*** and ***nitrous oxide*** produced by livestock and rice paddies.
Humans have been eating more meat than ever before.

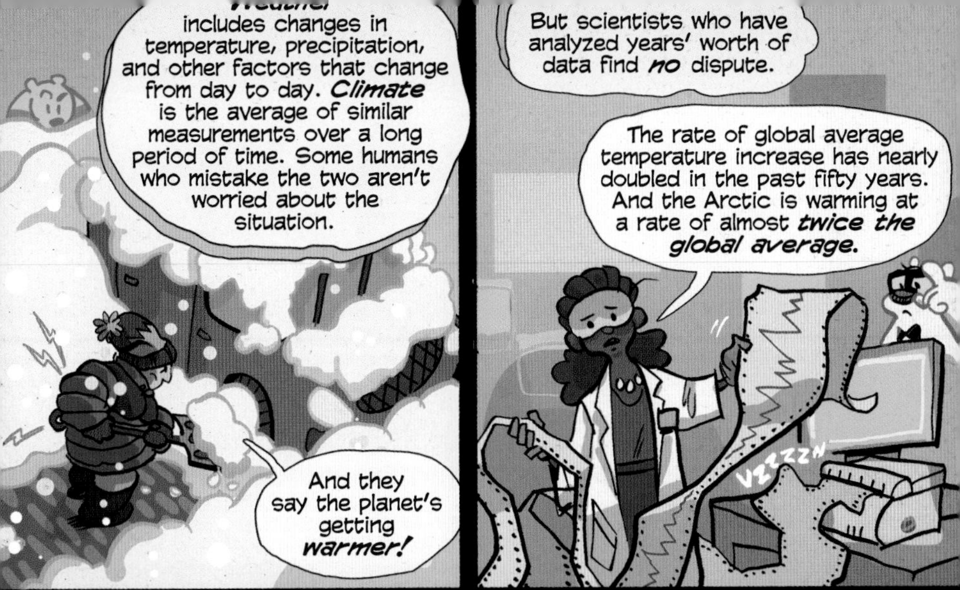
includes changes in temperature, precipitation, and other factors that change from day to day. *Climate* is the average of similar measurements over a long period of time. Some humans who mistake the two aren't worried about the situation.
And they say the planet's getting *warmer!*
But scientists who have analyzed years' worth of data find *no* dispute.
The rate of global average temperature increase has nearly doubled in the past fifty years. And the Arctic is warming at a rate of almost *twice the global average.*
VZZZZN

WHY THE ARCTIC?

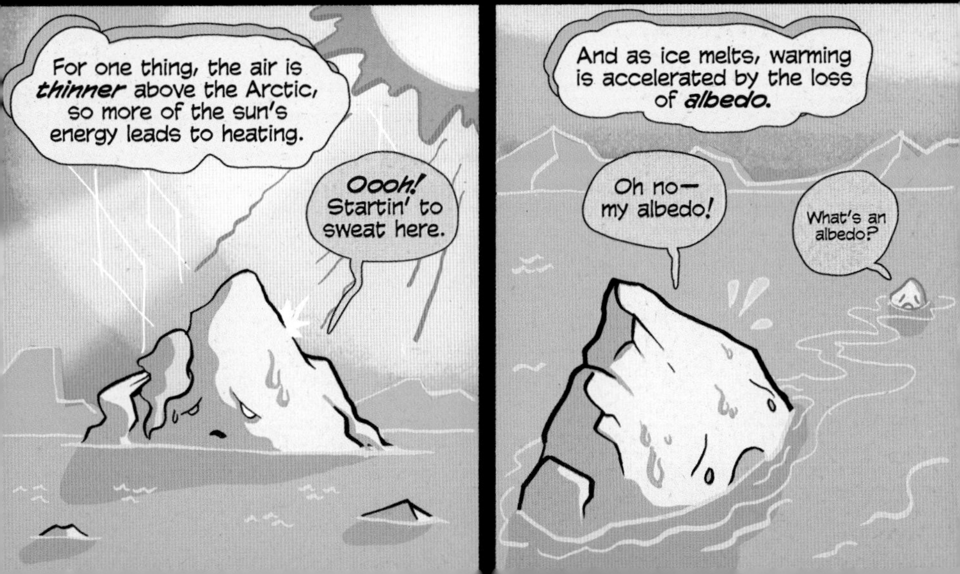
For one thing, the air is *thinner* above the Arctic, so more of the sun's energy leads to heating.
Oooh! Startin' to sweat here.
And as ice melts, warming is accelerated by the loss of *albedo.*
Oh no— my albedo!
What's an albedo?

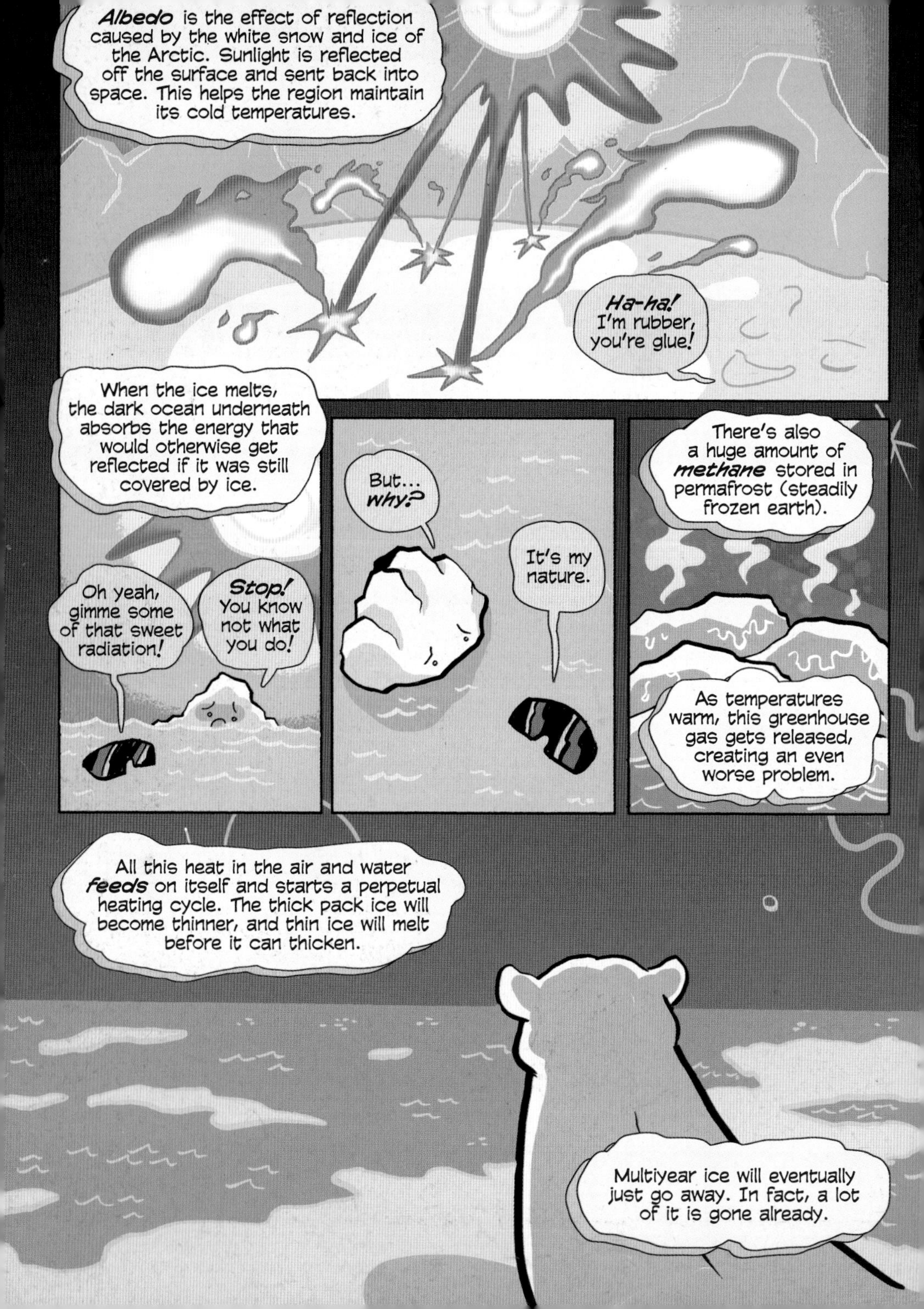

Albedo is the effect of reflection caused by the white snow and ice of the Arctic. Sunlight is reflected off the surface and sent back into space. This helps the region maintain its cold temperatures.
Ha-ha! I'm rubber, you're glue!
When the ice melts, the dark ocean underneath absorbs the energy that would otherwise get reflected if it was still covered by ice.
Oh yeah, gimme some of that sweet radiation!
Stop! You know not what you do!
But... *why?*
It's my nature.
There's also a huge amount of *methane* stored in permafrost (steadily frozen earth).
As temperatures warm, this greenhouse gas gets released, creating an even worse problem.
All this heat in the air and water *feeds* on itself and starts a perpetual heating cycle. The thick pack ice will become thinner, and thin ice will melt before it can thicken.
Multiyear ice will eventually just go away. In fact, a lot of it is gone already.

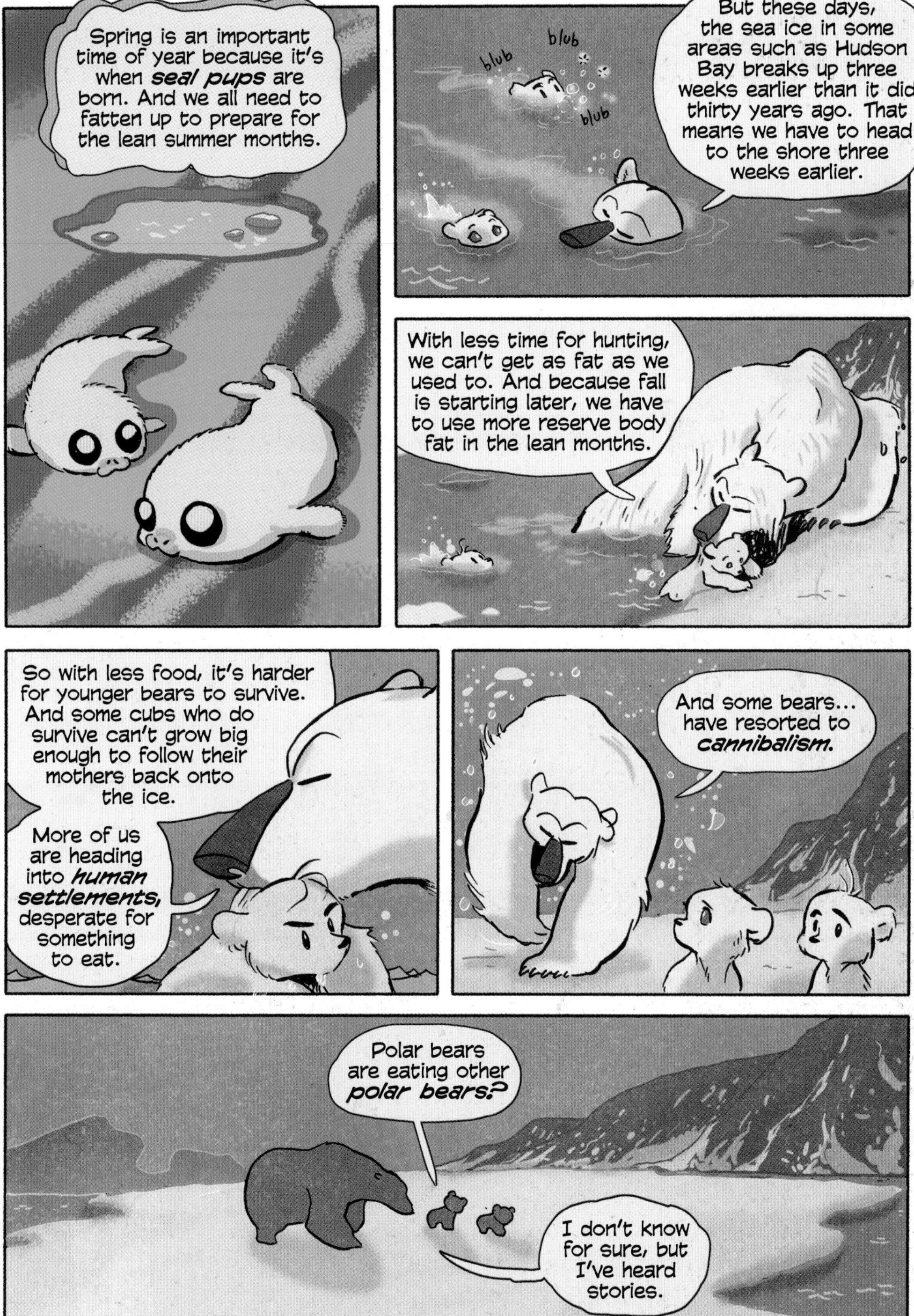
Spring is an important time of year because it's when *seal pups* are born. And we all need to fatten up to prepare for the lean summer months.
blub
blub
blub
But these days, the sea ice in some areas such as Hudson Bay breaks up three weeks earlier than it did thirty years ago. That means we have to head to the shore three weeks earlier.
With less time for hunting, we can't get as fat as we used to. And because fall is starting later, we have to use more reserve body fat in the lean months.
So with less food, it's harder for younger bears to survive. And some cubs who do survive can't grow big enough to follow their mothers back onto the ice.
More of us are heading into *human settlements*, desperate for something to eat.
And some bears... have resorted to *cannibalism*.
Polar bears are eating other *polar bears?*
I don't know for sure, but I've heard stories.

Melting snow can also make our dens unstable.

Because the ice floes in the pack are moving and turning and not leaving an easy trail, it's harder for males to follow a female's scent.

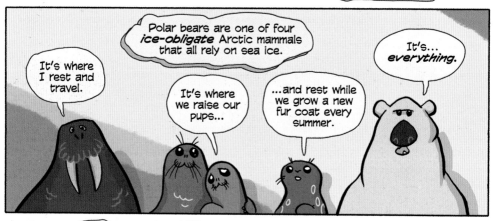

Polar bears are one of four *ice-obligate* Arctic mammals that all rely on sea ice.

It's where I rest and travel.

It's where we raise our pups...

...and rest while we grow a new fur coat every summer.

It's... *everything*.

Remember that the formation of pack ice creates the conditions for algae to bloom, while it attaches itself to the underside.

Forget the futility of hunting for food without pack ice—

Pack ice is the *foundation* of the entire Arctic food web.

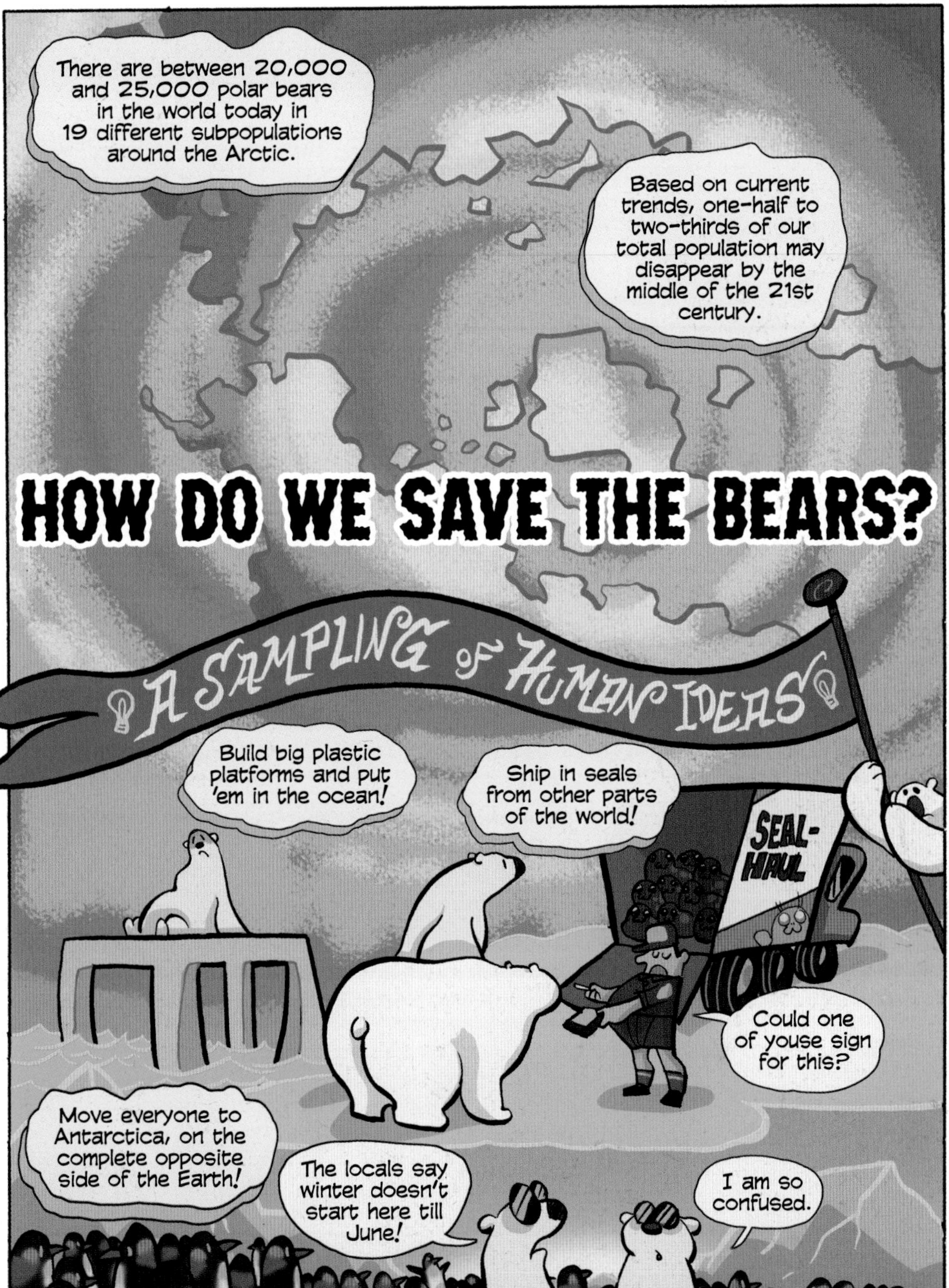
There are between 20,000 and 25,000 polar bears in the world today in 19 different subpopulations around the Arctic.
Based on current trends, one-half to two-thirds of our total population may disappear by the middle of the 21st century.
HOW DO WE SAVE THE BEARS?
A SAMPLING OF HUMAN IDEAS
Build big plastic platforms and put 'em in the ocean!
Ship in seals from other parts of the world!
SEAL-HAUL
Could one of youse sign for this?
Move everyone to Antarctica, on the complete opposite side of the Earth!
The locals say winter doesn't start here till June!
I am so confused.

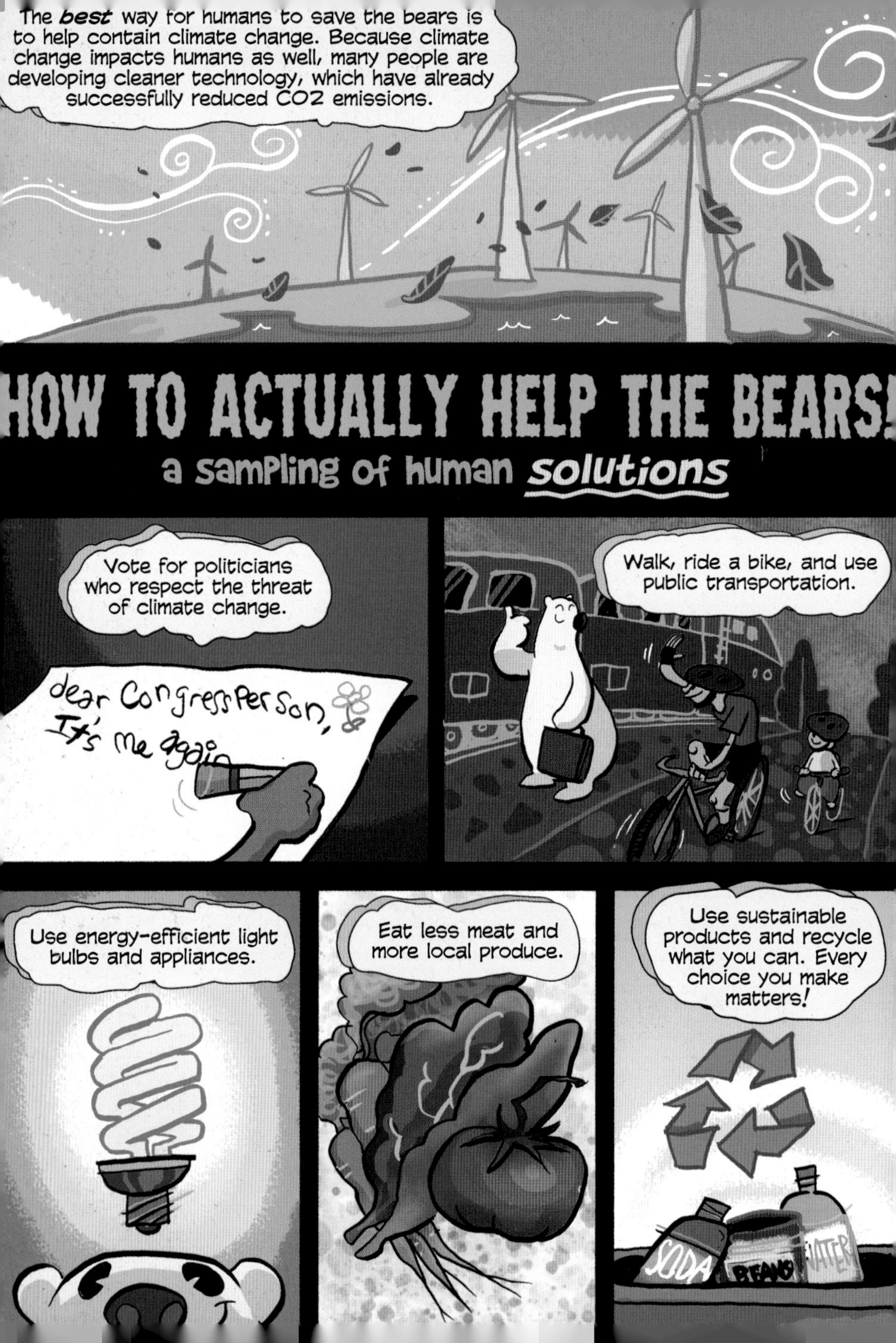
The best way for humans to save the bears is to help contain climate change. Because climate change impacts humans as well, many people are developing cleaner technology, which have already successfully reduced CO2 emissions.
HOW TO ACTUALLY HELP THE BEARS!
a sampling of human solutions
Vote for politicians who respect the threat of climate change.
dear Congressperson, It's me again
Walk, ride a bike, and use public transportation.
Use energy-efficient light bulbs and appliances.
Eat less meat and more local produce.
Use sustainable products and recycle what you can. Every choice you make matters!
SODA
BEANS
WATER

Mama, these are all things humans can do. But what can *we* do?

Well, some say we will have to figure it out.

How?

Nobody knows.

Spending more time off the ice means we have more encounters with grizzly bears.

Have we met before?

This has led to some romantic pairings.

Polar bears already share *some* genes with the grizzlies.

Scandalous!

Polar bear and grizzly hybrids end up with traits from both their mothers and fathers.

Those raised by polar bear mothers learn to become polar bears.

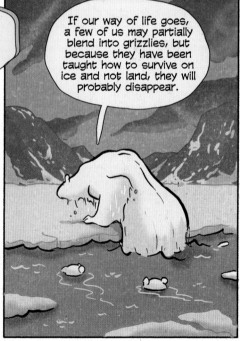

If our way of life goes, a few of us may partially blend into grizzlies, but because they have been taught how to survive on ice and not land, they will probably disappear.

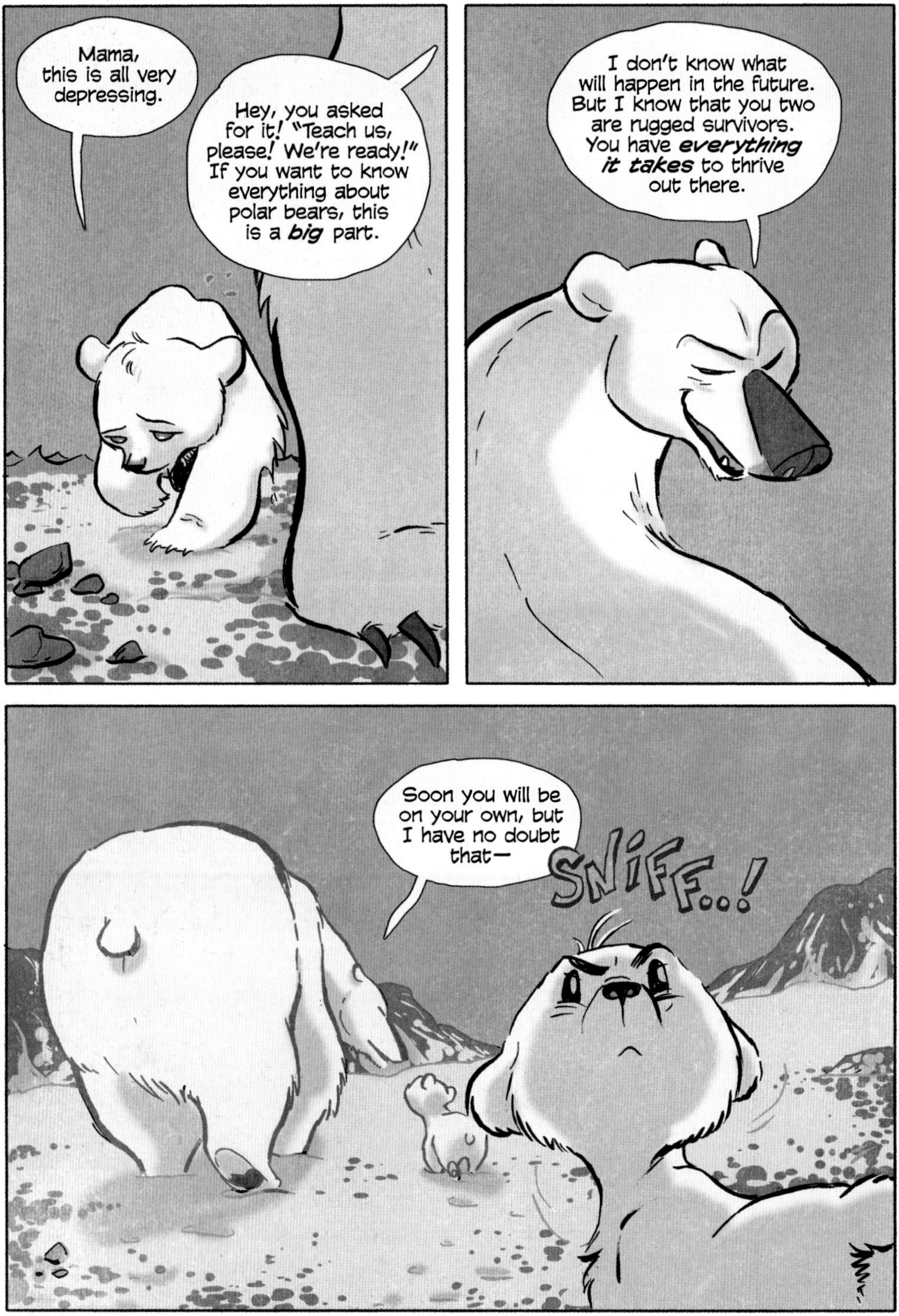
Mama, this is all very depressing.
Hey, you asked for it! "Teach us, please! We're ready!" If you want to know everything about polar bears, this is a ***big*** part.
I don't know what will happen in the future. But I know that you two are rugged survivors. You have ***everything it takes*** to thrive out there.
Soon you will be on your own, but I have no doubt that—
SNIFF..!

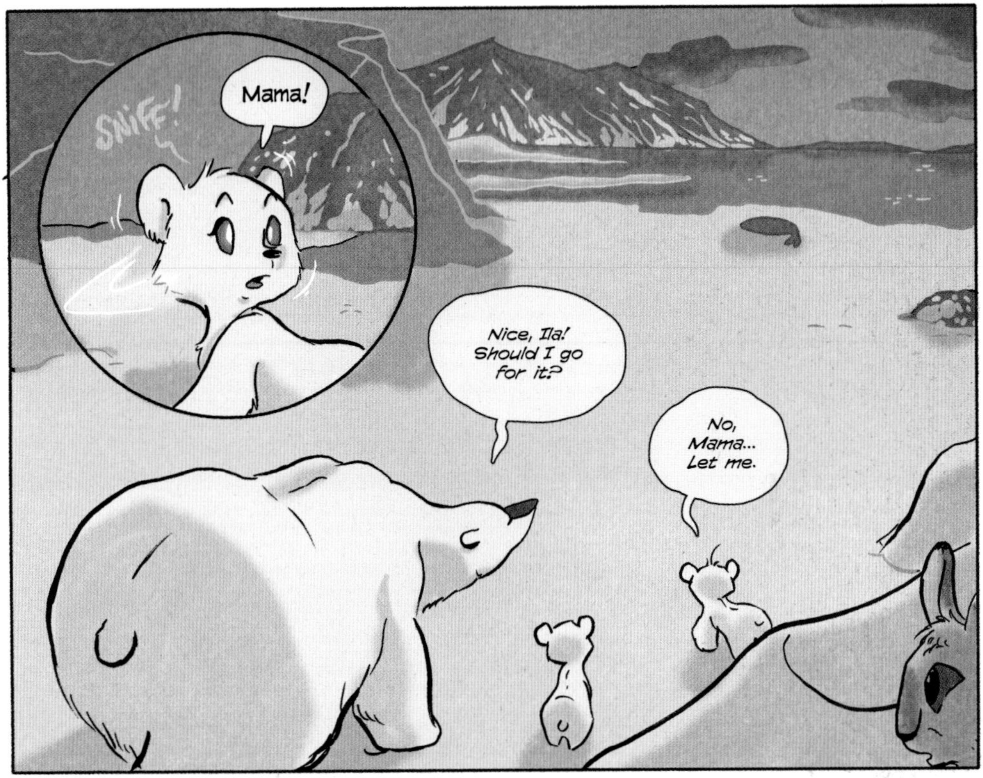
SNIFF!
Mama!
Nice, Ila! Should I go for it?
No, Mama... Let me.

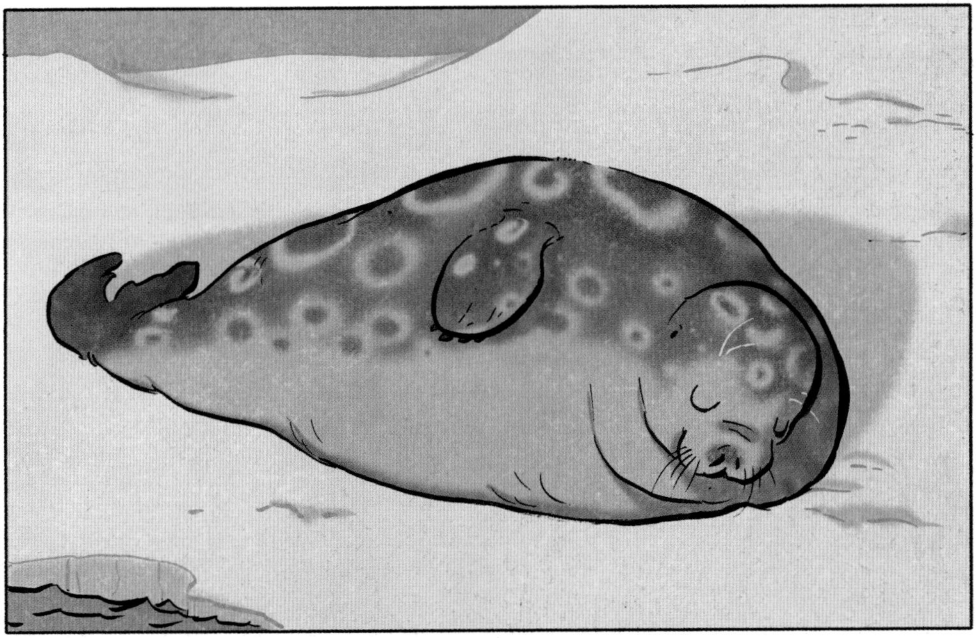

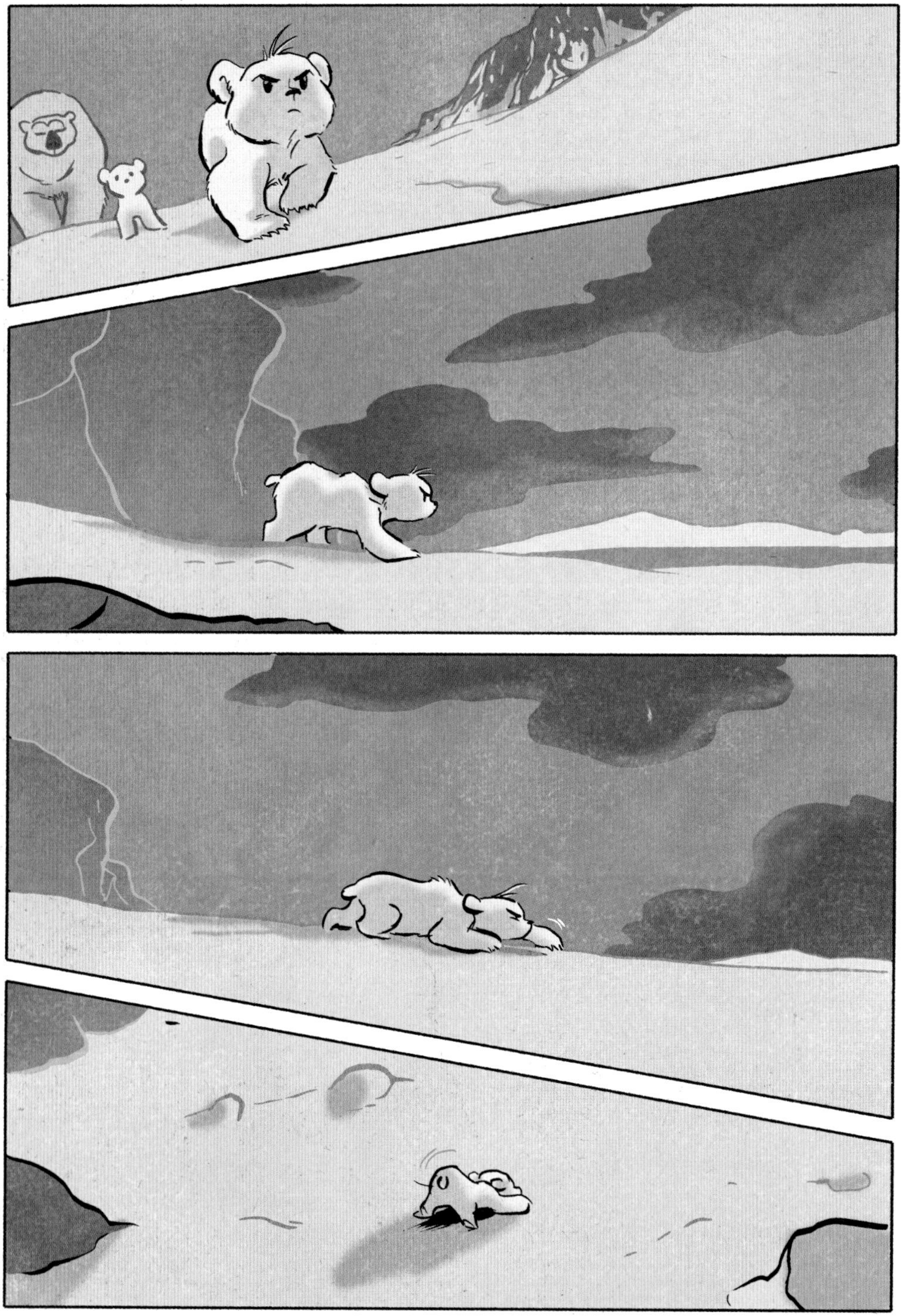

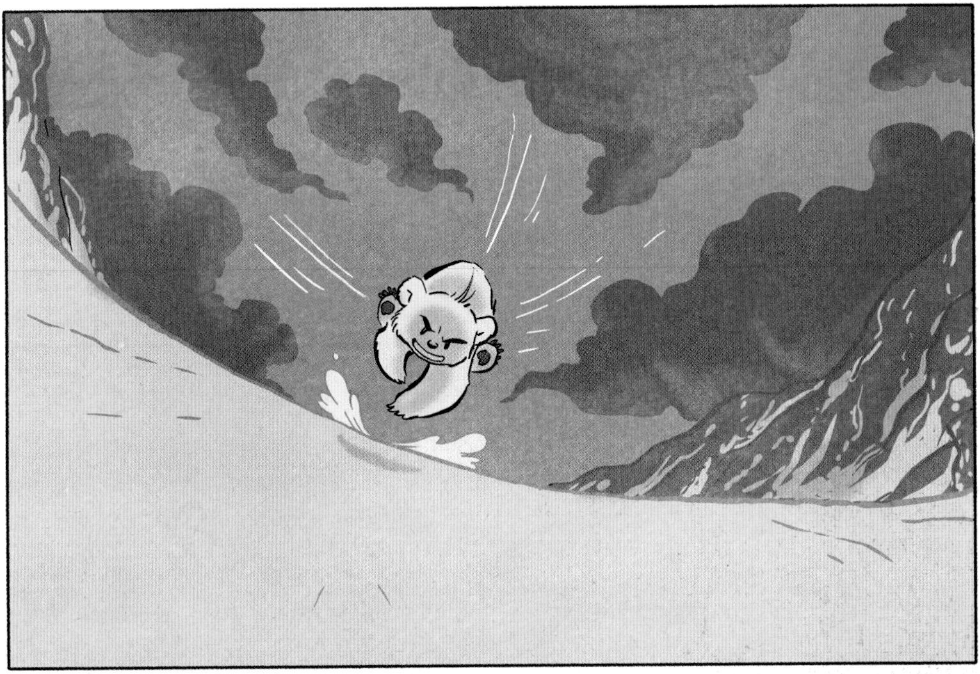

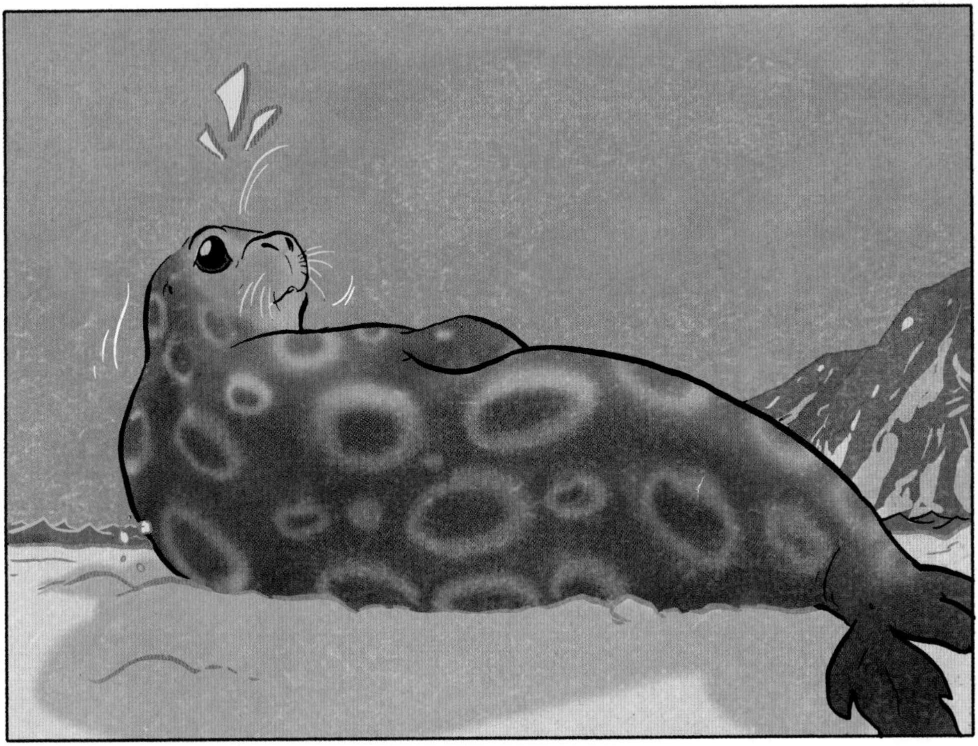

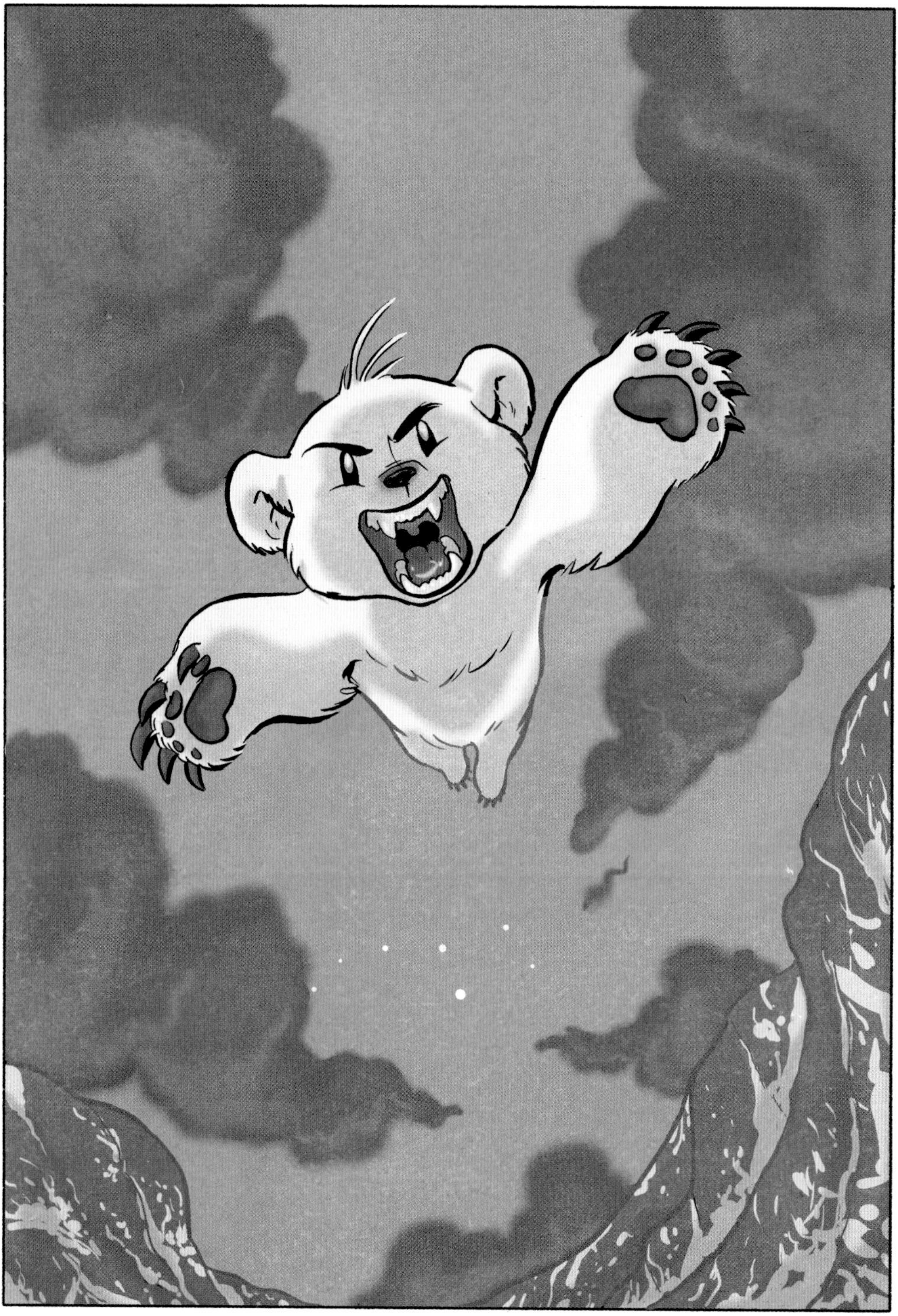

—GLOSSARY—

Albedo

A measure for the reflection of a surface like snow and ice. Surfaces with a higher albedo reflect more light and absorb less.

Biomagnification

A process that describes the increasing concentration of a substance as it moves up the food chain.

Carnivoran

A member of the Carnivora order, which includes mammals with sharp claws and teeth, a digestive system built for meat, and at least four toes on each foot. Not to be confused with "carnivore," which refers to any animal that eats mostly meat.

Climate

The average atmospheric conditions of a region over a long period of time. Scientists study climate to identify trends and changes in temperature, precipitation, and other measures over decades and centuries.

CO2

Carbon dioxide, the primary gas emitted through human activity. Scientists are concerned that the increase of CO_2 and other "greenhouses gases" that absorb and emit radiant energy are causing harmful effects on Earth's ecosystem.

Estrus

The recurring period of time for a non-primate female mammal when her body is most receptive to sexual reproduction.

Greenhouse effect

The warming process that occurs when some of the solar energy that has passed through the Earth's atmosphere is trapped by certain gases (such as carbon dioxide and methane) instead of being released back into space.

Home range

An individual bear's territory. A large area with boundaries that can shift depending on the availability of food and other habitat conditions.

Lipophilic

Describes the capability of a compound to dissolve into or combine with lipids such as fats. Lipophilic chemical pollutants make their way into the seal fat that is an essential part of a polar bear diet.

Mammal

A member of the vertebrate class Mammalia. Mammals have hair, mammary glands, and a neocortex. Mammals are warm-blooded and give birth to live young (with a few exceptions) who are nursed with milk.

PCBs

Polychlorinated biphenyls, a group of man-made organic chemicals. Despite recent bans, PCBs are still some of the most abundant pollutants in the Arctic.

Salinity

A measure of the concentration of salt in a body of water.

Subadult

According to one definition, an animal that has grown some adult characteristics but is not yet an adult. Polar bear cubs have grown into subadults when they are about two and a half years old. The subadult stage generally lasts three years. It's important to note, though, that some researchers define subadult to be anything younger than reproductive age; in other words, any bear that is not yet an adult is a subadult.

—ICE TERMINOLOGY—

Frazil ice

Loose, slushy ice that forms in a body of water and floats to the surface.

Grease ice

A thin layer of frazil ice that is formed by cold, turbulent water.

Ice floe

A large sheet of ice floating in the water.

Land-fast ice

Sea ice that is attached to the ground in some way, like on the coastline or the sea floor.

Nilas ice

Thickened sea ice made from grease ice in calm water.

Pack ice

A mass of frozen seawater.

Pancake ice

Round pieces of ice formed either when nilas ice breaks apart or when water covers textured frazil and grease ice.

—NOTES—

Page 4:

In some areas in the Arctic, the pack ice melts completely in the summer, so polar bears must fast on their stored fat reserves while they wait for the freeze to return in the fall. However, there are other populations of bears that are able to remain on the ice, moving north as the southern edge of the pack ice recedes. Unfortunately, sea ice far north isn't very productive and has very few seals. So the bears return south when freeze-up occurs in the spring because the water there is more biologically productive.

Page 11:

Just as the dawn bear was an offshoot of a complex evolutionary tree, there is no path from her to the polar bear that doesn't include all of the other bear species that resulted, including extinct bears like the European cave bear. While they can all trace their roots back to the dawn bear, today the polar bear has more in common genetically with the brown bear than with any other bear. In evolutionary history, polar bears appeared at the point when they diverged from their brown bear cousins.

Page 33:

The record-breaking trip was made by a female polar bear who swam for nine days straight in the Beaufort Sea. The long swim caused her to lose her cub and 22 percent of her body weight. Scientists say that polar bears have rarely had to face long swims before because large stretches of open water did not use to occur very often.

Pages 90–91:

Research programs are essential to collecting vital information about polar bears and their reaction to climate change, pollution, and other anthropogenic threats. The bear in our story is disturbed by his experience for comic effect only; in reality, he would be just fine! Several studies have investigated the long-term effects of wild polar bears being tagged multiple times, and none have found adverse effects.

Page 94–96:

The common name for these chemical compounds is Persistent Organic Pollutants (POPs). As the name suggests, these pollutants are extremely persistent in the environment, as well as in the bodies of the bears. Compounding the problem is that many of the POPs are even more harmful in their metabolized state (after they are incorporated into the polar bear's body).

Page 103:

Every year, the National Oceanic and Atmospheric Administration (NOAA) publishes an Arctic Report Card, which reports the latest scientific findings and compiles trends over time. In 2017, it reported that the average surface air temperature was the second warmest since 1900 (the first warmest year was 2016). The older, thicker sea ice comprised only 21 percent of the ice cover (compared with 45 percent in 1985), which means that 79 percent of the ice was only a year old. Trends show that Arctic sea ice is melting at the fastest pace in 1,500 years. When the report was released, research program director Jeremy Mathis said, "The Arctic is going through the most unprecedented transition in human history."

Page 109:

Researchers studying brown bears living on the ABC Islands in Southeast Alaska have discovered polar bear DNA in bears with the physical characteristics of grizzlies. They hypothesize that the bears descend from polar bears that were stranded at the end of the last ice age and brown bears that migrated to the islands.

—FUTHER READING—

Derocher, Andrew E. *Polar Bears: A Complete Guide to Their Biology and Behavior*. The John Hopkins University Press: Baltimore, 2012.

Ellis, Richard. *On Thin Ice: The Changing World of the Polar Bear*. Alfred A. Knopf: New York, 2009.

Mulvaney, Kieran. *The Great White Bear: A Natural and Unnatural History of the Polar Bear*. Houghton Mifflin Harcourt: New York, 2011.

Polar Bears International. http://www.polarbearsinternational.org.

Stirling, Ian. *Polar Bears: The Natural History of a Threatened Species*. Fitzhenry & Whiteside: Brighton, Massachusetts, 2011.

Thomas, David N. *Frozen Oceans: The Floating World of Pack Ice*. Firefly Books: Buffalo, New York, 2004.

GET TO KNOW YOUR UNIVERSE!

SCIENCE COMICS

"An excellent addition to school and classroom libraries."
—School Library Journal

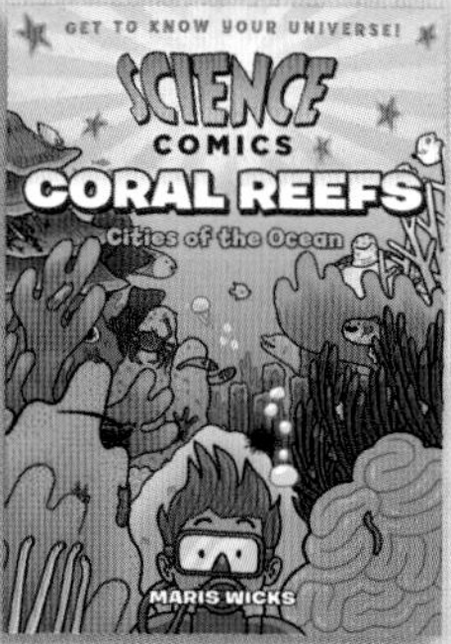
GET TO KNOW YOUR UNIVERSE!
SCIENCE COMICS
CORAL REEFS
Cities of the Ocean
MARIS WICKS

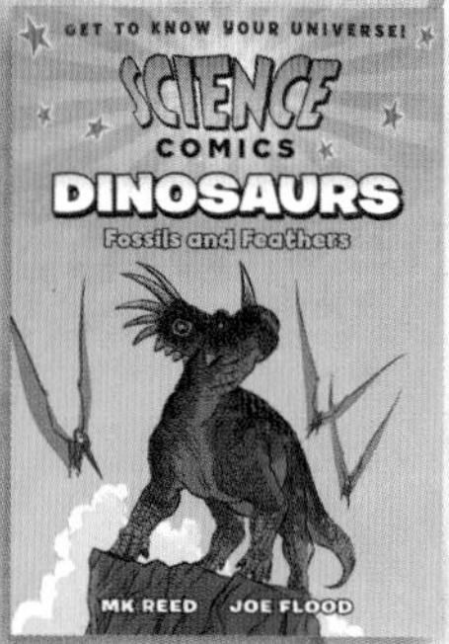
GET TO KNOW YOUR UNIVERSE!
SCIENCE COMICS
DINOSAURS
Fossils and Feathers
MK REED
JOE FLOOD

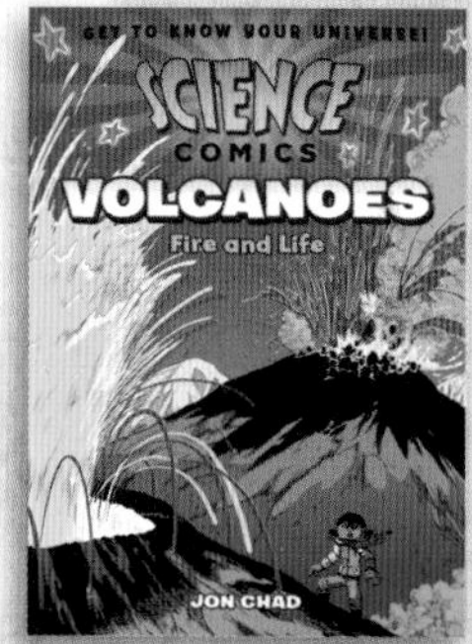
GET TO KNOW YOUR UNIVERSE!
SCIENCE COMICS
VOLCANOES
Fire and Life
JON CHAD

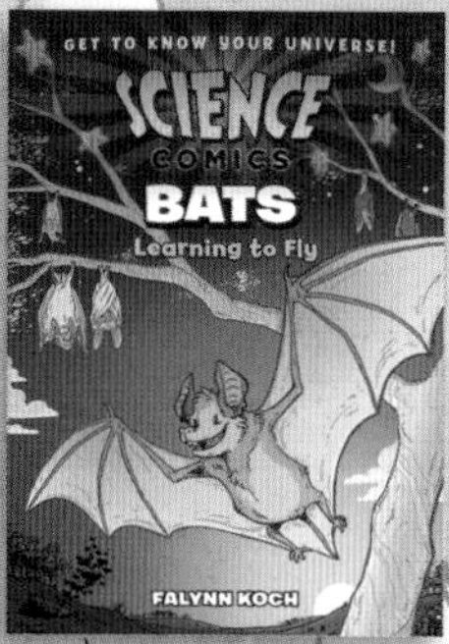
GET TO KNOW YOUR UNIVERSE!
SCIENCE COMICS
BATS
Learning to Fly
FALYNN KOCH

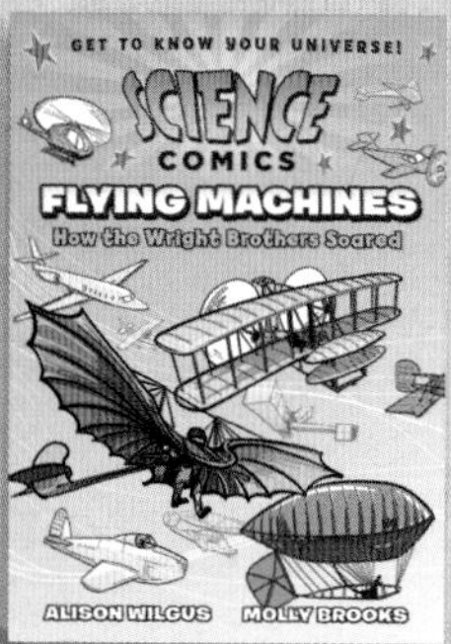
GET TO KNOW YOUR UNIVERSE!
SCIENCE COMICS
FLYING MACHINES
How the Wright Brothers Soared
ALISON WILGUS
MOLLY BROOKS

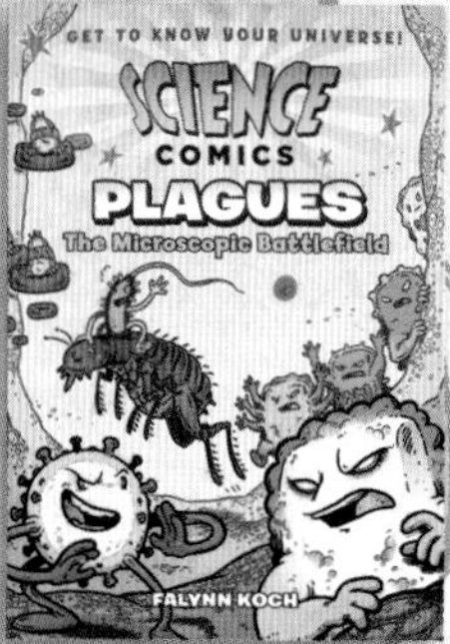
GET TO KNOW YOUR UNIVERSE!
SCIENCE COMICS
PLAGUES
The Microscopic Battlefield
FALYNN KOCH

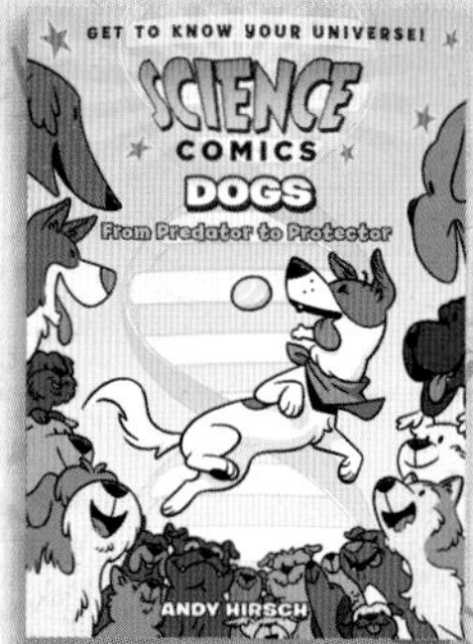
GET TO KNOW YOUR UNIVERSE!
SCIENCE COMICS
DOGS
From Predator to Protector
ANDY HIRSCH

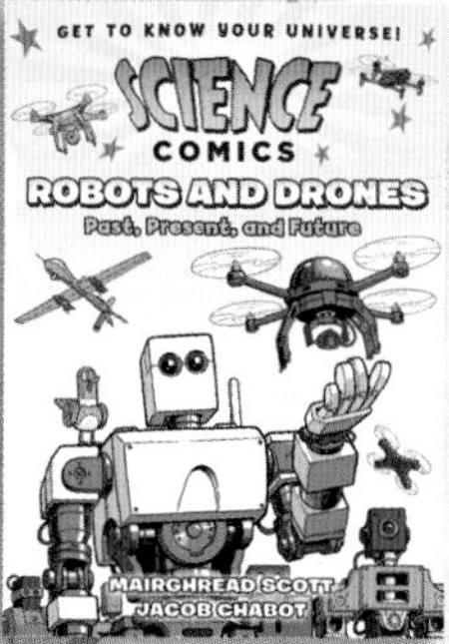
GET TO KNOW YOUR UNIVERSE!
SCIENCE COMICS
ROBOTS AND DRONES
Past, Present, and Future
MAIRGHREAD SCOTT
JACOB CHABOT

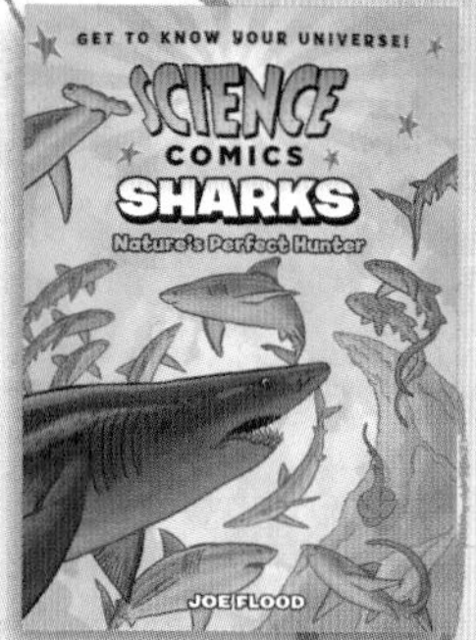
GET TO KNOW YOUR UNIVERSE!
SCIENCE COMICS
SHARKS
Nature's Perfect Hunter
JOE FLOOD

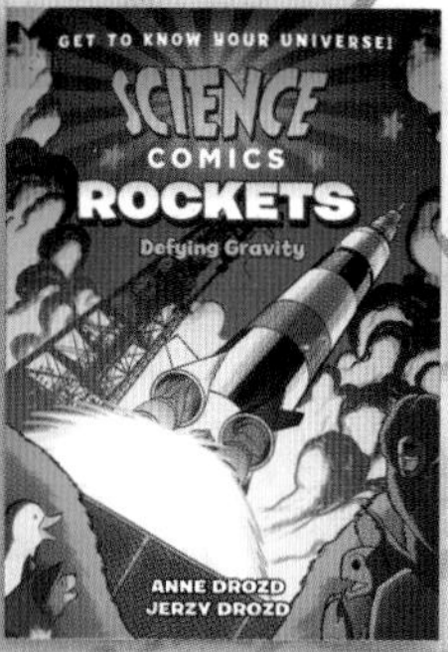
GET TO KNOW YOUR UNIVERSE!
SCIENCE COMICS
ROCKETS
Defying Gravity
ANNE DROZD
JERZY DROZD

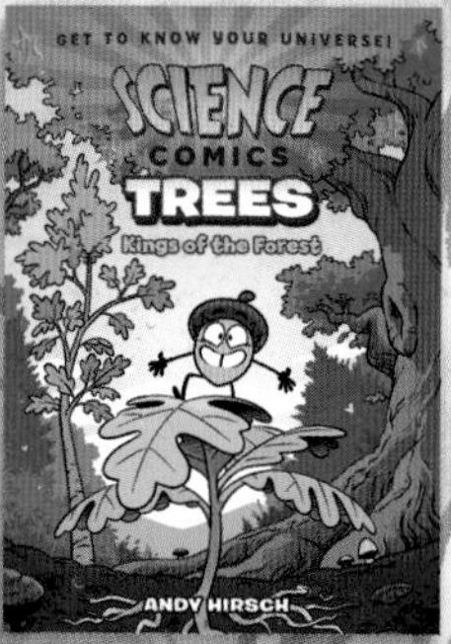
GET TO KNOW YOUR UNIVERSE!
SCIENCE COMICS
TREES
Kings of the Forest
ANDY HIRSCH

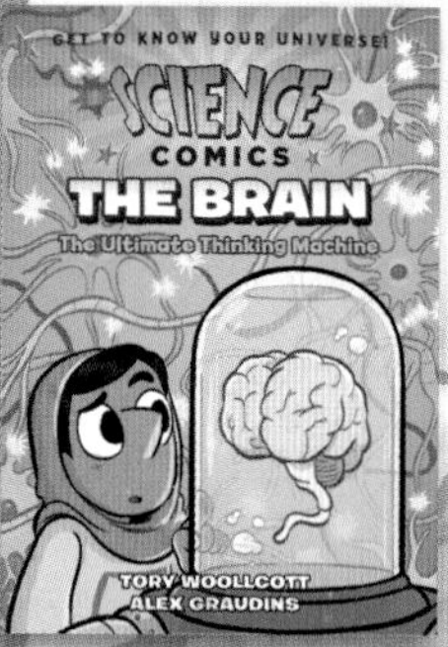
GET TO KNOW YOUR UNIVERSE!
SCIENCE COMICS
THE BRAIN
The Ultimate Thinking Machine
TORY WOOLLCOTT
ALEX GRAUDINS

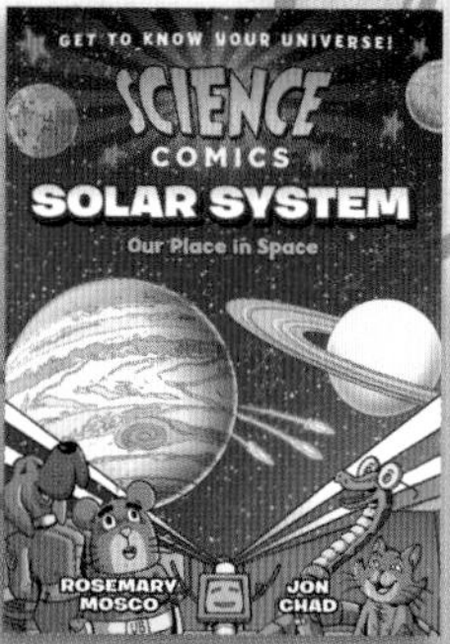
GET TO KNOW YOUR UNIVERSE!
SCIENCE COMICS
SOLAR SYSTEM
Our Place in Space
ROSEMARY MOSCO
JON CHAD

...And more books coming soon!